Estate Planning Through Life Assurance

BY

PETER HARRIS

*Managing Director of SCH Financial
Services Ltd.*

LONDON
SWEET & MAXWELL
1977

Published in 1977 by
Sweet & Maxwell Limited of
11 New Fetter Lane, London,
and printed in Great Britain
by The Eastern Press Limited
of London and Reading

ISBN 0 421 22150 X

Estate Planning Through Life Assurance

AUSTRALIA

The Law Book Company Ltd.
Sydney : Melbourne : Brisbane

CANADA AND U.S.A.

The Carswell Company Ltd.
Agincourt, Ontario

INDIA

N. M. Tripathi Private Ltd.
Bombay

ISRAEL

Steimatzky's Agency Ltd.
Jerusalem : Tel Aviv : Haifa

MALAYSIA : SINGAPORE : BRUNEI

Malayan Law Journal (Pte.) Ltd.
Singapore

NEW ZEALAND

Sweet & Maxwell (N.Z.) Ltd.
Wellington

PAKISTAN

Pakistan Law House
Karachi

PREFACE

THE writer of this present volume was the co-author of a book from the same publishers in 1970, dealing broadly with the same subject-matter. Since the earlier book was written, there have occurred profound changes in the economic and political climate, and those changes naturally affect the value and utility of life assurance as an investment medium. Substantial changes in taxation have occurred, notably the replacement of estate duty by capital transfer tax in the Finance Act 1975 and the little-remarked extensive recasting of the rules relating to qualification of life policies, availability of income tax relief and liability to taxation, in the Finance Acts 1975 and 1976. Finally, upstart entrants into the traditionally impregnable world of life assurance have at long last led to the industry as a whole being touched by the hand of financial failure, which has led to the Policyholders Protection Act 1975, and to greater stringency in the exercise of Government powers of control over the industry.

This book is intended as a practical guide for practitioners, both within the life assurance industry and in the professions. The real problem of writing it therefore was in deciding what to omit, rather than what to include. For example, the massively detailed legislation on qualifying policies and chargeable events, introduced in 1968 but significantly amended in 1975 and 1976, must be borne in mind constantly, but in practical terms all that the practitioner probably needs to know are the basic rules, the reasons for them, and the consequences of obeying or ignoring them. Where this topic is considered in the body of the book therefore, comment has been restricted to what is considered necessary to leave the practitioner in no doubt of the practical effect of a chosen course of action. It is really for individual insurance companies, who liaise closely with the Inland Revenue through the Life Offices' Association, to assist in the interpretation of the practical consequences of any non-standard policy or variation. Again, many life policies which were taken out with an eye on the estate duty legislation are affected by the Finance Act 1975 transitional legislation, at least in respect of premiums paid seven years or more before March 27, 1974. Practitioners are now far more likely to be concerned with the capital transfer tax consequences of premium payments, so the appropriate chapters in this book ignore estate duty, which is now historical, and concentrate on capital transfer tax, which is very much of the present day.

The role of life assurance as an essential tool in the tax planner's kit seems more than ever secure. Dramatic falls in equity, property and even gilt-edge prices in recent years have served a double purpose. First, they have demonstrated forcibly that the value of unit-linked insurances can go down just as well as they can go up, a factor which with the benefit of hindsight many insurance companies must now wish they had made greater attempts to emphasise in earlier advertising. Secondly, they have placed the proper emphasis on the virtues of traditional policies, particularly with profits, issued by the old-established and often maligned life offices.

The burden of taxation, particularly on the individual, is not reduced. There seems no realistic prospect of the introduction in the United Kingdom of index-linked taxation such as has been tried successfully elsewhere, so that the burden makes itself felt proportionately even more, the higher the rate of inflation. Given the apparent impossibility of turning back the tides of taxation on income and on capital, the proper husbandry of resources becomes an imperative. The individual who imagines he can afford to forego the annual Treasury subsidy which is available to all taxpayers through life assurance relief is more likely to be suffering from bad advice than from an over-abundance of assets.

Perhaps the most vital function which life assurance can fulfil is in encouraging the smooth transition of capital assets from one generation to another. Where the asset in question is a family or closely controlled business, the proper harbouring of limited resources through life assurance can make all the difference between the continuance or the winding up of the business. All too often, no alternative remedy is available. This is perhaps the best practical example of the part which life assurance plays, and will surely play on an increasing scale, in encouraging individuals, partnerships and corporations to manage their financial affairs to the greatest possible advantage.

It is impossible to over-stress that this book is not about the avoidance of taxation. It certainly points the way to the reduction or mitigation of tax liabilities, but does so from the standpoint that it is legitimate and proper for taxpayers to choose to arrange their affairs so as to attract the minimum rather than the maximum amount of tax. The guidance given by a life assurance counsellor is above all advice on sound management. It is hoped that this book will make some contribution towards the proper understanding of a complex subject which has many benefits to offer the hard-pressed taxpayer, but where bad advice can leave the taxpayer a financially poorer if wiser man. The book appears at a time when those in the professions and in management as well as the self-employed are suffering from the tightest financial squeeze for decades: a carefully arranged life assurance programme can help to alleviate immediate and short-term problems, but the quality of advice can literally mean the difference between financial survival and failure.

PETER HARRIS.

Shovelstrode Farm,
East Grinstead,
Sussex.
1977.

CONTENTS

CONTENTS

TABLE OF CASES

ix

TABLE OF STATUTES

[Figures in bold refer to the paragraphs on which sections are set out in full.]

xi

CHAPTER 1

GENERAL BACKGROUND

1–01   BY way of introduction, it is as well to explain what this book does not cover. As it is intended mainly as a handbook for professional advisers and the life assurance industry, it generally excludes consideration of industrial insurance, friendly societies and pensions. The first two of these subjects are excluded mainly on the grounds that the maximum permitted legal size of contract per taxpayer is hardly likely to make them burning topics with professional advisers. The third is excluded on the other hand because it is an enormously important subject in its own right which therefore has its own literature. Neither is the book intended to be an exposition of the general law of life assurance, which subject was tackled supremely well many years ago by the late Mr. David Houseman and whose book on the subject is likely to remain the standard reference work for very many years to come. The special contractual nature and tax treatment of life assurance is however an implicit part of the book, and probably the chapter dealing with the use of life assurance in settlements is the best example of the need in this book specifically to consider life assurance within the framework of the general law.

General tax background

1–02   Life assurance and annuity funds which provide the ultimate policy claim value are more lightly taxed than is the investment income and trading or investment profits of non-insurance companies. The amount received at maturity of an insurance policy will normally be exempt from capital gains tax [1]; premiums paid in respect of a policy on the life of the taxpayer or his spouse will generally attract a direct Treasury subsidy in the shape of life assurance relief; and unless it is paid directly to the estate of the deceased, the policy death benefit will usually not attract capital transfer tax. In the case of annuities, a pension should be taxed as earned income, and the greater part of each instalment of a purchased life annuity will be exempt from taxation. So far as benefits attributable to policyholders are concerned, annuity and pension funds in the hands of the insurance company are tax free.

1–03   Before March 20, 1968, taxpayers were unfettered in the ways they could benefit financially from taking advantage of the generally favourable tax treatment of life assurance in the hands of the company and of the individual policyholder. However, by that time an increasing number of insurance companies, not all of them by any means new-

---

[1] F.A. 1965, s. 28.

comers to the scene, were producing a gradually increasing range of policies designed as much to achieve avoidance of taxation as to fulfil the traditional and proper role of life assurance, namely the provision of protection. As a result, the Finance Act 1968 introduced a new taxation framework, designed *inter alia* to ensure that life assurance relief and freedom from taxation on policy proceeds would only be granted in relation to contracts with a minimum premium paying period of 10 years. However, the legislators at that time omitted also to make it a pre-condition for tax benefits that all types of policy should carry a minimum amount of mortality benefit, so that it remained possible in effect to purchase units in tax-privileged investment funds whilst still enjoying a Treasury subsidy in the form of life assurance relief. The Finance Act 1975 remedied this and other shortcomings of the 1968 legislation.

The practical effect of the 1968 and 1975 legislation is covered in detail in the appropriate chapters, but this is a convenient point to contemplate the tax treatment of policyholders' funds held by insurance companies.

Taxation of insurance companies

1–04 The exact taxation position of any life assurance company, whether mutual or proprietary, will depend *inter alia* on the composition of the various funds (life assurance business; general annuity business and pension business) and its liabilities in relation thereto. Shareholders' profit, in the case of a proprietary company, will be arrived at after unusually complex computations, which will often take account of actuarial factors such as mortality tables. Largely for this reason, it is unusual for the life assurance fund to be taxed on the conventional Case I of Schedule D basis, since for the purpose of a Case I computation, profits allocated to, reserved for, or expended on behalf of policyholders are excluded, although any profits so excluded as reserves which cease to be reserved are then taxed as profits.[2]

1–05 Since the Revenue have the option to charge on the basis which will attract the largest assessment, most life assurance companies are in practice taxed on the basis of investment income and realised capital gains less management expenses (I–E).[3] Corporation tax on profits is limited to the special rate of 37·5 per cent. on unfranked income[4]; and dividend income which is reserved for policyholders (which will have been received with the benefit of the tax credit) does not attract any further taxation, so the practical effect is that policyholders' dividends are taxed at 35 per cent. The insurance company cannot offset tax credits against its own corporation tax liability, to the extent that

---

[2] Taxes Act 1970, s. 309.
[3] See *Liverpool and London and Globe Insurance Company* v. *Bennett*, 6 **T.C.** 327.
[4] Taxes Act 1970, s. 310.

dividends received are channelled into policyholders' funds.[5] In the case of chargeable gains reserved for policyholders, tax is charged at the lower of 37·5 per cent. and the maximum rate payable by individuals, currently 30 per cent.[6] However, insurance companies are often able to postpone the realisation of capital gains for long periods of time, and because of this they may be able to make a smaller deduction than 30 per cent. when paying out the policy benefit. Many unit linked policies thus will give an undertaking to deduct capital gains tax at a concessionary rate, and this is certainly a factor which should be taken into account in deciding which policy to effect.

1–06   In the case of general annuity business, profits are charged under Case VI of Schedule D, although the method of computation follows Case I principles.[7] The company's liabilities to policyholders under all policies are treated as charges on income to the extent that they do not exceed the investment income and realised gains of the general annuity fund.[8] Therefore, there is only a corporation tax liability if the fund's investment income and realised gains exceed annuity payments. This as much as anything explains the wide variations which are encountered in annuity rates, and the manner in which particular offices enter the market from time to time offering especially attractive annuity rates. There will be no corporation tax liability so long as the insurance company can balance its annuity payments against its annuity fund income. Franked investment income which is set off against annuity payments for this purpose cannot be utilised to frank dividend distributions made by the company.[9]

1–07   Pension business enjoys total tax exemption for all investment income and realised gains.[10] There will only be a corporation tax liability in respect of any pension business profits which are paid out to shareholders.

In the exceptional case where the life assurance fund is taxed under Case I, management expenses will be allowed as a deduction in computing the corporation tax liability.[11] No such deduction is allowed in the case of computing profits in respect of general annuity and pension business, where the Case VI computations in each case are carried out on Case I principles.[12]

Development land tax, which relates to the disposal after July 31, 1976, of land having a development value, is payable in full irrespective of which of the three possible classes of life assurance fund disposes of the land.[13]

In the case of composite insurance companies (those which carry on

---

[5] *Ibid.*
[6] F.A. 1974, s. 26.
[7] Taxes Act 1970, s. 312.
[8] *Ibid.* s. 313.
[9] *Ibid.* s. 313 (4).
[10] *Ibid.* s. 314.
[11] *Ibid.* s. 305.
[12] *Ibid.* s. 312.   [13] Development Land Tax Act 1976, s. 34, Sched. 6.

all classes of business) the life assurance business is treated for corporation tax purposes as a separate business. Ordinary life assurance business and industrial life assurance business also are treated as separate businesses.[14] In the case where the insurance company does not segregate different classes of business, a division is made for corporation tax purposes on the principle of allocating premiums in respect of approved pension policies to pension business; allocating all other annuity premiums to general annuity business; and regarding what is left as being the insurance company's life assurance fund.[15]

Insurable interest

1–08   The Life Assurance Act 1774, s. 1, states that no insurance is to be made on the life of any person when the person for whose use, benefit or on whose account such policy is made shall have no interest, otherwise the insurance shall be null and void. Section 2 of the same Act requires there to be inserted in the policy the name or names of the person or persons interested in the policy for whose use, benefit, or on whose account, the insurance is effected As regards *quantum*, section 3 of the same Act provides that no greater sum shall be recovered under the policy than the amount or value of the interest of the person effecting the policy.

The Life Assurance Act 1774 was introduced because it had ". . . been found by experience, that the making of insurances on lives, or other events, wherein the assured shall have no interest, hath introduced a mischievous kind of gambling. . . ." The statute thus was introduced to deal with what the legislators more than 200 years ago clearly regarded as being a growing social evil. Evidence from countries with thriving life assurance industries, but no equivalent of the English law of insurable interest requirements, suggests that the Life Assurance Act 1774 has long outlived its practical usefulness. There seems to be a strong case for repeal of the Act, perhaps replacing it with a measure stipulating that the only requirement for establishing insurable interest should be the written acknowledgment and approval of the life to be insured. There would have to be, as now, specific legislation to avoid the risk of unscrupulous persons insuring minor lives where they have control of children,[16] but the general moral risk, as now, would be covered by the general common sense approach of the insurance company upon receipt of a life of another proposal form. As is noted below, it is simplicity itself to avoid the Life Assurance Act 1774 provisions by assignment of a policy, but even so it is necessary to have an understanding of the practical consequences of the law as it now stands.

---

[14] Taxes Act 1970, s. 307.
[15] *Ibid.* s. 323 (3).
[16] See Children Act 1958, s. 9; Adoption Act 1958, s. 46.

1–09 The great majority of all insurance policies are effected by the proposer on his own life for his own benefit, when the pecuniary interest is incapable of valuation, so has no limit. Similarly, spouses are considered to have insurable interests in the life of each other without limit. In all other cases, as noted above, section 3 of the Act restricts the level of insurance which may be effected to the pecuniary interest of the proposer in the life to be assured. It should however be noted that *Dalby* v. *India & London Life Assurance Co.*[17] decided that the requirement of section 1 was that the person for whose benefit the policy is taken out only needed to show insurable interest at inception of the policy: thus, the policy remains valid even though the interest may have ceased at the date of the death of the insured. It is also considered to be the case that the *quantum* of insurable interest depends on the facts at the moment the policy is effected; any subsequent reduction in the *quantum* does not void the insurance. It should also be noted that *obiter* in the *Dalby* case *infra* almost certainly refutes the statement at paragraph 362 of *MacGillivray on Insurance Law* (5th ed.) that the statute would not be satisfied unless the assured had, at the date of the contract, an insurable interest to the extent of the amount claimed. Thus, if a policy is effected for £2,000 but subsequently the limit of insurable interest at inception is established to be £1,000, the policy would only be void to the extent of £1,000, and not in its entirety.

1–10 It is noteworthy that the decided cases relating to insurable interest were mainly heard at the end of the nineteenth century, although there appears to be no authority before the 1962 case of *Carter Bros.* v. *Renouf*[18] confirming that the Life Assurance Act 1774 merely makes the policy void as between the insurance company and the insured, so that if the insurance company paid out under the policy in any event any question of title would be decided ignoring the provisions of the Act. The significance is that no reputable insurance company, having once accepted the risk, would be likely to refuse payment on the grounds of lack of insurable interest, unless of course it had a clear duty under public policy to refuse payment.

1–11 In practice, policies are frequently effected on insured lives by third parties for a variety of reasons, all of which can be seen to satisfy the requirements of the Act. Thus, insurable interest exists and is quantifiable *inter alia* in the following common cases:

    (i) An employer can insure the life of a key employee, to the extent of the anticipated monetary loss to the employer following the employee's death until such time as a suitable replacement could be found.

    (ii) Where there are rights under a pension scheme giving an

---

[17] [1843–60] All E.R.Rep. 1040.
[18] (1962) 36 A.L.J.R. 67.

employee enforceable benefits, those benefits may be effected through life assurance effected by the employer or by the pension scheme trustees.

(iii) A creditor has insurable interest in the life of his debtor up to the full extent of the debt, and because the insurance would not be effected by way of indemnity, the creditor could sue the deceased debtor's estate for the debt as well as enjoying the policy proceeds.

(iv) A parent or guardian may effect insurance on the life of a minor child *qua* bare trustee for the absolute benefit of the child, the only limitation being the availability of funds: as a rule, insurance companies will restrict the return on death under age 14 or 16 to no more than premiums previously paid. Generally, parents have no insurable interest in the lives of their children for the benefit of the parents, although this is not the case in Scotland where a parent does have the legal right to be supported by his child.

1–12   Where there is a problem of insurable interest, it can usually be overcome by using the simple expedient of assignment. For example, if trustees, having the powers under the trust instrument, wished to effect insurance on the life of a beneficiary, but had no insurable interest, the beneficiary could effect a policy on his own life, probably at a monthly premium initially, and forthwith assign the policy to the trustees either gratuitously or for value. The trustees could then pay all future premiums and of course the policy eventually would enure as an asset of the trust fund. Such procedure in the case of trustees could have certain tax consequences, which are considered elsewhere.[19]

1–13   In summary then, although it is necessary always to keep the provisions of the Life Assurance Act 1774 in mind, if there are sound commercial grounds for wanting to effect life assurance, the Act is unlikely to be an inhibiting factor.

---

[19] §§ 11–02—11–20.

CHAPTER 2

INVESTMENT

Introduction

2–01   The practitioner must approach the subject of investment in relation to life assurance with hesitancy, perhaps tinged with awe. It is estimated that at the present time institutional investors, comprising to all intents and purposes solely insurance companies, pension funds and unit trusts, control in excess of 60 per cent. of all of British industry through their holdings of ordinary shares either directly in the companies concerned, or indirectly by virtue of the institutions' share stakes in the financial sector (which provides finance for industrial investment), and in themselves. Furthermore, all indications are that in recent years the private investor has been a net seller of ordinary shares, whereas the institutions have become net purchasers. Whether or not the institutions concerned make a proper use of this immense economic power is currently at the heart of the continuing debate concerning economic strategy, and fortunately it is not the task of this book to comment on that debate. The practitioner must however have some kind of guide to the practical significance of the economic power wielded by insurance companies, since the manner in which that power is exercised will usually have some practical outcome so far as the policyholder is concerned, and depending on the type of policy selected, the performance of the investments which underpin the policy's value can be crucial.

Types of policy

2–02   In the early days of life assurance, all policies were issued on a non-profit basis. Life offices then gradually adopted the competitive practice of distributing a portion of the life fund surplus at each actuarial valuation to the policyholders. From this developed the system of having non-profit and with profit policies, a higher rate of premium being charged for policies entitled to participate in profits. This means in effect that particularly in the case of with profits contracts, the life offices were offering their services as investment managers as much as providers of straightforward life assurance cover. In the case of an endowment policy with profits, only a small proportion of each annual premium would be required to fund the mortality risk. The balance of each premium, after expenses, was available for investment, and although a relatively cautious investment philosophy needed to be followed (because of the guarantee to pay a minimum sum at the end of the endowment term) there was theoretically no legal restriction on the way in which the insurance company chose to invest its policyholders' funds. The ability to follow an investment course uninhibited by legal restraint concerning the make-up of policyholders' funds is one of the U.K. life assurance industry's most jealously guarded assets: Government intervention or control in this area is common in other countries.

2–03   Because of the generally cautious investment methods of insurance companies, the return at maturity of with profits contracts generally improved from decade to decade. Increasing prosperity, particularly during the post-war years, led to increased competition for the investing public's funds, which in turn prompted the insurance companies to follow a more adventurous, although still generally cautious, investment philosophy. Whereas in pre-war days the vast majority of all insurance company funds were invested into Treasury stock and other fixed interest securities, by 1971 only 38·5 per cent. of insurance company investments was in British government securities, the balance being in ordinary shares, company debentures, loans, and mortgages, land and other property. By the end of 1975, and largely thanks to the unprecedented stock market slump in 1974, the proportion of insurance company investments in British government securities had however increased to no less than 60·0 per cent.

Profit and non-profit

2–04   With profit and non-profit changes in the composition of insurance company funds, in so far as they relate to life and pension as opposed to general business funds, reflect largely a constant striving to ensure that no major insurance company is the first one to be forced to announce a reduction in its rate of reversionary bonus declared to with profits policies at each actuarial valuation. It must be acknowledged that by the end of 1976, the major insurance companies, most of which have been established for well over 100 years, could register the remarkable achievement that over a period of unprecedented invest-ment turmoil no significant with profits policy bonus rate had been reduced. This is of profound significance, since the yield to redemption on premiums paid into a competitive with profits endowment assurance, ignoring income tax relief on premiums, currently averages between 6 per cent. and 7½ per cent. annually. This return will generally be received free of all taxation, and if the true net investment cost is calculated after allowing for life assurance relief, the rate of yield commonly is in the area of 8½ per cent. Although this is hardly a spectacular investment result, it does mean that the return under such policies taking periods of 10 or 15 years to end-1976 has comfortably bettered the average rate of inflation. Considering how very difficult it is to find any long-term investment capable of achieving the objective of only maintaining the value of regular savings in real terms, it is clear that the adviser is not likely to be in danger of castigation by his client if he recommends taking out a good with profits policy.

2–05   Bearing in mind the long-term nature of most insurance contracts, it is manifestly vital that the prospective policyholder is advised to effect a contract likely to give him the best possible investment return at the end of the day. For this reason, non-profit policies cannot generally be recommended, especially in days of high inflation. It is true that non-profit cover will provide the cheapest form of insurance where all that is desired is a particular level of life assurance protection, for some specific purpose, such as repaying a mortgage advance, or providing collateral for some other reason. However, the yield to redemption on premiums paid into even the most competitive non-profit endowment policies is unlikely to exceed 6 per cent after income tax relief, whereas it is as near as certain as it is ever possible to be in the investment world that the comparable yield under a good with profits policy would be significantly greater. Premium cost is of course an important factor, but as a general rule the prospective client should be urged to effect a with profits contract for a smaller sum assured, rather than paying the same premium to effect a non-profit contract with a higher guaranteed basic sum assured. Some kinds of cover, such as term assurance, are only available on a non-profit basis, and in such cases it is clearly the duty of the practitioner to ensure that his client obtains the cover required from the reputable insurance company which offers the lowest premium rate.

Unit-linked policies

2–06   The obvious success of the traditional insurance companies in attracting regular savings from the investing public led to the emergence of competing policies which were neither non-profit nor with profits. Rather, the policy value was linked to investment units in specialised investment funds. Initially, these specialised funds invested wholly in equities, but gradually the range of investment spread to embrace property investment and fixed interest investment, including building society deposits. The logical development was to be able to link the policy to units in any one of a number of specialised funds, the policyholder or the insurance company retaining the ability to switch from fund to fund as investment circumstances, or perhaps fashions, demanded. Although the present writer is unconvinced that any special benefit has obviously accrued to the public from the existence of unit-linked policies, as compared with the indisputable benefits which have been enjoyed by generations of conventional with profit and even non-profit policyholders, it is important that the practitioner should have a basic understanding of what is involved.

Equity-linked policies

2–07   Throughout the 1950s and 1960s, it was accepted wisdom in the investment world that investment into the equity capital of publicly quoted companies was a sure hedge against inflation. This was the main reason for the comparatively rapid expansion of the unit trust industry; investment managers set out to make profits for themselves by acting as the wholesaler of ordinary shares, which were sold on to the public in a unitised form. The inevitable and logical development was for similar units to be sold to the public under the umbrella of an insurance policy which could offer the investor an apparently attractive package. In exchange for his commitment to save regularly by paying life assurance premiums the policyholder enjoyed the benefit of life assurance relief on his investment as well as whatever level of insurance cover was provided. The first equity linked policy was on general sale to the public in 1957. The bear market of 1974, culminating with the *Financial Times* Industrial Ordinary share index falling to 146·0 in January 1975 compared with its all-time high of 543·6 reached less than three years earlier, finally convinced many investors that the cult of the equity had perhaps led to an over-statement of the benefits flowing from such investment. Calculations based on the actual movement of the *Financial Times* Industrial Ordinary share index for the 120 months from January, 1966 to December, 1975 make interesting and very relevant reading.

2–08   Assuming the type of policy structure where 100 per cent. of all premiums paid was used to purchase units, the insurance company's costs being met out of income attaching to the units, this typical policy, assuming a monthly investment of £10 making total premiums paid of £1,200, would have had a value at maturity of £1,325, which represents a net yield to redemption on the premiums invested of a little under 2½ per cent. annually, ignoring income tax relief. This is significantly worse than the return which could have been enjoyed over the same period under a non-profit endowment assurance.

2–09   It is never advisable to be dogmatic on matters relating to investment, and in the case of equity linked life assurance policies not a great deal of evidence is available. Since March 20, 1968, the vast majority of all equity linked contracts have been for minimum periods of 10 years, so as to fulfil the qualifying policy conditions, and of course no policy effected on or after that date has yet matured. However, a comparison of the price of units to which the 35 most widely sold policies were linked at the end of 1976 showed that over the preceding five years the unit price movement had been at best an improvement of 75 per cent., and at worst a reduction of 70 per cent. Also, the unit price which had moved upwards by 75 per cent. over five years had, over periods of two and three years respectively, appreciated by less than the average of the group of 35. These figures lend support to the following general propositions:

(i) It is not proven that the value of an equity-linked endowment assurance will usually have more success than a good conventional with profits policy in protecting the value of premiums against erosion through inflation: indeed, evidence to date suggests the contrary conclusion.

(ii) The quality of investment management varies enormously, and one of the practitioner's main difficulties lies in trying to determine how good investment management is going to be: he has to make his assessment by reference to a minimum period of 10 years. This does in practice impose a quite impossible burden on the practitioner, since investment management groups sometimes have good years and sometimes have bad years, but no group consistently manages its funds so well that unit prices for example invariably improve on the movement of the *Financial Times* All Share Index.

(iii) Given the fact that equity investment is basically risk investment, the practitioner should probably guide the client who wants to combine an element of investment with the provision of life assurance cover towards a good with profits policy.

(iv) If the client is insistent that investment rather than protection is the main criterion, he should be warned that on the basis of past performance, it is most unlikely that if he maintains his contractual obligations to pay equity-linked policy premiums throughout he will be better off than had he effected a with profits policy. It should also be explained to him that as he is interested mainly in the investment content, his equity-linked policy should be regarded in exactly the same way as an ordinary share or portfolio of shares. If the unit price at some time in the life of the policy is so high as to show a good profit, the policy should be forthwith surrendered. If this occurs within 10 years of inception, or within three-quarters of the term of an endowment policy for 11, 12 or 13 years, this may result in a liability to higher rate income tax and the investment income surcharge, depending on the policyholder's own tax position. It is however better to accept a tax charge on a certain profit rather than to run the profit thus giving rise to the probability, based on all precedent, that at the end of the day there will be a smaller profit, or none.

(v) Finally, some unit-linked policies provide a guarantee of a definite minimum return of capital at the end of the endowment period and some do not. Bearing in mind the risky nature of equity investment, the client should be guided towards policies which do provide a minimum guaranteed maturity benefit.

Property-linked policies

2–10   This is the most popular category of unit-linked policy, after those with an equity link. The unit value is calculated by reference to a fund comprising industrial and commercial property; some funds may also invest in property company shares. Because rental incomes belonging to these funds are taxed only at the insurance company's rate, and bearing in mind that provided the qualifying policy rules are followed there is no further tax liability in respect of the income, there is a persuasive case for claiming that the investor who wants a stake in the commercial property market should invest through a life assurance property bond, rather than directly into a property company.

2–11 An attribute claimed for property investment is that it should be relatively more stable than investment into equities. This claim was certainly substantiated on balance throughout the traumas which followed the general economic collapse starting in December 1973; whether it will remain true for the future must be a moot point. It has always been the case that investment into bricks and mortar is less risky than investment into ordinary shares of industrial companies, if only because people always need somewhere to live and commerce and industry need somewhere to work.

Property unit-linked policies did not arrive on the scene until long after equity-linked policies, so that it is really too early to comment on actual or prospective returns under existing property-linked policies. Based on such information as is available, it does again seem unlikely that the eventual return under property-linked policies will be significantly worse or significantly better than the return under a comparable good with profits policy.

Multi-unit or managed bond policies

2–12 As was mentioned earlier, a policy of this kind has an ultimate value dependent on units in a variety of specialist funds. The simplest type of policy will give a choice between equity- and property-linked units: the more sophisticated will give a choice of perhaps half a dozen or more funds. As well as the more conventional equity and property based funds, such an exotic range might include a money fund; a fixed interest fund; a government securities fund; an overseas equities fund; a building society deposit fund; and so on.

2–13 The objective is to enable new premiums to be invested into which of the available funds the policyholder nominates: also there is often the facility for the investment value of past premiums to be switched from one fund to another. Where this facility is available the switch from fund to fund may be permitted without charge. Some policies vest absolute discretion as to the initial choice of funds, and any subsequent switching, in the hands of the insurance company. Others may give the policyholder the option to decide on the investment strategy to be followed. Most policyholders will in practice take the view that once they have decided to remit funds to professional money managers, those managers should be left with a free hand since presumably they can generally be expected to know rather more about the subject than does the policyholder.

Multi-unit policies seek to offer the potential policyholder the best of all possible worlds. Such idealism is to be commended in theory, but in practice what is being offered is really no more than a highly sophisticated, and therefore more expensive to operate, version of a traditional with profits policy, which would usually be based upon exactly the same investment mix of United Kingdom and overseas equities, commercial property and fixed interest securities.

Policy charges

2–14   The professional adviser should always check what it is going to cost his client to enter into any contract of life assurance. In the case of unit-linked policies, the prospectus and/or the policy itself will provide the answers. Usually in the case of unit-linked policies, the insurance company makes a relatively large initial deduction from all premiums paid: the minimum deduction is likely to be 5 per cent. of the single or each annual premium. In addition, there may be a further charge for entry into the investment fund or funds to which the policy is linked, and in extreme cases this can amount to a further charge on all premiums of 5 per cent. or even more. In addition, there will generally be an annual administrative charge levied by the managers of the underlying investment fund and/or levied by the insurance company. Finally, depending on the type of contract, there may be further charges to pay for the inclusion of death benefit, which in the case of policies issued after April 1, 1976, *must* be provided if the policy is to be qualifying.

2–15   It can be seen that the charges levied can amount to a significant proportion of each premium: in extreme cases the charges could amount to as much as the income tax relief on all premiums paid, currently 17·5 per cent. The practitioner must be aware of the fact that there can be wide variations in total policy charges. Generally speaking, charges will be lower in the case of insurance companies which operate their own investment funds, whether or not those funds are formally constituted as unit trusts. The most expensive type of policy tends to be that where the investment management is independent of the insurance company. Such independence can be a very positive factor. Bearing in mind the vital importance of good investment management, there may in principle be much to be said for insurance policies linked to units which are not managed by the life office's captive investment management team.

2–16   In the case of non-profit and with profit policies, it is very difficult to take a view on management and other expenses. There is no particular problem in the case of non-profit contracts, where the practitioner merely needs to secure the lowest premium rate available from a reputable insurance company, for a given sum assured. In the case of with profits policies, management expenses is clearly an important item in determining overall profitability of the business, and hence in establishing what level of bonus will be paid out over the life of the policy. Past performance is probably as sure a guide as any in this area, since offices with a record of higher than average management expenses will generally be found to have a less impressive bonus record. Those insurance companies which do not pay commission for the introduction of business tend to have a better bonus record than most, but this is by no means invariably true.

CHAPTER 3

CAPITAL TRANSFER TAX

3–01 IN this chapter, it is intended to examine ways in which life assurance can assist in estate conservation. The two major taxes on capital today are capital gains tax, introduced by the Finance Act 1965, and capital transfer tax, introduced by the Finance Act 1975. Insurance policies which have not been dealt with commercially are exempt from capital gains tax: the practical effect of this is that in all instances mentioned throughout this chapter, no capital gains tax is payable [1] even though a life policy which comes to maturity, is surrendered or enures to the estate of a deceased life assured, or to a third party then entitled, will usually show a handsome profit as compared with premiums paid.

3–02 Capital transfer tax replaced the old estate duty, first introduced by the Finance Act 1894, and also removed formally from the Statute Book certain other obsolete death duties. The major political motivation behind capital transfer tax was the general acceptance that estate duty in too many cases justified the sobriquet of a " voluntary tax." It was possible to transfer assets during one's lifetime and live for seven years, the prize for achieving this longevity being the knowledge that there would be no tax liability at one's death after having survived for seven years from the date of gift. Capital transfer tax is intended to make the imposition of capital taxation on the transmission of assets from generation to generation less arbitrary by taxing dispositions *inter vivos* as well as the transfer of value of a whole estate which takes place every time a death occurs. Capital transfer tax is chargeable by reference to two separate scales of duty. The first applies to the value transferred by a chargeable transfer made on or at any time within three years of the death of the transferor; the second, generally lower, scale of duty applies to all other transfers.[2] Thus, a taxable transfer of value will bear a lower rate of duty if the transferor lives for three years, and to this extent capital transfer tax still contains an element of " voluntariness," which must surely surprise those responsible for the introduction of the tax in the first place.

3–03 In the days of estate duty, the proceeds of life assurance policies which became a claim by death were often treated favourably. Although the historical origins of this favourable treatment were accidental, being based on an interpretation of the proviso to section 4, Finance Act 1894, which can hardly have been in the minds of the legislators, it was gradually accepted by successive governments that the provision

---

[1] F.A. 1965, s. 28 (2).
[2] F.A. 1975, s. 37.

of funds through life assurance, *inter alia* to help discharge estate duty liabilities, was socially acceptable. Unfortunately, this relatively benign attitude led ultimately to large-scale abuse, since what originally had been intended as relieving legislation was adapted to blatant and large-scale avoidance. Inevitably, this meant that the duty treatment of policies becoming claims by a death was made less generous, and by the time of the abolition of estate duty in 1975, life assurance played a much less vital role in estate planning than had applied in the days prior to the Finance Act 1968. The capital transfer tax legislation, hardly surprisingly, offers little by way of specific concession to those who choose to use life assurance as part of their estate planning. Despite this, there can be no doubt that life assurance does continue to play an important role in this area.

3-04 Capital transfer tax is similar to estate duty in many respects, particularly in so far as it affects the taxation of property to which a deceased was beneficially entitled immediately before his death. The prime utility of life assurance is for the provision of cash sums when death occurs. The art of the tax planner is to ensure that such funds are so directed that, when an estate owner dies, they are forthwith available in the right hands to discharge as much as possible of the capital transfer tax which then becomes payable in relation to the deceased's estate. Ideally, the claim value of the insurance policy should itself be exempt from capital transfer tax, and indeed the way the capital transfer tax charging sections are framed makes it unlikely that the mere fact of policy proceeds enuring to a third party at death will *per se* result in a tax charge.

The charge to capital transfer tax is by virtue of Finance Act 1975, ss. 19 and 20. The basic charging subsection 20 (2) states that " . . . a transfer of value is any disposition made by a person (' the transferor ') as a result of which the value of his estate immediately after the disposition is less than it would be but for the disposition; and the amount by which it is less is the value transferred by the transfer."

3-05 It can be seen that the basic test for imposing capital transfer tax is the diminution of the estate of the person making the transfer of value. If therefore, as will commonly occur in the case of a life policy drawn up under trust, when the taxpayer dies a benefit enures to third parties which does not have the effect of reducing the deceased's estate below its level immediately prior to the death, no capital transfer tax is payable prima facie. It is only if the terms of the policy trust are such that the death itself terminates or changes existing, or creates new, interests in possession that capital transfer tax could become payable. The ramifications of this are considered elsewhere.

3-06 The most common way in which a transfer of value for capital transfer tax purposes will be related to a life policy is where the life assured, or a third party, pays a premium in order to keep up a policy for the benefit of others. This will most usually occur when the policy is the subject of a trust. Under the estate duty legislation there was a complicated formula for calculating the value transferred (known under estate duty as " gifts of rights ") each time a premium was paid. The general result of this legislation was that the " transfer of value " procured by each gift of rights was in the early years of a typical policy considerably less than the premium, but in later years the value transferred by each successive premium progressively increased. Under capital transfer tax, the position is simpler, as for most practical purposes the *quantum* of the transfer of value each time a premium is paid is no more and no less than the premium itself. There is no equivalent in the capital transfer tax legislation to the special legislation, such as the Finance Act 1959, s. 34, which usually determined the *quantum*, if any, of estate duty liability.

3–07   Under estate duty, the charge was usually calculated by reference to the value of the policy at death of the life assured. This is not the case with capital transfer tax, although in the case of policies which fall into the life assured's own estate, there could be a problem if the normal capital transfer tax valuation rule were followed. The normal rules are that on the death of any person tax is charged as if immediately before his death he had made a transfer of value equal to the value of his estate immediately before his death, and that the value of any property so deemed to be transferred is its open market value at the time. A life policy, especially a term policy, immediately before the death of the life assured might well have only a speculative value, yet the life assured's death would result in the full death benefit accruing to his estate. The capital transfer tax legislation does in fact ensure that a life policy or any other asset which increases in value by virtue of the deceased's death falls into the taxable estate. Finance Act 1975, Sched. 10, para. 9 (1) (*a*) and 9 (2) ensure that what falls into the estate is not merely the policy market or surrender value immediately before the death, or the total of premiums paid prior to the death, but rather the full policy death benefit.

3–08   A transfer of value can naturally be related to a life policy in circumstances other than the payment of premiums—for example, where an existing policy on the life of the taxpayer is assigned to a third party. In such cases, the value transferred is calculated in accordance with Finance Act 1975, Sched. 10, para. 11, the broad effect of which is that the value transferred is taken as the greater of (a) all premiums paid before the transfer of value, less any value taken out of the policy by way of surrender prior to the transfer, and (b) the market value (which generally will be the surrender value) of the policy at the time of the transfer. However, term assurance policies which comply with certain simple rules are exempt from this provision, and in the case where the policy which is the subject of the transfer

17

of value is unit-linked, the value transferred is reduced by any reduction in the value of those units between the time they were allocated and the time of the transfer of value.

3–09 Under capital transfer tax, the broad principles in the case of a life policy drawn up under trust for others are (i) that the taxable *quantum* each time a premium is paid is the premium itself,[3] and (ii) provided that the death does not result in the creation or alteration of interests in possession in the policy proceeds, no capital transfer tax is payable when the death of the life assured occurs. How then can these broad principles be applied in order to provide financial benefits within the context of estate conservation?

It is sometimes overlooked that certain capital transfer tax exemptions and concessions are considerably more favourable to the taxpayer than were comparable provisions under estate duty. The range of exempt transfers found in Finance Act 1975, Sched. 6, Pt. I, as amended by Finance Act 1976, is of particular relevance within the context of the regular payment of life assurance premiums for the benefit of others. These exemptions are now considered individually.

Transfers between spouses

3–10 An outright gift from one spouse to another is an exempt transfer, with no limitation as to amount, provided that both spouses are domiciled in the United Kingdom.[4] The practical effect of this is that a spouse can insure his or her life for any amount and provided that the policy is expressed as a trust for the absolute benefit of any other spouse, no capital transfer tax will be payable irrespective of the size of the annual premium. This exemption would have particular utility in cases where one spouse is possessed of substantial assets, such as close company shares or agricultural land, which he or she wishes to will directly to children. Although capital transfer tax will be payable on the testamentary transfer of value to the children, estate planning will be considerably eased if it is known that when the insured spouse dies a substantial tax-free cash sum will become available to the surviving spouse.

Values not exceeding £2,000

3–11 " Transfers of value made by a transferor in any one year are exempt to the extent that the values transferred by them (calculated as values on which no tax is payable) do not exceed £2,000." [5]

3–12 If the transfer of value takes the form of the payment of a premium to keep up a life policy for donees, very substantial benefits may accrue. Indeed, it is probably true to state that the use of the " values not

---

[3] *Ibid.* s. 20 (2).
[4] *Ibid.* Sched. 6, para. 1.
[5] *Ibid.* Sched. 6, para. 2 (1) and F.A. 1976, s. 93 (1).

exceeding £2,000 " exemption represents the most significant way in which life assurance can be adapted within the framework of capital transfer tax so as to aid estate conservation. As has been noted above, when a transferor pays a premium to keep up a life policy for the benefit of others, the *quantum* of value transferred by payment of the premium will always be the premium itself. Also, provided that any policy trust is appropriately worded, no capital transfer tax will be payable on the policy claim value when death of the transferor occurs.

A young man of 30 might insure his life for the benefit of others, paying a gross annual premium of £2,000. This would buy whole life cover of about £200,000, or term assurance cover well in excess of £1 million, depending on the term in question. This question is considered in greater depth later in the chapter.

It should be noted that if part or all of the £2,000 exemption is not used in one tax year, it may be carried forward and utilised in the following tax year, but no later.[6]

Small gifts to same person

3-13   " Transfers of value made by a transferor in any one year by outright gifts to any one person are exempt to the extent that the values transferred by them (calculated as values on which no tax is chargeable) do not exceed £100." [7]

3-14   It will be noted that the wording of this exemption sub-paragraph is clearly intended to make the small gifts exemption available in addition to any other exemption which might be available. Therefore, if a life policy is drawn up under trust for one individual, or the transferor in some way keeps up the policy for the benefit of one person, it would be possible to pay an annual premium of up to £2,100, and no capital transfer tax would arise by virtue of the annual premium payment. The £100 small gifts exemption is added to the values not exceeding £2,000 exemption for this purpose.

3-15   The small gifts exemption does have one particular practical application in the life assurance field. There is available a wide range of policies designed to build up life assurance or investment benefits for minor children. Such policies are usually known by some such name as " child's deferred " policies, and typically a policy of this kind will give the child an option, on attainment of age 18 or 21, either to continue the policy as an insurance on its own life for its own benefit and on special terms, or to take as a cash sum the then investment value which the policy has built up during the child's minority.

3-16   It will be seen that a parent, grandparent, godparent or any other person having affinity with a child could effect a child's deferred policy

---

[6] *Ibid.* Sched. 6, para. 2 (2).
[7] F.A. 1975, Sched. 6, para. 4 (1).

for its benefit, paying an annual premium of up to £100, without in any way affecting the availability of other capital transfer tax exemptions. As there is no limitation to the number of persons who can be benefited by any one transferor, it can be seen that in the case, for example, of parents with five children, each spouse could transfer £500 annually to the children in this manner. Indeed, as each parent could also use up the values not exceeding £2,000 exemptions each year by paying premiums for the benefit of the children, it can be seen that in these circumstances the parents could between them transfer £5,000 annually to the children, and the whole of such annual transfer would be exempt assuming that no other taxable transfers of value were made. Over a period of 20 years, therefore, the parents could transfer £100,000 to their children without paying a penny of capital transfer tax.

Normal expenditure out of income

3–17   " A transfer of value is an exempt transfer if, or to the extent that it is shown—

   (a) that it was made as part of the normal expenditure of the transferor; and

   (b) that (taking one year with another) it was made out of his income; and

   (c) that, after allowing for all transfers of value forming part of his normal expenditure, the transferor was left with sufficient income to maintain his usual standard of living." [8]

It is never satisfactory when the incidence of taxation can depend upon the outcome of a subjective test. To that extent, the normal expenditure out of income exemption for capital transfer tax purposes is indeed unsatisfactory, since the closer the taxpayer moves to the margin between what is and what is not normal expenditure out of income, the more uncertain must be the fiscal consequences of his generosity.

3–18   The capital transfer tax normal expenditure exemption is more or less on all fours with the equivalent estate duty exemption provided by Finance Act 1968, s. 37 (1). Both exemptions, although wholly dependent on the concept of subjectivity, are at least an improvement on the original equivalent exemption from estate duty provided by section 59 (2) of the Finance (1909–10) Act 1910. It will be recalled (hardly with nostalgia) by practitioners of long standing that the wording of the 1910 exemption was such that it was necessary to prove that the deceased's largesse was " reasonable " provision for his beneficiaries. However, it was never finally established under the 1910 legislation whether " normal and reasonable " expenditure out of

---

[8] *Ibid.* Sched. 6, para. 5 (1).

capital, rather than income, did or did not qualify for the exemption. It might perhaps appear churlish to complain that the capital transfer tax "normal expenditure" exemption depends on a subjective test, when the wording is a model of clarity as compared with the ambiguity of the old (pre–1968) estate duty wording.

3-19 In a book of this kind to make the observation that the test of what is normal expenditure out of income is a subjective one is really to say all. However, it is perhaps worth noting that whereas it might be normal for a person with a net income after tax of £4,000 to be in the habit of giving away say £1,500 of that income each year, it might also be quite abnormal for a person with an income after tax of £12,000 to give away even £100 of that income. On the other hand, presumably it would be accepted by the courts, if not by a sceptical Revenue, as quite normal for a taxpayer with an after-tax income of £12,000 annually to give away one half of that income. However, it is fairly obvious that availability of the normal expenditure exemption is another factor to be considered in advising a taxpayer on what level of insurance he should effect for estate conservation purposes. We have noted so far that on a cumulative basis, a person with five children might pay premiums of up to £2,500 annually, without risk of there being any capital transfer tax liability. Perhaps it is a pious hope that a person with five children might also be in a position to make regular gifts out of his income, but certainly in cases known to the author it has been considered that even leaving out of account the small gifts exemption, a father could pay a premium of £4,000 to build up an insurance benefit for his family, with every confidence that £2,000 of that premium would qualify for normal expenditure exemption.

3-20 Finance Act 1975, Sched. 6, para. 5 (2) contains an anti-avoidance measure specifically aimed at certain types of life assurance based arrangement. The measure in question is that where a life assurance premium or a gift of money or money's worth which is applied directly or indirectly in payment of such a premium, is paid to keep up a policy on the transferor's life, the payment of the premium is not to be regarded as normal expenditure out of income if a purchased life annuity is in existence on the life of the transferor. This measure is intended to counteract a favourite estate duty avoidance measure, whereby it was possible for an estate owner significantly to increase his after-tax income by buying an annuity on his life, and to devote part or all of the enhanced income to keeping up duty free life assurance for the benefit of members of his family.

3-21 This anti-avoidance provision does not apply if it is shown that the effecting of the insurance policy and the purchase of the annuity were not associated operations. It is understood that the official Revenue view of the meaning of this is that the transactions will not be considered as associated operations if it can be demonstrated that the insurance company concerned would have granted the life assurance on the same terms, irrespective of the annuity being purchased from the same insurance company. This whole question is considered in greater depth in Chapter 5 which deals with back to back schemes.

It should be noted that whether or not the effecting of the life policy and the granting of the annuity are associated operations, it is not possible for the purpose of the normal expenditure exemption to include in the transferor's net income the non-taxable capital element contained in the annuity. This applies in every case where the annuity was purchased after November 12, 1974, and in relation to transfers of value made after April 5, 1975.[9]

Gifts in consideration of marriage

3–22   " (1) Transfers of value made by gifts in consideration of marriage are exempt to the extent that the values transferred by such transfers made by any one transferor in respect of any one marriage (calculated as values on which no tax is payable) do not exceed—

(*a*) in the case of gifts within sub-paragraph (2) below by a parent of a party to the marriage, £5,000;

(*b*) in the case of other gifts within sub-paragraph (2) below, £2,500; and

(*c*) in any other case £1,000;

any excess being attributed to the transfers in proportion to the values transferred.

(2) A gift is within this sub-paragraph if—

(*a*) it is an outright gift to a child or remoter descendant of the transferor, or

(*b*) the transferor is a parent or remoter ancestor of either party to the marriage, and either the gift is an outright gift to the other party to the marriage or the property comprised in the gift is settled by the gift, or

(*c*) the transferor is a party to the marriage, and either the gift is an outright gift to the other party to the marriage or the property comprised in the gift is settled by the gift;

and in this paragraph 'child' includes an illegitimate child, an adopted child and a step-child and 'parent,' 'descendant' and 'ancestor' shall be construed accordingly." [10]

3–23 So that each of the parents of each party to a marriage can make transfers of value of up to £5,000 to his or her child, and those transfers are exempt from capital transfer tax. The putative parents-in-law and ancestors other than parents, are restricted to exempt transfers of value not exceeding £2,500. Finally, relatives who are not direct ancestors of the parties to the marriage, and all other persons, may

---

[9] *Ibid.* Sched. 6, para. 5 (3).   [10] *Ibid.* Sched. 6, para. 6 (1), (2).

make transfers of value not exceeding £1,000 and fall within the exemption.

3–24　　Since the 1968 legislation which imposed potential charges to higher rate income tax on the proceeds of maturing single premium policies, there has been comparatively little incentive to make gifts in consideration of marriage comprising such policies. Although a single premium whole of life policy with profits effected on the life of a parent of one of the parties to the marriage would often be an attractive commercial proposition, in most cases uncertainty as to the amount of higher rate tax payable on the profit element when the parent eventually dies [11] makes this kind of marriage consideration gift less attractive than in former years.

3–25　　It is suggested that the best tactical use of the marriage consideration exemption so as to provide life assurance benefit would be if a parent gifted to his or her child on marriage an annual premium life assurance policy, coupled with a covenant to keep up the premiums. For example, a father aged 55 could effect on his own life a whole life policy with profits for a sum assured of £16,000 at a gross annual premium of £500. The policy might be drawn up as a trust for the absolute benefit of his son about to be married, the trust stating that it was effected in consideration of the son's marriage. Simultaneously, and for the same consideration, the father would covenant to keep up renewal premiums for a term of not less than nine years. The initial premium payment, plus the payment of each of the nine next annual premiums, would represent transfers of value totalling £5,000, which would be wholly exempt from capital transfer tax as a gift in consideration of marriage, assuming that no other marriage consideration gift was made by the father to his son at or around the time of the marriage.

3–26　　At the end of the tenth policy year, the policy could be converted to a paid up contract, when the reduced death benefit inclusive of accrued bonuses might typically be around £12,000. This death benefit would increase progressively with the addition of further bonuses, and if the father died say at age 80 the tax free sum then received by his son could be of the order of £20,000. Of course, it would not be imperative for premiums to cease after 10 years. The father could continue paying them, and as the premium in any event is only £500 annually, premium payments after the tenth year might well not attract capital transfer tax because of falling in one of the other exemptions. Alternatively, the son could elect to meet premiums himself from the eleventh year onwards. As a matter of interest, if premiums were maintained for a further 10 years after the marriage consideration exemption was exhausted by the payment of the tenth annual premium, the approximate value of the policy if the father died at age 80 could be of the order of £36,000.

---

[11] Taxes Act 1970, ss. 394, 395.

Life assurance relief

3–27   As was noted earlier in this chapter, the *quantum* of value transferred for capital transfer tax purposes is the reduction in the estate
of the disponer. In the case where the transfer of value relates to rights
under a life policy which the transferor is keeping up for the benefit
of others, the value transferred each time a premium is paid may be
reduced by the incidence of income tax relief. For example, if the
transferor pays a gross annual premium of £2,000 to keep up a policy
on his life for the benefit of his children, he may be entitled to income
tax relief of up to £350.[12] The maximum relief of £350 would be
available if his taxable income in any year that he paid a premium
was at least £12,000 and he paid no other insurance premiums qualifying
for income tax relief. It seems therefore that the value transferred
each time a premium paid would be £1,650, and not the full £2,000
represented by the gross premium. Indeed, in the case of qualifying
premiums paid after April 5, 1979, the life assured transferor is permitted to deduct 17½ per cent. of gross premiums totalling no more
than £1,500, paying only the appropriate net premium over to the
insurance company.[13] If total premiums exceed £1,500, income tax
relief of up to 17½ per cent. on any excess will continue to be available
as now, subject to the usual statutory limitation that relief is not
granted on premiums in excess of one-sixth of the taxpayer's total
income. However, whether or not income tax relief on premiums paid
is available, and the extent (if any) to which it in fact is limited in the
case of any one policy because the person paying the premium has
other qualifying assurance premium expenditure will very much depend
on individual circumstances from year to year. Also, it must remain a
moot point how income tax is apportioned as between policies kept
up for the benefit of others, and policies for the taxpayer's own benefit,
in cases where some premiums would be transfers of value for capital
transfer tax purposes and some would not.

For simplicity in this chapter and throughout the book generally,
the possible impact of life assurance relief on the value transferred by
the payment of life assurance premiums which rank as a gift is ignored,
but it must be remembered that in appropriate circumstances the relief
undoubtedly will reduce the quantum of value transferred. The point
is particularly significant in considering availability of the various
capital transfer tax exemptions.

FUNDING THE LIABILITY AT DEATH
Introduction

3–28   As applied with the old estate duty, capital transfer tax payable at
death is more often than not a potential liability which if properly

---

[12] *Ibid.* s. 19.
[13] F.A. 1976, Sched. 4, para. 5.

planned for, can be met without undue strain on family finances. The fact that in far too many cases payment of death duties results in financial stringency or even difficulty is all too often a reflection of the deceased's refusal to make proper arrangements during his lifetime to ease the financial burden at his death. Although it is the fashion to suppose that a book which deals with taxation matters is *per se* based on advice as to legitimate methods of tax avoidance, it will be seen that this book, and this chapter in particular, is concerned much more with tax *mitigation*. This means the easing of the burden of the liability, as opposed to its avoidance. In other words, the true role of the estate planner is not at all to show how tax can be avoided: rather it is to encourage estate owners and taxpayers to manage their financial affairs by reference to the highest rather than the lowest standard of efficiency. It is a source of constant surprise and gratification to the author how frequently taxpayers seem to be convinced that through careful planning a magic wand has been waved over the management of their affairs, whereas in fact all that has happened is that the taxpayer has been shown how the practical application to his affairs of certain fundamental principles can transform an apparently hopeless position into one where the next generation of taxpayers will, after all, still require to take advice on estate conservation.

3–29 Capital transfer tax which becomes payable at a death amounts to one thing only: the need for there to be tax-free cash available in the right hands and as quickly as possible to discharge the tax liability. Until tax which may not be postponed is paid, probate cannot be granted so that the deceased's assets are frozen. If the estate is relatively illiquid, for example, because a large proportion comprises agricultural land or close company shares, probate can only be obtained by borrowing money from the bank or in effect from the Treasury at 6 per cent. perhaps with no income tax relief,[14] which throws yet another financial burden on the successors in title. A properly arranged life policy produces cash in the right hands immediately upon receipt by the insurance company of proof of death and of title to the policy; cash therefore can be available in good time before the granting of probate. This is one of the features of life assurance which makes it an especially appropriate medium for capital transfer tax funding.

3–30 Another reason why life assurance is so useful within this context is to be found in the whole structure of a typical life assurance contract. It is essentially a contract whereby an insurance company agrees to pay out a certain sum of money, in exchange for the annual payment of a premium which is fixed in amount at the outset of the contract. Usually, the insurance company's financial commitment is substantially in excess of the policyholder's total premium commitment. Particularly in the case of a with profits policy, it is usually impossible to envisage

---

[14] F.A. 1975, Sched. 4, para. 19 (1).

any circumstance where the return under the policy in the shape of the death benefit, will not very substantially exceed the total number of premiums paid. Because an insurance policy represents a unique financial investment in this sense, it is perhaps only surprising that life assurance is not much more widely used in estate conservation exercises than in fact it is. A with profits whole life policy is certainly a unique commercial contract, being entirely the product of actuarial reasoning, yet the fact is that it is as good as capable of *guaranteeing* that when the contract comes to an end by death of the life assured, the cash paid out will invariably exceed very substantially the cash paid in by way of premiums. Hence, the contract comes to maturity and produces a very substantial tax-free cash profit, at precisely the time when cash is most needed.

Typical Policy Return

3-31   The best way to illustrate the point that whole of life assurance is a uniquely suitable tool for funding capital transfer tax payable at death is to quote some typical figures. The figures shown below show typical returns under what has already established itself as one of the most appropriate contracts for use as an estate conservation aid. The contract in question is a " joint life and survivorship " policy. This is a contract dependent on each of two lives, which does not make any payment until the death of the surviving life. It is commonly referred to simply as a joint life policy, and that is the description which will be used throughout this chapter.

3-32   For very many years, the joint life policy was one of those contracts which most life offices were prepared to underwrite, but which was rarely issued in practice, for the simple reason that there were relatively few practical applications requiring a policy which would not pay out until the death of the survivor of two lives. The reason for the contract emerging from this obscurity and now forming a prominent part of the sales kit of every insurance salesman, is to be found in the capital transfer tax legislation. Transfers *inter vivos* or at death between spouses both of whom are domiciled in the United Kingdom are exempt from capital transfer tax, with no limitation to the exemption. In the case where the transferor spouse is United Kingdom domiciled, and the transferee spouse is not, there is a quantum restriction of £15,000 which qualifies for the exemption.[15] It is probably true that in the majority of all estates involving significant assets, it is now sensible for spouses living together to have reciprocal wills whereby each leaves to the other absolutely or in trust the greatest possible proportion of his or her estate. Capital transfer tax will then not become payable until the death of the surviving spouse, and the most obvious financial benefits arising from this are

---

[15] *Ibid.* Sched. 6.

first that the survivor has the use of more assets than would apply if tax were payable by reference to the first death, and secondly that estate planning becomes rather more certain.[16] One technique which has immediately evolved as a result of there being greater certainty as to *when* capital transfer tax will strike, as compared with the position under the old estate duty, is the funding of tax payable at the death of the survivor, through life assurance.

3-33   In the table of figures below, it is assumed in each case that a husband and wife, the wife being five years junior in age, decide to pay between them a gross annual premium of £1,000 in order to maintain a joint life policy with profits, effected on their own lives. It is assumed for illustration purposes that in the case of each policy the wife survives her husband and dies at the age of 75. As throughout this book, with profits figures quoted are based on good typical with profits contracts such as are available from a very wide selection of reputable insurance companies.

Ages of male/ female lives at inception	Initial sum assured	Claim value at age 75 of survivor	Total Premiums Paid	Crude Profit
	£	£	£	£
35/30	55,000	280,000	45,000	235,000
45/50	42,000	144,000	35,000	109,000
55/50	31,000	71,000	25,000	46,000
65/60	21,000	32,000	15,000	17,000

So that in every case, provided premiums are kept up until the death of the surviving spouse, the expected death benefit amounts to at least twice the sum paid in by way of premiums. It is difficult to envisage any mode of investment more suited to the funding of capital transfer tax than a good insurance policy.

3-34   There is usually available a choice as to the contractual liability to pay premiums under a joint life policy. Specifically, premiums may and may not be limited to cease after a fixed number of years, say 20 or 30: and perhaps of greater significance, they may continue at the same level after the death of the first life, or may be reduced to say one-half or two-thirds of the original level. In the case where the premium reduces after the first death, it is obvious that the initial sum assured is bound to be lower than in the case where premiums are maintained at the same level throughout. Since the whole point of a joint life policy will in most cases be to fund capital transfer tax, planning should be based on maintaining the highest possible level of cover throughout. After all, one of the risks which life assurance is ideally suited to protect against is that of both of the two spouses

---

[16] See however the example at § 3-37 which highlights a *taxation* disadvantage of " reciprocal " wills.

dying close together or simultaneously, for example as the result of an accident. If that happens and there are young children to be cared for, the greater level of life assurance protection which is available the better.

3–35   The reason usually put forward for premiums reducing after the death of the first spouse is that the survivor might find it more difficult to continue meeting the premium. It is hard to follow this reasoning as in practically all cases living expenses will reduce following the first death, and it is suggested that if estate owners do find this point worrying, then provision should be made in the wills giving trustees of the estates powers to apply trust assets (whether capital or income) to the payment of life assurance premiums. Better still would probably be a discretionary power specifically to advance capital to the extent that the surviving spouse could use that capital to keep up an insurance on the spouse's life, whether or not the policy is for the personal benefit of the spouse. Payments which in practice are made out of the estate by the trustees, in accordance with this power, would not attract capital transfer tax since the transfer of value would be an exempt transaction.

Funding from Capital

3–36   A vital principle involved here is that by taking a conscious decision regularly to rearrange a small proportion of capital, it is possible for the estate owner to take highly effective action ensuring the conservation of most, if not all, of the estate for the benefit of future generations. Time and again, when it is suggested that an insurance policy should be considered as part of an estate planning exercise, the estate owner objects that he cannot afford to pay the premium. Invariably, what he means is that if he was asked to regard the premium as a regular charge against his net income he might indeed have great difficulty in meeting the commitment. Yet in fact, there is nothing more logical than regarding the regular payment of life assurance premiums as being a planned transfer of capital designed solely to protect the very capital from which the premium payments are met. The fact that by transferring capital in this fashion the taxpayer will very often enjoy life assurance relief which otherwise he might never have claimed is in more cases than not an unexpected bonus. It is, however, worth making the point that within the normal limitations, life assurance relief means that whilst basic rate income tax is 35 per cent., up to 17·5 per cent. of the cost of premiums to fund capital transfer tax liabilities is recovered from the Revenue by way of income tax relief. The very thought of this should be sufficient to inspire many a recalcitrant estate owner to do something rather than nothing about conserving his assets.

3–37   Consider an estate of £500,000 divided equally between husband and wife, who have three children. If, at the first death, the deceased in his will leaves the entire estate directly to the children, the estate of £250,000 will suffer capital transfer tax of £114,750, leaving a net amount of £135,250 to the children. If, on the other hand, at the first death the deceased's estate devolves absolutely or in trust for life to the surviving spouse, no capital transfer tax will be payable at the time of the death. Ultimately however, at the death of the surviving spouse, the combined estate of £500,000 will at that point suffer capital transfer tax, and the amount of tax payable on the estate of £500,000 would significantly exceed that which would have applied to two separate estates of £250,000 taxed separately. The differences in amounts of tax payable are shown below, the first column being based on the wills of each spouse leaving everything directly to the children, the second column being based on reciprocal wills leaving the whole of the estate of the first to die to the surviving spouse:

	Nothing to Survivor	*All to Survivor*
	£	£
Combined estates	500,000	500,000
Less: Capital transfer tax	229,500	264,750
NET ESTATE TO SUCCESSORS	£270,500	£235,250

The addition of the deceased spouse's assets for capital transfer tax to the assets of the surviving spouse is known as "bunching." The foregoing figures demonstrate that in the case of an estate of £500,000 equally divided between husband and wife, a decision to accept bunching of the estates is a decision in principle to pay approximately £35,000 more capital transfer tax by the time the estate of the surviving spouse has been settled.

3-38   Assume that husband and wife possessed of combined assets of £500,000 decided to insure their lives on a joint life basis, paying a gross annual premium of £3,000. The policy is effected as a simple trust for the absolute benefit of the three children of the marriage in equal shares. The present age next birthday of the husband is 55 and the wife is five years younger. The initial level of life cover provided on a with profits basis, is £93,000. This basic level of life cover increases annually with the accrual of bonuses and it is projected, based on past records and the insurance company's expectations for the future, that if premiums are fully maintained until the death of the survivor, that death occurring in the twenty-fifth policy year, the death benefit payable under the with profits policy will actually be £210,000 or thereabouts. However, husband and wife each contributes £1,500 annually towards the premium cost, and each £1,500 is raised out of capital so that there is no strain on spouses' joint income position throughout the policy term.[17] Payment of each premium is a transfer of value in favour of the children of the marriage who are the three beneficiaries under the policy trust, but the *quantum* of value transferred annually is restricted to the premium, the practical effect being that no capital transfer tax is payable by virtue of the premium payments. Indeed, each spouse is in the position to give away annually up to an extra £500 before exhausting his or her values not exceeding £2,000 annual exemption.

3-39   Assuming that the surviving spouse dies in the twenty-fifth policy year—*i.e.* either husband survives wife and dies at age 80, or wife survives husband and dies at age 75—the approximate estate position will be:

	£
Original taxable estate	500,000
Insurance premiums	75,000
Reduced taxable estate	425,000
Less: Capital transfer tax	219,750
Estate net of tax	205,250
Add: Tax-free policy proceeds	210,000
TOTAL AMOUNT TO SUCCESSORS	415,250
Net estate if no life policy	235,250
GAIN TO SUCCESSORS	£180,000

3-40   On the assumptions stated then, the capital inheritance of the children at the death of their surviving parent is improved by approximately 80 per cent. It must be noted first that the removal of £75,000 from the taxable estate into a whole life policy reduces the amount of capital transfer tax actually payable at the second death by £45,000; secondly that the projected policy claim value equates almost exactly to the reduced capital transfer tax liability on the estate; and thirdly, that these figures are calculated assuming level values, taking no account of inflation.

Inflation

3-41   The impact of inflation on future asset values is a crucial consideration; undoubtedly some attempt should be made to take this issue into account in estate planning. In the example under consideration, it might be assumed that inflation will result in the value

----

[17] Indeed, joint income after tax would usually increase since life assurance relief (maximum £525) will substantially exceed net income lost from the realised capital.

of the combined estate increasing by 3 per cent. annually on average
for a term of 25 years. In that case, the impact of the with profits
life policy costing £3,000 per annum would be somewhat as follows:

	Without Policy £	*With policy* £
Taxable estate	1,047,000	933,000
Less: Capital transfer tax	622,650	546,200
	424,350	386,800
Add: Tax-free policy proceeds	—	210,000
NET ESTATE TO SUCCESSORS	£424,350	£596,800

3–42   On this basis, the improvement to estate to successors brought about
by the policy is about 40 per cent. whereas assuming that values remain
constant, the improvement is in excess of 80 per cent. To be on the
safe side, the foregoing illustration assumes that inflation would not
result in an increase in the claim value of the policy after 25 years,
although in practice the value would probably be well in excess of
£210,000. Nevertheless, any increase in the projected policy benefit
is unlikely to affect the fundamental principle illustrated by these
figures—which is that estate planning certainly should take account
of inflation. It will be seen from the example that whereas assuming
a level estate throughout, the capital transfer tax problem is comfortably contained by a life policy, if one assumes a very modest future
inflation rate, the policy proceeds could well be quite inadequate to meet
the full amount of tax. Although in dealing with an estate of this size
it is most unlikely that life insurance would be the only method of
capital transfer tax mitigation utilised, it would certainly seem that
there is a strong case for increasing the agreed annual premium commitment as much as possible above the tentative figure of £3,000.

Although level figures are used throughout this book for illustration,
the crucial impact which inflation is liable to have on any estate conservation exercise must never be overlooked. The extent to which
allowance is made for the inevitable distortion which would be brought
about by inflation would always be a matter for personal judgment,
but there is no doubt that the practitioner has a duty to take the factor
into account when framing his advice.

Short-term protection

3–43   In the earlier example, it was noted that a gross annual premium of
£3,000 would secure initial with profits cover of about £93,000, steadily
increasing over 25 years, at which point the death benefit is projected
to be £210,000. In the event of the early death of both insured spouses,

31

the death benefit under the policy would be relatively low, and would probably be inadequate to meet even one-half of the capital transfer tax liability. One way of dealing with this problem would be to effect a second insurance policy on the joint lives. The policy would be decreasing term, commencing with a relatively high level of cover in the early years but gradually reducing, roughly mirroring the build-up of bonuses under the main with profits whole life policy.

3–44 As an example, £100,000 of decreasing term assurance reducing by £5,000 annually for 20 years might be effected. The cost of such cover is comparatively low. In the case of the spouses in the illustration (husband 55 and wife 50 next birthday) the level of decreasing term cover can be provided at an annual premium of about £220 payable for 13 years only. Thus, by increasing the annual premium commitment from £3,000 to £3,220, the parents could provide substantially greater protection of their estate for the children, the immediate death benefit being increased to £193,000. By the end of the twentieth year, when the decreasing term cover would expire, the claim value under the with profits joint life policy should have increased to somewhere in the region of £185,000. Naturally, it would be desirable for decreasing term cover effected for this purpose to be drawn up under trust, the trust being identical to that which determines the destination of the main joint life policy proceeds.

Separate estate basis

3–45 There will frequently be perfectly good reasons why a husband and wife would prefer that at death the whole of each estate should go directly to the children or other beneficiaries. This is perhaps most likely to be the case where an estate is made up largely of family company shares, an interest in an agricultural partnership, or some other asset where awkward questions of control could be thrown up if the asset in question passed into the hands of professional or family trustees who had the task of administering a trust for the lifetime benefit of the surviving spouse. Also, many a parent will take the view that he or she knows that the surviving spouse will have more than sufficient assets to look after his or her material wellbeing, so can see no reason why the children should have to wait until the death of the survivor before inheriting assets.

Another relatively common family position would be where one spouse is significantly younger than the other, in which case the children's chances of ultimate inheritance could be greatly reduced, if the surviving spouse decided to remarry. It would then be perfectly understandable that he or she would wish to leave his or her own estate to the step-parent, in which case the children of the first marriage could in any event find their expectations of inheritance curtailed.

3-46   Finally, there is the point made earlier in this chapter concerning bunching of estates. It may be recalled that additional transfer tax of £35,000 can be payable on a combined estate of £500,000 if, at the first death, the whole of the deceased's assets goes for life or absolutely to the surviving spouse, rather than missing him or her entirely. No matter how careful the estate planning, the possibility of having to pay an extra £35,000 of tax at the second death must be a very strong incentive for parents seriously to consider each cutting the other entirely out of his or her will. A prerequisite for this rather drastic action would often be the levelling up (or down) of estates by tax-free transfers between the spouses.

Reverting to our separate estates of £250,000 each owned by a father aged 55 and a mother aged 50 next birthday, suppose that each decides to insure his or her own life for the direct benefit of the children. Instead of a joint life policy premium of £3,000 as previously, it is now the case that each parent pays a premium of £1,500 out of his or her own capital to insure his or her own life. In the case of the husband, the initial level of life cover is about £29,000, whereas in the case of the wife it is about £40,000. On the assumptions that each spouse has a will leaving the whole of the estate directly to the children, and that the husband dies at age 75 whereas the wife survives to age 80, the approximate revised estate positions will become:

	Husband £	Wife £
Original taxable estate	250,000	250,000
Less: Insurance premiums	30,000	37,500
Reduced taxable estate	220,000	212,500
Less: Capital transfer tax	106,750	92,250
Estate net of tax	113,250	120,250
Add: Tax-free policy proceeds	68,000	134,000
TOTAL AMOUNT TO SUCCESSORS	181,250	254,250
Net estate if no life policy	135,250	135,250
GAIN TO SUCCESSORS	£46,000	£119,000

3-47   Whereas in the earlier illustration involving a joint life policy there was an improvement of about 80 per cent. in the net estate to successors, in this case the overall improvement under the two separate estates is about 61 per cent. The reduction in benefit is explained by the fact that the husband, in the case of the separate estate exercise, dies five years earlier than his wife, so that the return on premiums under his policy is comparatively modest. Even so, the life policy which falls in at his death will produce sufficient cash in the hands of the children to discharge about 65 per cent. of the tax liability on their father's estate.

Large Estates

3–48   A correctly arranged insurance policy tends to provide a greater proportionate benefit the larger the size of the taxable estate. For example, consider two estates, equally divided between husband and wife who are currently aged 65 and 60 respectively, with reciprocal wills leaving the whole of each estate to the surviving spouse. It is decided in each case to build up capital transfer tax funds by a regular annual transfer by way of premium into a joint life policy of 1 per cent. of the capital value of the combined estates. In each case, the wife survives the husband and dies at her age 75, so that premiums have been kept up for 15 years up to the time of death. In the first case, the combined estate is £500,000; in the second case it is £1 million. The revised estate positions, assuming of course that the life policies are drawn up under trust so that the policy proceeds do not attract tax when the second death occurs, are as follows:

	£	£
Original taxable estate	500,000	1,000,000
Less: Insurance premiums	75,000	150,000
	425,000	* 844,375
Less: Capital transfer tax	219,750	488,595
Estate net of tax	205,250	355,780
Add: Tax-free policy proceeds	160,000	320,000
TOTAL AMOUNT TO SUCCESSORS	365,250	675,780
Net estate if no life policy	235,250	410,250
GAIN TO SUCCESSORS	£130,000	£265,530
Percentage improvement	55·26	64·72

    * Allowing for tax already paid by transferor on *inter vivos* transfers of value relating to first 12 years' premiums.

3–49   In the case of the smaller estate, the gross annual life assurance premium is £5,000, and it is assumed that £4,000 of this will be exempt, absorbing the spouses' combined annual transfers not exceeding £2,000 exemptions. It is further assumed that the extra £1,000 of annual premium is exempt under the normal expenditure from income exemption. In the case of the larger estate, it is assumed that £5,000 of the annual premium is exempt for the same reasons, but that the balance of £5,000 each year attracts capital transfer tax as an *inter vivos* transfer of value. The reasons why there is a proportionately greater benefit in the case of the larger estate, even though the premium paid in each case amounts to exactly 1 per cent. of the combined taxable estates, are as follows:

(1) The general principle that where capital is transferred out of a potentially taxable estate and into tax-free life policy proceeds, the higher the potential overall rate of tax on the estate, the greater must be the potential benefit.

(2) In the case of the larger estate, a proportion of each year's premium transfer of value is taxable. However, the transfer attracts tax at the lower *inter vivos* transfers rate. This means that a proportion of each premium enjoys the benefits for tax purposes of this lower rate, instead of being retained as part of the combined taxable estate which suffers the higher rate of capital transfer tax at the death of the surviving spouse.

3–50   This final illustration of the use of life assurance as a capital transfer tax funding vehicle has purposely been calculated so as to illustrate what must be something like an optimum benefit scheme. In particular, it will be noticed that the illustration was based on the husband's age 65 at commencement, when the joint life expectancy is comparatively short, yet even so it is possible to postulate an increase of something like 65 per cent. in the ultimate inheritance of successors in title, merely through the rational rearrangement of no more than 1 per cent. of the combined estate capital. That benefits of the level indicated can be achieved through the careful use of life assurances is irrefutable, yet it is surprising how very infrequently estate owners and their advisers are disposed to embrace life assurance as the lynchpin of an overall estate conservation exercise.

Funding from Income

3–51   The practical significance of the capital transfer tax normal expenditure out of income exemption in relation to life assurance was considered earlier in this chapter. It is therefore only necessary at this point to stress that since effecting a life policy involves entering into a regular income commitment, probably on a monthly or yearly basis, the mere effecting of the policy should *per se* establish the normality of the expenditure by way of insurance premium for the purpose of this exemption.

3–52   The availablity of this exemption in relation to the payment of life assurance premiums should never be overlooked, although experience in the short time since capital transfer tax became operative in March 1974 shows that in practice it often is. The real importance of the normal expenditure exemption within this context is to be found in its interaction with other exemptions, and specifically the values not exceeding £2,000 annual exemption. Consider an example where husband and wife each has a substantial income, either from investments or from earnings, and where between them they pay a premium of £4,000 to keep up a joint life policy. There is no doubt that the annual £4,000 transfer of value is exempt, if the payment is regarded as absorbing each spouse's annual £2,000 exemption. It might however be difficult for either spouse to establish, if he or she wished to make occasional gifts of say £1,000 to children or grandchildren, that those additional transfers of value were exempt. Even though in practice the spouses might be capable of making such transfers out of their income, the occasional nature of transfers of value over and above the insurance premiums could call in question whether the additional expenditure was normal.

3-53   It is preferable in this case that as much as is practicable of the £4,000 joint annual premium should be established firmly as qualifying for the normal expenditure exemption from outset. This will mean that only that proportion of the £4,000 annual premium which is not normal expenditure will count against the joint annual transfers not exceeding £2,000 exemption which in this case totals £4,000. The balance of the combined annual £2,000 exemption will then be available to enable the spouses to make occasional additional transfers within the £2,000 annual limits, without any risk of those transfers being taxable.

3-54   It will be necessary for an account to be submitted every year with a specific view to claiming the normal income exemption in relation to the appropriate proportion of the £4,000 annual premium which is considered so to qualify. Reference was made earlier to the subjectivity of the test for normal income exemption, and in all cases where it is considered that the exemption is applicable, it is essential that the position be negotiated and agreed with the Inland Revenue so as to avoid the possibility of *ex post facto* dispute.

Funding a Liability Inter Vivos

3-55   The same principles which have been considered in relation to transfers of value which occur at a death can be applied to help ease the burden of tax where it is wished to pass assets on during an estate owner's lifetime. In principle, it must be right not only to absorb as fully as possible all annual and other capital transfer tax exemptions, for which purpose life assurance is particularly well suited, but also it must be right to make the greatest possible practical use of the lower tax scale applicable to lifetime transfers.

3-56   Consider an estate with a market value well in excess of £500,000 but including agricultural land valued for capital transfer tax purposes, after agricultural rate relief, at £200,000. Application of the agricultural relief has the effect of reducing the total potential transferable value, for capital transfer tax purposes, to exactly £500,000. It is particularly desired that the agricultural land remains intact within the family, and at the moment there is a 10-year-old son who shows every prospect of shaping up to be a fitting recipient of the estate in due course. For simplicity, it will be assumed that the total taxable estate is owned by the father, the mother being of independent means, to the extent that the spouses have agreed that neither will should leave any interest to the surviving spouse.

3–57   If no action were taken, and it was decided that the agricultural land would pass to the son under the father's will the total amount of duty payable at the death would be £264,750, leaving a net estate of £235,250. Ignoring the relatively small amount of deferment which would be available if it were elected to pay the tax relating to the agricultural land by instalments, it can be seen that only about £35,000 of assets other than the agricultural land would be left. The tax specifically apportionable to the agricultural land would be £105,900.

3–58   If on the other hand it were decided to transfer the agricultural land to the son during the lifetime of the father, the amount of tax payable on the transfer should not exceed £51,375 after agricultural relief, assuming that the father had made no other chargeable transfers during his lifetime. The father might therefore decide to effect an endowment assurance with profits on his own life, drawn up as a trust for the absolute benefit of his son, paying a gross annual premium of £2,500. The expected maturity value of the policy, at the end of 15 years, would be £56,000, so that at maturity of the policy the son would receive a tax-free payment of that amount, thus placing him in funds to discharge the capital transfer tax on the transfer to him of the agricultural estate. He will also have available a small surplus, which should be adequate to meet the stamp duty payable on the transfer.

3–59   Assuming that the payment of the annual premium of £2,500 is an exempt transfer (absorbing the father's transfers not exceeding £2,000 and normal expenditure exemptions) the land worth well in excess of £200,000 will have passed from one generation to the next without the payment of any capital transfer tax by the father. Further, by making the transferee (the son) liable for the tax, the necessity to gross up the transfer of value by the father for tax purposes is avoided. In the case of lifetime transfers, the calculation of the tax is by reference to the reduction in the value of the estate of the transferor, and in making the calculation it is necessary to cumulate any capital transfer tax borne by the donor as a result of his transfers of value. Putting the prospective transferee in funds so that he can discharge the liability can be of crucial significance. Thus, in the present case the amount of capital transfer tax payable by the transferor if it were decided that the father should pay the tax, would be no less than £109,687, compared with £51,375 if the son pays.

3–60   It was noted above that if no transfer of value out of this estate took place until the father's death, the tax payable would be £264,750. Assuming that no other transfers take place apart from the £200,000 agricultural estate going to the son, the capital transfer tax payable on the father's retained £300,000 at his death will be £180,000, and adding in the tax of £51,375 paid in respect of the lifetime transfer to the son, the total tax payable on the estate becomes £231,375. Hence, by taking advantage of the lower scale of tax applicable to lifetime transfers, there is in this instance a tax saving of £33,375. In practice, the saving might well be greater if part at least of the cost of the endowment assurance premiums was met out of the father's capital, since this naturally would have the effect of reducing his retained taxable estate below the level of £300,000.

3–61   It is always necessary to allow for the way in which capital transfer tax interacts with other taxes. In the case just considered, there may well be a capital gains tax liability when the farm is transferred to the son. On the other hand, were the farm retained by the father until his death, and then left to the son, no capital gains tax would be payable. However, if on the lifetime transfer it is decided that the son will meet the capital gains tax, the taxable value transferred to him for purposes of capital transfer tax will be reduced by the amount of capital gains tax which the son pays.[18] It would no doubt be appropriate in trying to calculate the optimum size of endowment assurance to be effected for the benefit of the son to ensure that he did in fact receive sufficient cash at maturity of the policy to discharge the capital gains tax as well as the capital transfer tax and stamp duty payable on the transfer to him.

Life of another policies

3–62   A policy on the life of A effected by B for his own benefit, or for the benefit of others, was a common arrangement in the days of estate duty. This device could often provide substantial estate duty savings, particularly as between husband and wife, where there was not the same total exemption as applies under capital transfer tax for lifetime or testamentary dispositions between spouses. It is probable that most pre-March 1974 life of another policy arrangements can sensibly be continued even where it is no longer necessary to keep up the policy so as to protect assets which are intended to be left by will from one spouse to the other. As was noted earlier in this chapter, insurance policies usually represent a very sensible investment, and before discontinuing existing policies which were arranged with estate duty in mind much thought should be devoted to the estate conservation role which an existing life of another policy might continue to play. For example, an existing policy effected by a wife on the life of her

---

[18] F.A. 1975, Sched. 10, para. 4, and F.A. 1965, Sched. 7, para. 19.

husband might be assigned to trustees to hold for the benefit of the children who in any event would be expected to inherit the estate at the death of the survivor or their parents. The future premiums, whether paid by the wife or by the life assured husband would be transfers of value for capital transfer tax purposes, the tax consequences being exactly as has been described earlier in this chapter. Depending on circumstances, it may be more sensible to deal with a pre-March 1974 life of another policy in this way, than for example to convert the policy to a paid-up contract and substitute for it a joint life policy payable at the death of the survivor of husband and wife.

3–63   Life of another policies will still have a role in the field of tax planning; for example, it may still be sensible for partners, or for share-holding directors of close companies, to insure each other's lives so as to give protection against the capital transfer tax and other pecuniary charges liable to arise at the death of any business colleague. No extra capital transfer tax will be payable in the hands of the policyholder at the death of the life assured, merely because the policyholder then receives the policy death benefit. There are two reasons for this. The first is that the death of the life assured merely means that the invest-ment of the policyholder, being an insurance policy on the life of the deceased, fructifies.[19] The second reason is that the essential circum-stance for a taxable transfer of value to occur, namely a reduction in the estate of a transferor, simply does not exist.

Attention is drawn to the comments in the first chapter of this book on the subject of insurable interest.

3–64   One of the most common uses for life of another policies in the days of estate duty was for a donee to insure the life of his benefactor against the estate duty which would have become payable, had the donor died within seven years of the time of making a gift. The need for life assurance cover to protect gifts still remains under capital transfer tax, although the amount of prospective tax payable will generally be much lower, and the risk period much shorter, than applied under estate duty. What life assurance will be needed to cover is the extra tax which will become chargeable on a gift *inter vivos* should the donor die within three years of the date of transfer. For example, take the case of an estate owner who, to celebrate his sixtieth birthday, transfers cash of £200,000 to his son. All previous transfers of value had fallen within the various exemptions, so this, being the first taxable transfer of value, attracts capital transfer tax on the " lifetime " scale amounting to £51,375. It is agreed between father and son that the son, as donee, will pay the tax. However, should the father die within three years from his sixtieth birthday, tax on the gift of £200,000 will be recalculated by reference to the higher scale of duty, which would increase the capital transfer tax on the £200,000 gift from £51,375

---

[19] *D'Avigdor-Goldsmid* v. *I.R.C.* [1953] A.C. 347.

up to £84,750. Therefore, the son could be called upon to pay a further £33,375 of capital transfer tax should his father die within three years, and the obvious way to cover this contingent liability is for the son to insure the life of his father for £33,375. The appropriate policy would be a straightforward term assurance, effected on the father's life by the son, which would pay out £33,375 if death should occur within the three-year term. At age 60 the cost of providing this cover would be relatively low (it should not exceed a single premium of £1,150) and the son would have insurable interest on the life of his father to the extent of £33,375 by virtue of the Finance Act 1975, s. 25 (2) (*b*).

CHAPTER 4

LIFE ASSURANCE AND INCOME TAX

Introduction

4-01 FOR very many years, life assurance in the United Kingdom as good as escaped the attentions of the legislature. As a result, it was used on an increasing scale as a home-based tax haven: in other words it was possible for the U.K. resident taxpayer to achieve many of the income tax and capital gains tax advantages inherent in transferring assets to overseas tax havens without actually having to bother with the transfer. This state of affairs was abruptly brought to an end from March 19, 1968, but the holders of insurance policies issued up to that date and who retain them are still in the unique position that for so long as the policy is not surrendered, assigned for value or materially altered no income tax liability will attach to the policy itself.[1] Liability to taxation is restricted to any which arises in the hands of the insurance company owning the assets to which the policy value is linked.

4-02 Prior to March 20, 1968, annual premium insurance policies could also be used, where the annual rate of premium did not exceed 12½ per cent. of the sum assured, so as to achieve drastic reductions in the policyholder's overall income tax liability. Premiums were regularly borrowed, and the loan interest counted as a charge against the policyholder's top taxable slice of income.[2] Taking an endowment assurance with profits for a term of say 10 or 15 years therefore, all premiums after the first could be borrowed at an effective net interest rate which for the top rate taxpayer would be well under 1 per cent., whereas the effective yield to redemption on all premiums paid under the policy would probably be at least 7 per cent. compound tax free. The ability for the top rate taxpayer so to transmute highly taxable income into tax free capital was severely circumscribed by the Finance Act 1968, and subsequent legislation, to the effect of emasculating policies which had been taken out previously with this specific tax avoidance intent. Residual income tax advantages will apply in the case of certain premiums paid out of borrowed money up until 1980, but the Finance Act 1974 legislation means that even where tax relief is still available in respect of policy loans taken before March 27, 1974, it will cease to apply to interest paid after April 5, 1980.

4-03 Also as from March 20, 1968, there was a considerable tightening up of the rules affecting the eligibility of life assurance premiums for income tax relief. Prior to that time, even a single premium paid to

---

[1] There could in exceptional circumstances be a liability to capital gains tax— see F.A. 1965, s. 28.
[2] See T.A. 1970, ss. 403, 404.

an insurance company could qualify for income tax relief, subject only to the statutory restrictions that relief did not apply to that proportion of the premium exceeding 7 per cent. of the sum assured at death and the usual one-sixth of taxable income rule. Now life assurance relief is only ceded where there are certain relationships between sum assured, premium and policy term *ab initio*. Furthermore, any attempt to manipulate life assurance relief so as to obtain a short-term profit, by surrendering a policy with a guaranteed high surrender value after the payment of a few premiums, or even one premium, is frustrated by Finance Act 1975 legislation.

4–04   Life assurance still does have a legitimate role to play in that area of financial planning where income tax considerations are important. It can still be useful as a medium for reducing immediate income tax liability on investment income, and provided the rules are followed, life assurance relief can still mean that the Treasury makes a healthy contribution. The days of watertight income tax planning amounting to no more than switching the largest possible slice of the taxpayer's investment capital into a single premium insurance policy have vanished, but insurance can still be a more tax-efficient investment medium than most.

LIFE ASSURANCE RELIEF

4–05   Relief from income tax in respect of premiums paid to keep up life assurance on the life of the taxpayer or his spouse is one of the longest standing of all taxation reliefs, and stems from the principle that the person who is prepared to devote a proportion of his income to the protection of his dependants should be encouraged. In recent years, particularly with the development of unit-linked policies, there was a steady increase of " life assurance " policies which in practice were little more than contractual savings arrangements. The actual life assurance element, in the shape of a minimum guaranteed mortality payment, disappeared altogether in many instances, so that there was no guaranteed minimum return at all at death of the life assured. The return on death was the then value of investment units allocated to the policy on the payment of premiums prior to the death, and if the unit value was low when death occurred, the return to the deceased's estate or to the policy beneficiaries could be significantly less than the total of premiums paid. This transmogrification of life assurance relief from an aid to the provision of protection to a direct subsidy for investment clearly could not continue indefinitely, if only because it gave unit-linked policies a Treasury-assisted benefit over all other kinds of contractual savings, including those directly sponsored by the Government.

4–06   As from March 20, 1968, the availability of life assurance relief was restricted to premiums paid on qualifying policies, as originally defined

42

in the Finance Act 1968,[3] although relief on policies effected before March 20, 1968, which failed to comply with the new rules was and is allowed to continue. However, the net effect of the 1968 legislation was to lend an unintended legitimacy to " maximum investment " endowment and open-ended life policies. Although the 1968 legislation imposed a requirement for the taxpayer to contract to pay premiums for a minimum period, it contained in the case of whole life and term assurances no stipulations regarding minimum mortality benefit: this state of affairs continued until March 31, 1976. By virtue of the Finance Act 1975, the rules for qualification were changed as from April 1, 1976, to the intent that premiums under such policies would only qualify for life assurance relief where the policy conveyed specified minimum levels of guaranteed mortality benefit. Premiums on policies issued before March 20, 1968, and on policies issued on and after that date but before April 1, 1976, which were qualifying policies under the 1968 legislation continue to attract life assurance relief. The Finance Act 1975 also introduced the concept of " clawback " having the effect that where a qualifying policy on which life assurance relief has been granted is surrendered, the whole relief, or a proportion of it, is recovered by the Revenue. Finally, the Finance Act 1976 changed the whole basis of granting life assurance relief, the general principle being that as from tax year 1979–80 relief on annual premiums of up to £1,500 in total per taxpayer will be deducted at source by the taxpayer before he pays his premium over to the insurance company.

Position before April 6, 1979

Availability of life assurance relief

4–07 It should first be observed that one of the effects of the Finance Act 1975 legislation is to remove one restriction on the availability of tax relief by reference to a relationship between guaranteed mortality benefit and premium.[4] Under the old legislation, tax relief was restricted to that proportion of annual premiums not exceeding 7 per cent. of the policy death benefit. In the case of policies issued before March 20, 1968, relief was also available on a single premium policy up to the extent of 7 per cent. of the sum assured. The effect of the Finance Act 1975 legislation is that in the case of qualifying policies eligible for life assurance relief (as well as in the case of policies issued before March 20, 1968, whether or not they are " qualifying ") the whole of the premium is allowable subject to the statutory restrictions noted in the next paragraph.[5]

4–08 The relief is one half of the basic rate of income tax,[6] the maximum premium or premiums which qualify for the relief being restricted to

---

[3] T.A. 1970, s. 19.
[4] F.A. 1975, Sched. 2, para. 6.
[5] *Ibid.*
[6] T.A. 1970, s. 19 (1).

one-sixth of total income.[7] For the purpose of calculating " income " in establishing the one-sixth limit, charges against income such as allowable interest are deducted but personal reliefs are ignored. If in any year of assessment the total premiums in respect of which relief falls to be granted do not exceed £20, the relief is a deduction equal to income tax at the basic rate on £10 or on the full amount of the premiums, whichever is the less.[8]

4-09   Although in general relief is not granted in respect of premiums under non-qualifying policies effected after March 19, 1968, there are certain very limited exceptions to this rule. Thus, the relief can be claimed in the case of mortgage repayment policies which do not comply with the qualifying policy rules; in the case of any policy issued in connection with a sponsored superannuation scheme as defined in section 226 (11), Taxes Act 1970 (" self-employed " annuities) provided that the taxpayer meets at least one-half of the cost of the scheme; and in the case of any policy issued in connection with an approved pension scheme.[9]

It should also be noted that in the case of policies effected before March 20, 1968, which are varied so as to increase the benefits secured or to extend the term of the insurance, relief will only continue to be granted if the policy, after the variation, complies with the qualifying policy rules.[10]

Clawback on early surrender

4-10   Until the passing of the Finance Act 1975, there was no procedure for the repayment of income tax relief where a policy was surrendered early in its life, notwithstanding the fact that the whole philosophy behind the granting of tax relief on premiums, particularly post-1968, was the long-term contractual nature of eligible premiums. This led to a certain amount of abuse. Qualifying policies with little or no guaranteed mortality benefit, and hence with very low expense ratios, could be effected linked to building society deposits, or some similar investment unit with a high yield and no risk of a downwards move-ment in the unit price. Income tax relief on annual contributions could be claimed, amounting to a subsidy of between 15 per cent. and 17·5 per cent. (depending on the basic rate of income tax in the relevant years) on the annual premiums which were actually paid. The policy could then be surrendered, and provided surrender took place at any time after the payment of at least two annual premiums, the taxpayer was assured of receiving back a sum substantially in excess of his premium investment net of life assurance relief. Although the gross profit on early surrender could be subject to the higher rates of income

---

[7] *Ibid*. s. 21 (1).
[8] *Ibid*. s. 19 (1) proviso.
[9] *Ibid*. s. 19 (4).
[10] *Ibid*. s. 19 (5).

tax and the investment income surcharge, any such charge would be calculated by reference only to the *gross* profit element (*i.e.* on any surplus of surrender over and above gross premiums paid to date) so that the net return to a top rate taxpayer could still be very attractive. For example, a taxpayer with a taxable income of £30,000 annually, £10,000 of which was investment income, could pay two gross annual premiums of £5,000 and if he received life assurance relief at an average rate of 16 per cent., his total gross investment of £10,000 would be reduced to £8,400 net. Typically, he might then have been able to surrender the policy for £10,500, and although the £500 surplus over and above the gross investment of £10,000 would be taxed at a rate in excess of 90 per cent., rendering the surplus of little value, the profit of £1,400 being the difference between premiums net of income tax relief and the £10,000 gross investment would be tax free. This type of arrangement was clearly an abuse of the system, and the clawback provisions of the Finance Act 1975 were the Revenue's answer.

4–11   The intent of the legislation is that if a qualifying policy is surrendered or converted to a paid-up contract within the first four policy years, the insurance company must " clawback " a sum related to the amount of income tax relief which might have been granted on the premiums previously paid.[11] The amount of clawback is the lower of (i) a percentage of the total of premiums payable under the policy up to the time of surrender or conversion, and (ii) the surrender value of the policy at that time, less the inverse ratio of those premiums. The amount of clawback in the case of a partial surrender cannot exceed the value surrendered; nor can it exceed the surrender value of the proportion of a policy which is converted to paid-up. The percentage to be applied for the purpose of calculation (i) above, if basic rate income tax is 35 per cent., is $17\frac{1}{2}$ per cent. if the event occurs in the first two years; $11\frac{3}{4}$ per cent. in the third year; and $5\frac{5}{8}$ per cent. in the fourth year. The inverse proportions to be applied, in the case of calculation (ii), are $82\frac{1}{2}$ per cent. in the first two years, $88\frac{1}{4}$ per cent. in the third and $94\frac{3}{8}$ in the fourth year.

4–12   The effect of these provisions is that where the policy surrender value equals or exceeds the total of premiums already paid, clawback is restricted to the appropriate percentage of those premiums. Where however the surrender value is less than the premium total by at least the amount arrived at through calculation (i) *supra*, the amount of clawback is nil. The insurance company is obliged to deduct the appropriate amount and pay it over to the Revenue: the taxpayer is then entitled to a refund of clawback, to the extent that he has not in fact enjoyed life assurance relief on the premiums in question.[12]

It is stressed that the same rules apply, with appropriate proportionate modifications, where policies are surrendered or converted to

---

[11] F.A. 1975, s. 7.   [12] *Ibid.* s. 9.

paid-up in part. Also, the encashment of a policy bonus is regarded as a partial policy surrender for the purposes of these provisions.[13] It thus ceases to be attractive for premiums to be paid with part or all of the cost being recouped immediately through the surrender of bonuses.[14]

4–13   If a qualifying policy is partially or wholly surrendered at any time in the fifth or any later year, or if a cash sum representing bonuses is received, clawback provisions again apply, the clawback being a percentage equal to one-half of the basic rate of income tax in force in the year of assessment in which the event happens.[15] This percentage is applied to the premium paid in the year in question, or to the cash sum received, whichever is the lower. Clawback provisions apply to policies effected after March 26, 1974, or in the case of earlier policies which are modified after that date so as to increase the premium by more than 25 per cent. (for example, by exercise of an option to convert from non-profit to with profits). The clawback provisions apply only to the additional rights attributable to the excess premium payable as a result of the policy alteration.[16] After four years, clawback applies *only* to the second and subsequent occasions on which surrender or encashment of bonuses occurs.

Position after April 5, 1979

4–14   Schedule 4, Finance Act 1976, introduces a radically new method for the granting of life assurance relief, as from tax year 1979–80. Some aspects of the Schedule 4 method were strongly resisted by the insurance companies, and it may be that significant amendments to the 1976 legislation will occur before tax year 1979–80, but this section deals with the proposals as they stand at June 30, 1977.

The broad principle is that with certain limited exceptions, the same rules for the granting of life assurance relief will continue to apply. However, the policyholder will have the right to deduct from a qualifying policy premium an amount equal to $17\frac{1}{2}$ per cent. thereof.[17] Premiums thus will be paid over net to the insurer, who will then recover the deficiency between gross and net premium from the Inland Revenue.[18]

4–15   The new system involving the payment of net premiums will apply to qualifying premiums which do not exceed £1,500 annually, or one-sixth of taxable income, as now. It was originally intended that premiums not exceeding £1,500 annually would be an absolute upper limit for relief for any one taxpayer, but this intention was altered during the passage of the Finance Bill 1976 through Parliament. In

---

[13] *Ibid.* s. 7 (1) (*a*).
[14] See also § 4–46 for the position concerning certain policy loans.
[15] *Ibid.* s. 8.
[16] *Ibid.* ss. 7 (7), 8 (5).
[17] F.A. 1976, Sched. 4, para. 5 (*a*).   [18] *Ibid.* Sched. 4, paras. 4 (1), 5 (*b*).

cases where premiums exceeding £1,500 annually are paid, and taxable income exceeds £9,000, the taxpayer may claim relief in respect of the excess premium over £1,500 in the same way as applies now, and subject to the one-sixth of taxable income rule.[19]

-16 In the event of any taxpayer over-claiming relief or over-deducting where premiums are paid net, the Revenue has the right to reclaim the excess relief by assessment, and also to require the taxpayer in future to pay premiums gross.[20] The requirement for future premiums to be paid gross would apply, for example, in any case where the taxpayer had premium commitments well in excess of one-sixth of normal taxable income. In such a case, rather than permitting the policy-holder to pay his premiums net, subsequently recovering life assurance relief over-allowed by assessment, the Revenue will be able to short-circuit this cumbersome procedure by requiring that some or all premiums be paid to the insurance company in full.

-17 It should be noted that the Finance Act 1976 legislation refers to the calculation of life assurance relief in terms of a definite percentage (17½ per cent.) of allowable qualifying premiums[21]: the relief is *not* apparently to be calculated after April 5, 1979, by reference to a proportion of the basic rate of income tax. The point is probably academic, since presumably at any time that the basic of income tax is altered, the Finance Act in question will also make provision for amending Finance Act 1976, Sched. 4, where it makes reference to 17½ per cent. of qualifying premiums. The new formula for calculating relief obviates the need for a special rule in the case of small premiums, so the proviso to Taxes Act 1970, s. 19 (1) (dealing with relief in the case of premiums of £20 annually or less under the present system) is repealed by Finance Act 1976, Sched. 4.

-18 It should be stressed that as from April 6, 1979, but subject to the safeguards mentioned above, every individual paying a qualifying life assurance premium will be entitled to relief, and hence to pay premiums net of life assurance relief, as of right and without making a specific income tax claim.[22] Also, it should be noted that the relief will not be available, commencing in 1979–80, where premiums are paid to non-resident insurance companies.[23] Thus, premiums payable to an insurance company resident in the Channel Islands, the Isle of Man, or the Republic of Ireland will no longer be eligible for life assurance relief, although the relief will still be available where payment is made to a United Kingdom branch of such a non-resident insurance company. It would clearly be difficult or impossible to administer the new life assurance relief system, whereby the deficiency

[19] *Ibid*. Sched. 4, paras. 6 (1), 15 (1).
[20] *Ibid*. Sched. 4, para. 14.
[21] *Ibid*. Sched. 4, para. 5 (*a*).
[22] *Ibid*. Sched. 4, para. 3 (1).
[23] *Ibid*. Sched. 4, para. 3 (2).

in premiums is recovered from the Inland Revenue, where payment is made to insurance companies outside the United Kingdom taxation jurisdiction.

Husband and wife

Position before April 6, 1979

4–19   In the majority of cases, relief is granted provided the premium is paid in respect of a policy on the life of the claimant or of his or her spouse. Thus, in the case of another policy maintained by a husband on the life of his wife, or by a wife on the life of her husband, the relief will be available in exactly the same way as if the premium was in respect of a policy on the spouse's own life.[24] In the case of an election for separate taxation of the earnings of a wife, relief is only allowed in respect of premiums paid by each spouse relating to policies on his or her own life. The reason for this somewhat peculiar rule is the statutory requirement in the case of a separate taxation election that personal reliefs are determined as if the husband and the wife were not married.[25] For the same reason, life assurance relief will not be ceded where husband and wife are separately taxed, and premiums are paid to keep up a joint life policy. The usual form of such policy will be a single contract payable at the second death, so during the joint lifetimes of husband and wife neither claimant can be said to have paid a premium exclusively on his or her own life. This is one of the comparatively rare examples of a policy which may satisfy all the tests of "qualification" but where life assurance relief invariably will be denied. The point may be an important one to bear in mind when counselling on arrangements designed to fund capital transfer tax.

Position after April 5, 1979

4–20   There is little doubt that the position described above as arising in the case of both single and joint life policies can be regarded as churlishly anomalous. The position will however be rectified as from 1979–80 since the relief to which either the husband or the wife is entitled in respect of an insurance on the life of the other will no longer be affected by the requirement that relief be determined as if the husband and the wife were not married.[26] Also as from April 6, 1979, it is made clear that life assurance relief is to be granted within the statutory limitation of one-sixth of taxable income, irrespective of whether premiums are paid by husband or wife on his or her own life or on the life of the other; whether husband or wife individually has taxable income; and whether or not an election for separate assessment has been made.[27] This is a useful clarification,

---

[24] T.A. 1970, s. 19 (2) (*b*), 19 (7).   [25] F.A. 1971, Sched. 4, para. 3.
[26] F.A. 1976, Sched. 4, para. 9.   [27] *Ibid.* Sched. 4, para. 10.

since although under the law as it stands up until April 5, 1979, the position just described has usually operated in practice, the wording of the relevant legislation is not wholly unequivocal.

QUALIFYING POLICIES AND THE CHARGE TO INCOME TAX

-21 As was noted at the beginning of the chapter, it was possible prior to March 20, 1968, to utilise policies of assurance almost without restriction with no risk of any adverse taxation consequence. Life assurance policies generally were excluded from the charge to capital gains tax in the original 1965 legislation,[28] on the perfectly logical grounds that the funds from which life policy proceeds are paid themselves attract capital gains tax. Also, there was no machinery for charging to income tax the profit element received under cover of a maturing or surrendered life policy. Therefore, the taxpayer could transfer assets without limit into the hands of an insurance company in the safe knowledge that the effective rate of taxation on income attracted by the assets for the future would never exceed the insurance company's rate, and knowing also that capital gains tax would almost certainly in practice be mitigated within the life fund so that the effective rate borne on realised and other gains would be well under the individual's maximum rate of 30 per cent.[29] There would be no question of any further tax liability at such time as the policyholder decided to encash his policy.

-22 It can be seen that insurance policies were a very attractive vehicle indeed to all taxpayers, but the greater the individual's personal income from earnings or investments the more attractive financially was the vehicle. Logically, a top rate income tax payer could switch the whole of his personal investments into the life fund of an insurance company, and never again bear any personal income tax liability in respect of investment income. Life assurance therefore was increasingly being used purely as a vehicle for tax-protected investment: there was no need for policies of this kind to provide any mortality benefit over and above the investment value, and indeed there was a great disincentive to the provision of such benefit, since it had to be paid for, and thus reduced the investment content of the contract.

-23 Aggressive marketing of these investment-orientated policies inevitably led to the Inland Revenue showing considerable interest, and on Budget Day 1968 the heyday of the single premium investment policy was abruptly terminated. The taxation advantages of life assurance contracts were preserved, but for the future it became necessary to observe certain rules in order to enjoy the full benefit. In essence, beneficial tax treatment of policy proceeds was and is

---

[28] *F.A.* 1965, s. 28.
[29] See § 1–05.

restricted to policies with a contractual obligation to maintain premiums for at least 10 years. If such a contractual obligation exists at outset of the policy, all premiums prima facie attract life assurance relief. However, if the contractual obligation to maintain premiums for a minimum term of years is dishonoured, any profit element at termination of the contract is charged to the higher rates of income tax and to the investment income surcharge. This same taxation liability on the profit element exists also in the case of policies which do not comply with the qualification rules for life assurance relief—the obvious example of such a policy is a single premium " bond."

4–24   Experience of the 1968 legislation showed that it left open various loopholes, which enabled the astuter members of the life assurance industry to develop a further range of contracts with income tax avoidance or the creation of income tax benefits, very much a prime objective. The Finance Act 1975 contained further extensive legislation aimed specifically at eliminating these residual areas where tax avoidance was encouraged by the life assurance legislation, and the taxpayer who wishes to use life assurance primarily or solely as a method for reducing his income tax liabilities now receives very little encouragement from the legislation.

Rules for qualification

4–25   It should perhaps be reiterated that in general two main consequences flow from whether or not a policy is qualifying:

(1) Subject to the comments at § 4–19 above, if the premium is in respect of a policy on the life of the taxpayer or of his or her spouse, it will be eligible for life assurance relief: no relief is available for premiums relating to non-qualifying policies.[30]

(2) If the policy is qualifying, no liability to the higher rates of income tax or the investment income surcharge will result, provided that the qualifying policy is not exceptionally dealt with so as to bring it within the charging provisions.[31] A non-qualifying policy will always prima facie attract higher rate income tax and investment income surcharge whenever its value is realised in part or in whole so as to give rise to an element of profit.

The legislation relating to qualification is found in Taxes Act 1970, Sched. 1 and in Finance Act 1975, Sched. 2. A summary of the main provisions now follows:

Whole life policies

4–26   The policy must secure a capital sum payable only on death (or on death or earlier disability) and must provide no other benefit.[32] How-

---

[30] T.A. 1970, s. 19 (4).
[31] *Ibid.* s. 394 (1).   [32] *Ibid.* Sched. 1, para. 1 (I) (*b*).

ever, so as to take account of the hybrid nature of many commonly issued contracts of assurance, the policy is not to be regarded as securing " other benefits " for this purpose by reason only of the fact that it confers a right to participate in profits, that it provides a surrender value, that it gives an option to receive payments by way of annuity, that it provides for the waiver of premiums by reason of a person's disability, or that it allows for the effecting of further insurance without further medical evidence.[33] Although the policy now must secure a capital sum payable only on death, in the case of policies issued prior to April 1, 1976, there was no minimum mortality requirement. However, policies issued after that date must provide as death benefit not less than 75 per cent. of the total premiums that would be payable if the death occurred at the age of 75 years.[34] In the case of lives assured under the age of 16, there is no need for the policy to secure a capital sum on death, but any payment under the policy in that event must not exceed the total premiums previously paid. In the case of joint life policies, the age of 75 relates to the older of the two lives if the sum assured is payable on the death of the first to die; if the sum assured is payable on the death of the survivor, the age of 75 relates to the younger of them.

4–27   Requirements relating to the payment of premium are:

    (i) Premiums must be payable at annual or shorter intervals over a period of at least 10 years or until the earlier death (or disability) of the life assured.

    (ii) The total of premiums payable in any period of 12 months must not exceed twice the total of premiums payable in any other such period.

    (iii) Premiums payable in any period of 12 months must not exceed one-eighth of total premiums payable (where premiums are limited in number); or one-eighth of premiums payable in the first 10 years (where premiums are payable throughout life).[35]

Term assurances

(i) *Term exceeding 10 years*

4–28   The basic requirements for qualification are the same as those noted at §§ 4–26, 4–27 relating to whole life policies. However, the 75 per cent. of premium requirements for sum assured is waived if the policy ceases before age 75 of the life assured, and has no surrender value.[36]

Premium payment requirements are:

    (i) Premiums must be payable at annual or shorter intervals for at least 10 years, *or* for at least three-quarters of the term, which-

---

[33] *Ibid*. Sched. 1, para. 5.
[34] F.A. 1975, Sched. 2, para. 4 (3), importing to T.A. 1970, Sched. 1 a new para. 1 (4A).
[35] T.A. 1970, Sched. 1, para. 1 (2).
[36] See reference at note 34.

ever period is the shorter. Thus premiums under a 12–year term assurance need be payable for nine years only.

(ii) Total premiums payable in any period of 12 months must not exceed twice the total premiums payable in any other such period, nor must they exceed one-eighth of the total premiums payable over the whole term.[37]

(ii) *Term 10 years or less*

4-29   There is no premium payment stipulation, the only significant requirement for qualification being that the policy must provide that any surrender value is not to exceed the total of premiums previously paid. As with longer term policies, the " 75 per cent. of premium " requirement is waived if the policy ceases before age 75 of the life assured, and has no surrender value.[38] Term assurances for less than one year issued after April 5, 1979, cannot qualify under any circumstances.[39]

Endowment assurances [40]

4-30   In order for the policy to be qualifying, it must secure a capital sum payable only either on survival to end of the endowment term or on earlier death (or disability). The term in question must be at least 10 years, and in the case of young lives, the policy will still be qualifying if it provides a specific mortality benefit only after the attainment of an age not exceeding 16. Unlike whole life assurances, endowment assurances have needed since March 20, 1968, to provide a specific minimum death benefit, that benefit being three-quarters at least of the total premiums which would be payable if the policy were to run for its full term. In the case of policies issued after March 31, 1976, the Finance Act 1975 alters the qualifying provisions to the extent that, if, at commencement of the policy, the life assured is aged more than 55 the guaranteed death benefit may be reduced, for each year of age in excess of 55, by 2 per cent. of 75 per cent. of all premiums payable. Again, in the case of joint life policies, the age to be taken is the older if the death benefit is payable on the first death, and the younger life if the benefit is payable at the death of the survivor.

Premium payment requirements are:

(i) Premiums must be payable at annual or shorter intervals over a period of at least 10 years, or until the earlier death or disability of the life assured.

(ii) Total premiums payable in any period of 12 months must not exceed twice the total premiums payable in any other such

---

[37] T.A. 1970, Sched. 1, para. 1 (3).
[38] See reference at note 34.
[39] F.A. 1976, Sched. 4, para. 2.
[40] T.A. 1970, Sched. 1, para. 2; and F.A. 1975, Sched. 2, para. 4.

period, nor must they exceed one-eighth of the total premiums payable over the whole term.

Contingency policies

4-31   Where the sum assured is expressed as being payable subject to a contingency (for example ". . . provided that X be then living . . .") the inclusion of a counter-life in this manner will not adversely affect qualification, provided that in all other respects the policy would be qualifying.

Other provisions

4-32   In applying the "premium" tests to determine qualification, no account is taken of (i) the premium "loading" usually charged where the policyholder has the option to pay premiums more frequently than once a year, or (ii) any provision for premiums to be waived because of disability.

In assessing the "capital sum" when testing the qualification of policies, which may pay out either a single lump sum or a series of sums, the 75 per cent. of premiums is compared with the smaller or smallest total claim value.[41]

Back dating

4-33   It is sometimes convenient (for example, when the life to be assured has just had a birthday) for the commencement date of a policy to be dated back. Thus, where an initial premium is paid on October 1, the policy might be back-dated to August 1, the main practical effect being that all premiums after the first would be payable on August 1 annually. This might result in policies which otherwise would be qualifying falling foul of the " one-eighth " rule, and provision is made for policies to be back-dated by up to three months without causing the policy *per se* to become non-qualifying.[42]

4-34   *Family income* policies are a special type of decreasing term assurance, where the sum assured is payable as a series of capital sums. For the purpose of qualification, family income policies are subjected to the same tests as are term assurances. In cases where family income benefit is attached to a whole life or endowment policy, the policy is qualifying if the policy taken as a whole fulfils the conditions for whole life or endowment qualification, or if both the basic policy and the income benefits taken separately would have been qualifying policies. Similar rules apply to *mortgage protection* policies, effected generally to secure after-death payments under a mortgage should the breadwinner die.[43]

---

[41] T.A. 1970, Sched. 1, para. 1 (6), (7); F.A. 1975, Sched. 2, para. 4 (4).
[42] T.A. 1970, Sched. 1, paras. 1 (6) (*b*) and 2 (3).
[43] *Ibid.* Sched. 1, para. 5.

Other special provisions

(i) *Exceptional mortality risk*

4–35   For the purpose of determining whether any policy is a qualifying policy, there is disregarded so much of any premium as is charged on the grounds that an exceptional risk of death is involved. This would apply in the case of a life to be assured in poor health, or one who indulged in some exceptionally hazardous pastime or occupation. If instead of increasing the premium, the life office placed a lien or debt against the policy this too would be disregarded for qualification purposes.[44]

(ii) *Connected policies*

4–36   " Where the terms of any policy provide that it is to continue in force only so long as another policy does so, neither policy is a qualifying policy unless, if they had constituted together a single policy issued in respect of an insurance made at the time of the insurance in respect of which the first-mentioned policy was issued, that single policy would have been a qualifying policy." [45] This is self-explanatory, a main reason for the provision being that before March 20, 1968, it was possible to use inter-connected policies so as to switch assets from donor to donee thus providing a substantial estate duty benefit. Whether or not such a technique would succeed in reducing the impact of capital transfer tax is now academic, since neither policy (or no policy if more than two were utilised) would be qualifying, and there could be a substantial income tax liability in the hands of the donee(s).

Premiums paid out of sums due under previous policies [46]

4–37   There is one circumstance under which a single premium policy can be qualifying. It is where payment of the single premium is discharged by the retention by the life office of the whole or a part of any sum which has become payable on the maturity of, or on the surrender more than 10 years after its issue of the rights conferred by, a previous policy. This has a particularly interesting tax planning connotation, as it does mean that in cases where it is desired to build up long-term tax advantages, the taxpayer can for example effect a 10-year endowment insurance and arrange for the insurance company, at the end of 10 years, to retain the maturity proceeds and use them to issue to the taxpayer a whole life or endowment assurance.

The same provision gives relief from the qualifying policy requirements in the case of the maturity or surrender proceeds of what is commonly known as a " child's deferred " policy. The maturity or surrender sum can be applied to effect a single premium qualifying

---

[44] *Ibid*. Sched. 1, para. 6.
[45] *Ibid*. Sched. 1, para. 7.
[46] *Ibid*. Sched. 1, para. 8.

whole life or endowment policy, provided that the original policy secured a capital sum not more than one month after the " child " attained age 25, or on the anniversary of the policy immediately following his attainment of that age.

4-38 These same provisions apply where the maturity or surrender proceeds of the previous policy are applied as the initial premium for a new annual premium policy: the size of initial premium is disregarded in applying the qualification tests for the new policy. Finally, it should be emphasised that this concessionary qualifying policy treatment is only available where the previous policy was itself a qualifying policy, or in the case of a policy issued before March 20, 1968, would have been a qualifying policy. There is however an exception to this rule where the new policy is an annual premium policy which otherwise would be qualifying apart from the size of the first premium, and the previous policy was a child's deferred policy.

Substitutions and variations [47]

4-39 Where a new policy is issued in substitution for, or on the maturity of and in consequence of an option conferred by, a previous policy, the question whether the new policy is a qualifying policy is determined by reference to both policies together. These provisions are most likely to be of practical relevance in the case of child's deferred policies, and once more this type of policy is given special protection. Whereas the general rule is that if the previous policy was not a qualifying policy, the new policy also is not, this is waived in the case of a child's deferred policy coming to maturity not later than one month after attainment of age 25, or on the anniversary of the policy immediately following attainment of that age.

4-40 As from April 1, 1976, the law relating to policies containing options is changed. Previously, an option was disregarded until such time as it was exercised, and the " new " policy as varied was then tested to determine whether or not exercise of the option still resulted in a qualifying policy. In the case of policies issued from April 1, 1976, the first policy must be tested at the time of issue on the basis that every possible option might be exercised. If a qualifying policy would still result after the exercise of every possible option, the new policy is a qualifying policy *ab initio*: if however the exercise of even one option would result in the new policy, as varied, not being qualifying, then the original policy also is not a qualifying policy.[48]

CERTIFICATION

4-41 Prior to April 1, 1976, the certification that a policy was a qualifying policy remained the exclusive responsibility of the insurance company

---

[47] *Ibid.* Sched. 1, paras. 9, 10. [48] F.A. 1975, Sched. 2, para. 3.

issuing the policy. The insurance company was required to give the policyholder a duly authenticated certificate within three months of the date of issue: there was the same liability following variation of an insurance policy. As from April 1, 1976, the Board of Inland Revenue became responsible for certification, to the effect that a policy issued or varied as from April 1, 1976, is only a qualifying policy if it is certified as such by the Board, or if it conforms with a form of policy certified by the Board as a standard form of qualifying policy, or varies from such standard form no more than to an extent certified by the Board as being compatible with a qualifying policy.[49] Similar responsibility for certification applies in the case of variations made as from April 1, 1976, although Finance Act 1976, s. 33 postponed reversion of responsibility to the Board in such cases until a later day to be appointed by the Treasury.

COMPUTATION OF INCOME TAX LIABILITY

4-42   The charge to the higher rate of income tax and investment income surcharge is imposed by Part XIV, Chapter III, Taxes Act 1970. There now follows a summary of the charging provisions as they affect life policies, together with examples and comments on the working of the legislation. Similar charging provisions apply also in the case of life annuities; those provisions are considered elsewhere.[50]

Chargeable events defined

4-43   In the case of a non-qualifying policy (the most common example of which will be a single premium bond) the happening of any of the undernoted eventualities is a " chargeable event ":

   (i) any death giving rise to benefits under the policy,
   (ii) the maturity of the policy,
   (iii) the complete surrender of the rights conferred by the policy,
   (iv) the assignment for money or money's worth of the whole policy, and
   (v) the arising of a chargeable excess (as explained below) at the end of any policy year.[51]

4-44   Qualifying policies are generally exempt from these provisions, unless operation of the policy fails to comply with the " 10 years " or " three-quarters " rules. Thus, death or maturity is a chargeable event if the policy has been converted to paid-up before 10 annual premiums have been paid, or if in the case of a qualifying endowment policy it has been converted to paid-up within three-quarters of its term. Similarly, surrender, assignment for money or money's worth, or the occurrence of a chargeable excess is only a chargeable event

---

[49] *Ibid.* Sched. 2, Pt. I.
[50] See §§ 6–22—6–27.
[51] Taxes Act 1970, s. 394 (1) (a).

within the first 10 years of a qualifying policy, or within three-quarters of the term of an endowment policy if less than 10 years.[52]

Assignments between spouses living together are disregarded for chargeable event purposes, as are assignments effected by way of security for or on a repayment of a debt.[53] In earlier days, the surrender of a right to a bonus could not of itself give rise to a chargeable event, but as from any policy year commencing after March 13, 1975, the encashment of bonuses is treated as a surrender of rights conferred by the policy or contract.[54]

4-45 The charging legislation does not apply to contracts effected on or before March 19, 1968, but such a policy which is varied after that date so as to increase the benefits secured or to extend the term of the insurance is treated for qualifying policy and chargeable event purposes as if the insurance had been made at the time the variation took effect.[55] Another earlier provision which was varied by the Finance Act 1975 occurs in the case of chargeable events in relation to policies which have at any time before the event been assigned for money or money's worth. Prior to December 10, 1974, once a chargeable event had occurred on an assignment, there could be no question of a further chargeable event. On or after December 10, 1974, this is still the case *provided* that the policy has not been reassigned to the original beneficial owner. A neat device for escaping the charging provisions, by assigning a policy for value immediately after its inception when the surrender value was little or nil, and forthwith reassigning to the original owner is no longer available.[56]

Policy loans

4-46 Loans made on policies effected after March 26, 1974, are treated as partial surrenders, except in cases where the loan is made against a qualifying policy, and either interest is payable at " a commercial rate " or the loan is to a full-time employee of the insurance company, and is made to help him buy or improve his main residence.[57] It is understood that the Revenue interpretation of interest at a commercial rate requires that the interest be payable within a band of interest rates which is the broad spectrum charged on policy loans by insurance companies generally. Policy loans which offend this rule and are treated as partial surrenders may also give rise to clawback —see §§ 4–10—4–13.

Excess aggregate value

4-47 In the case of policy years commencing after March 13, 1975, the old chargeable event rules relating to a partial surrender of rights

---

[52] *Ibid.* s. 394 (1) (*b*).
[53] *Ibid.* s. 394 (5).
[54] F.A. 1975, Sched. 2, para. 15.
[55] T.A. 1970, s. 393 (5).
[56] F.A. 1975, Sched. 2, para. 10.
[57] *Ibid.* Sched. 2, para. 16.

under a policy are replaced by a system which is much simpler to understand. Previously, if there was any element of profit in the entire policy above the premium(s) previously paid at the time of a partial surrender, a proportion of that profit was automatically attributed to the partial surrender. The old law is superseded, in the case of all policies (including those issued after March 19, 1968, and before March 13, 1975) by the following system:

(i) At the end of each policy year the taxpayer receives a " credit " equivalent to one-twentieth of the premium paid in that or any earlier year. If this " credit " is not utilised by reference to that year, it is carried forward on a cumulative basis for a maximum of 20 years: the maximum total " credit " in respect of any premium therefore is 100 per cent.

(ii) Each time a partial surrender takes place, the amount of cash received is compared at the end of the policy year with the cumulative total of credits.

(iii) If the amount of cash received on partial surrender is less than the cumulative total of previously unused credits, no chargeable event occurs, but the cash received on the partial surrender becomes a " debit."

(iv) If at the end of any policy year the sum surrendered plus any accrued " debits," exceeds the cumulative " credits," a chargeable event occurs. The excess of cumulative debits over cumulative credits is chargeable, and is known as the " excess aggregate value."

(v) Once a chargeable excess has occurred, the cumulative totals of credits and debits up to the end of that policy year are regarded as exhausted, so that the whole process of credits and debits occurs again.

(vi) At the occurrence of a terminal chargeable event (death of the life assured; total surrender of the policy; or total assignment for value) a final calculation occurs. The terminal value of the policy, plus the total of any earlier partial surrenders, becomes the " debit " item; the initial premium(s) plus all previous taxable excess values, if any, is the " credit " item. If as a result of this formula there is still a surplus, that surplus is chargeable to tax. If on the other hand there is a debit balance, that deficiency is allowed as a deduction (but not for basic rate income tax) in the relevant year of assessment, to the extent that the deficiency does not exceed the total of any previously taxed " excess aggregate values." [58]

4-48   In the case of policies issued before March 13, 1975, but after March 19, 1968, there is excluded from the " debit " calculation any cash received in respect of a partial surrender or assignment occurring

---

[58] *Ibid.* Sched. 2, paras. 9, 19.

before the first policy year falling wholly after March 13, 1975. In the case of the " credit " calculation at (i) above there is deducted one-twentieth of any premium or consideration paid in the policy year immediately preceding the first policy falling immediately after March 13, 1975; two-twentieths of the premium paid in the second preceding year; and so on. Such policies are thus " neutered " with regard to all payments in and out occurring before the first " after March 13, 1975 " policy year.

Calculation of charge

4–49   On the happening of a chargeable event there is treated as a gain:

(i) If the event is a death, the excess of the *surrender* value of the policy immediately before the death, *plus* the amount of any relevant capital payments, over the amount previously paid under the policy by way of premiums *plus* the total of any earlier excess aggregate values.

(ii) If the event is maturity of the policy or the complete surrender of the policy, the chargeable gain is any excess of the amount then received, *plus* any relevant capital payments, over the total amount of the premiums *plus* the total of any earlier excess aggregate values.

(iii) If the event is an assignment, the chargeable amount is any excess of the consideration, *plus* any relevant capital payments or any previously assigned policy share, over the total of premiums *plus* the total of any earlier excess aggregate values.[59]

" Relevant capital payments " for this purpose means in effect any amount previously paid out under the policy, excluding any disability benefit. Finally, in any case where the taking of a policy loan has been treated as a partial surrender of the policy, any amount of such loan which has been repaid prior to the terminal chargeable event also is treated as if it were a premium for this purpose.

Calculation of tax liability

4–50   Where a chargeable gain does occur, it is liable only to the higher rates of income tax and the investment income surcharge, if appropriate: no basic rate tax liability arises.[60] Further it will not usually be the whole of the gain which is added to the taxpayer's income during the year of assessment when the chargeable gain occurs. Top slicing relief is available, which can have the effect of usefully reducing, or eliminating, any liability.[61] Thus, suppose a policy has been in force for five years when it is surrendered, showing

---

[59] T.A. 1970, s. 395 (1).
[60] *Ibid.* s. 399 (1), (4).
[61] *Ibid.* s. 400.

a profit of £10,000. The whole amount of profit is divided by the number of complete policy years prior to surrender, which in the case of this example produces a figure of £2,000. This amount of £2,000 is then added to the taxpayer's income for the year of assessment in which the chargeable event has occurred, and is regarded as the top slice of his taxable income. The next calculation is to see what average rate of tax would be paid by the taxpayer in relation to that top £2,000 regarded as investment income. From this average figure is deducted basic rate income tax (currently 35 per cent.) and the resultant figure is the rate of tax which is applied to the whole £10,000 gain.

4-51 As can be seen, if notwithstanding the top slicing relief the whole of the £2,000 would fall to be taxed at the maximum possible rate of 98 per cent., the whole of the £10,000 gain would bear tax at 63 per cent., so the tax liability would be £6,300. If on the other hand the addition of £2,000 to the taxpayer's income in the relevant year failed to make him subject to any higher rate of income tax or to the investment income surcharge, the rate of tax charged on the whole £10,000 profit would be nil. Supposing that the individual's taxable income in the final year, after allowances and reliefs, were £2,500, all investment income, the addition of a further £2,000 would result in no higher rate tax liability. However, the entire £2,000 would then be subject to the investment income surcharge of 15 per cent., and that rate would be applied to the entire £10,000 gain, resulting in a tax liability of £1,500.

In the case of " chargeable excess values," the period of spread for top slicing purposes is the number of years since the start of the policy, in the cases of the first chargeable event and of the terminal chargeable event. For intermediate chargeable events, the period of spread is the number of policy years since the previous chargeable event.[62]

Practical examples

Example 1

4-52 One of the most popular practical applications of non-qualifying policies is still the acquisition of a single premium bond, with a view to taking regular annual withdrawals. These withdrawals might be required to supplement annual spendable income, or to meet some specific regular commitment such as school fees. Provided that annual withdrawals do not exceed the 5 per cent. of premium annual credit, no immediate tax liability will arise in respect of annual encashments: the day of reckoning will be postponed until the happening of the terminal chargeable event, which in practical terms will probably mean the death of the life assured or total surrender of the policy.

---

[62] F.A. 1975, Sched. 2, para. 18.

4–53   Consider an investment of £20,000 with a regular annual withdrawal of £800. This is £200 less than 5 per cent. of the initial premium, so no annual taxable excess will occur. Assuming that investment units underlying the policy grow at a level average of 8 per cent., and that the policy is finally surrendered in the twelfth year, the figures would be as follows:

Investment:	£20,000
Initial policy charge:	5 per cent.
Withdrawn annually:	£800
Assumed annual growth rate:	8 per cent.

End of policy year	Value £	Encashment £
1	20,520	800
2	21,297	800
3	22,136	800
4	23,042	800
5	24,021	800
6	25,078	800
7	26,220	800
8	27,453	800
9	28,785	800
10	30,223	800
11	31,776	800
12	33,454	—
		£8,800

Terminal calculation	£
Surrender value:	33,454
Total of annual part surrenders	8,800
	42,254
Less: Initial premium	20,000
TAXABLE GAIN	**£22,254**

The taxable gain of £22,254 would be divided by 11, leaving the amount of £2,023 to be added to the policyholder's taxable income for top slicing purposes. There will thus be an income tax liability of between nil and £14,020, depending on the policyholder's income in the twelfth policy year.

Example 2

4–54   Consider now the position if instead of withdrawing £800 annually, the policyholder withdraws £1,200. This gives rise to an annual taxable excess of £200, and based on the same growth assumptions as before, the position becomes:

Investment:	£20,000
Initial policy charge:	5 per cent.
Withdrawn annually:	£1,200
Assumed annual growth rate:	8 per cent.

End of policy year	Value £	Encashment £	Taxable excess £
1	20,520	1,200	200
2	20,865	1,200	200
3	21,238	1,200	200
4	21,641	1,200	200
5	22,076	1,200	200
6	22,546	1,200	200
7	23,053	1,200	200
8	23,601	1,200	200
9	24,193	1,200	200
10	24,832	1,200	200
11	25,522	1,200	200
12	26,267	—	—
		£13,200	£2,200

Terminal calculation

Surrender value	26,267	
Total of annual part surrenders	13,200	39,467
Less:		
Initial premium	20,000	
Excess values	2,200	22,200
TAXABLE GAIN		£17,267

Each year, the taxable excess of £200 will be treated as the policyholder's top slice of income for higher rate income tax and investment income surcharge purposes. Also, in the last year, £17,267 will be taxable subject to top slicing giving rise to a tax liability of between nil and £10,878.

Example 3

4–55   In this case, the same growth assumptions as before are made, but it is assumed that it is the intention to take substantial annual withdrawals of £2,600, giving rise to an annual taxable excess of £1,600 and more or less exhausting the bond by the end of the twelfth year. The position becomes:

Investment:	£20,000
Initial policy charge:	5 per cent.
Withdrawn annually:	£2,600
Assumed annual growth rate:	8 per cent.

End of policy year	Value	Encashment	Taxable excess
	£	£	£
1	20,520	2,600	1,600
2	19,353	2,600	1,600
3	18,093	2,600	1,600
4	16,732	2,600	1,600
5	15,262	2,600	1,600
6	13,674	2,600	1,600
7	11,959	2,600	1,600
8	10,107	2,600	1,600
9	8,107	2,600	1,600
10	5,947	2,600	1,600
11	3,614	2,600	1,600
12	1,095	—	—
		£28,600	£17,600

Final calculation

Surrender value	1,095	
Total of annual part surrenders	28,600	29,695
Less:		
Initial premium	20,000	
Excess values	17,600	37,600
ALLOWABLE DEFICIENCY		(£7,905)

4–56   In this case, £1,600 annually for 11 years has been regarded as the policyholder's top slice of taxable income, giving rise to an annual income tax liability of between nil and £1,008. When the policy is surrendered in the twelfth year, there is a deficiency available as a deduction against the policyholder's other taxable income for that year,[63] so that his higher rate income tax and investment income surcharge liabilities only would be reduced by a charge of £7,905. It is difficult to envisage circumstances in which the operation of a bond in this fashion could be recommended, as the charge against income in the final year of £7,905 is hardly compensation for a total of £17,600 having been subject to taxation in earlier years.

In summary, it is clear that the 1968 and 1975 legislation achieves its purpose of preventing the use of single premium life assurance so as to engender large-scale tax avoidance. However, single premium policies still have a useful role to play in financial planning, especially where the policyholder is subject to income tax only at the basic rate, or to the low bands of higher rate income tax; or expects to be at termination of the policy.

Underlying investment units: a cautionary note

4-57   The foregoing examples were all based on the somewhat unrealistic assumption that unit prices would increase at a level average rate of 8 per cent. In practice, units linked to equities, to property or to managed funds are likely to move unevenly in price; furthermore, that movement will not necessarily always be upwards. For example, in a case known to the writer, a single premium of £20,000 was paid to one of the major unit-linked specialist companies in June 1971 with a view to £2,000 annually being withdrawn for " income " purposes and the position under the bond as at July 1976 was as follows:

Investment:	£20,000
Initial policy charge:	5 per cent.
Withdrawn annually:	£2,000
Annual growth rate:	Actual

End of policy year	Value £	Encashment £	Remaining Value £
1	19,000	2,000	17,000
2	17,740	2,000	15,740
3	9,129	2,000	7,129
4	10,073	2,000	8,073
5	8,051	2,000	6,051

The value of the policy when the various encashments of units were made largely reflected the extreme fluctuations in U.K. equity prices over the period, but the example is a graphic reminder of the pitfalls which await the unwary. This practical illustration is perhaps the best possible argument for single premium policies where it is intended to operate a withdrawal system to be linked to a money or fixed interest fund.

---

[63] *Ibid.* Sched. 2, para. 19.

Capital redemption policies [64]

4-58   Because of the generally unfavourable tax treatment of capital redemption business, it is unusual for a policy of this kind to be encountered in circumstances likely to give rise to a chargeable event. It will usually be possible to achieve a more attractive investment yield through a conventional endowment policy. Capital redemption policies are however still occasionally encountered in connection with partnership funding and amortisation arrangements, and in limited other commercial circumstances, so it should be noted that maturity or complete surrender of the policy; assignment for value; or the occurrence of an excess aggregate value will give rise to a chargeable event, except in the case of maturity where the policy provides annual payments taxable as income.

Method of charging gain to tax [65]

4-59   Where a chargeable event in relation to life, annuity or capital redemption business occurs, the gain is taxed by reference to the circumstances of the beneficial owner of the policy. Where the policy was held on trust (including trusts arising under section 11, Married Women's Property Act 1882 and the equivalent Acts in Scotland and Northern Ireland) any tax liability is calculated by reference to the settlor's circumstances. If the settlor is dead when the chargeable event occurs at any time after the year of his death, there can be no assessment. This circumstance is unlikely to arise in the case of a policy held on one of the statutory trusts, but could well do so in cases where settlement trustees effect or accept the assignment of a policy as a trust asset.

If the policy was owned by a close company, or held on trusts created, or as security for a debt owed, by a close company, the company's distributable income for the purpose of Finance Act 1972, Sched. 16, (apportionment) is increased by the amount of the gain. If the policy is owned by personal representatives, the amount of the gain is treated as part of the aggregate income of the estate of the deceased. Where the policy was in joint ownership, any chargeable gain is apportioned accordingly.

---

[64] Taxes Act 1970, s. 398.
[65] *Ibid.* s. 399.

CHAPTER 5

BACK TO BACK ARRANGEMENTS

5–01   IN the wider commercial sense, a back to back arrangement usually involves a banking facility, whereby cash secured against or guaranteed by the assets of one party can be used to secure a commercial proposition in the name of the same or another party. Most practitioners are likely to be familiar with the concept in the areas of property financing or back to back loans used to overcome exchange control problems. In the world of life assurance, a back to back arrangement is one whereby an annuity or life policy secured by a single payment is used, at least in part, so as to fund an annual premium policy. The heyday of back to back schemes was undoubtedly during the period before the 1968 anti-avoidance legislation made both the procurement of single premium bonds and the combination of an annuity for life plus a whole life policy much less attractive in the areas of surtax saving and estate duty avoidance respectively. Subsequent anti-avoidance measures and the replacement of estate duty by capital transfer tax have further altered the background, yet the fact remains that back to back arrangements still have a very useful part to play in some areas of financial planning.

ANNUITY SCHEMES

5–02   The main tax reason for using an annuity as part of this kind of financial exercise is that a large part of each instalment of a purchased life annuity approved under Taxes Act 1970, s. 230, is tax free. A question often asked by anxious taxpayers is whether this tax treatment of purchased life annuities is likely to be altered in future, to the detriment of existing annuitants. The answer must be that any adverse alteration is most unlikely, since the method of taxing such annuities was introduced in 1965, following specific recommendations of a Royal Commission on Taxation. Although there is a tendency for taxpayers to regard the purchased life annuity tax treatment as a " concession," in logic and in equity it is no such thing, amounting as it does to formal recognition that part of each annuity instalment is no more than a return to him of part of the purchaser's capital investment into the annuity contract.[1]

Whole life annuities

5–03   An annuity payable for the remainder of the taxpayer's lifetime can be used as a basis of planning to achieve either of two objectives, or a combination of the two. Those objectives are to reduce the impact of capital transfer tax and to increase the taxpayer's income for the

---

[1] See the very explicit wording in Taxes Act 1970, s. 230 (1).

remainder of his lifetime whilst preserving his capital, at least in terms of present day values. The examples in this section assume a taxpayer who will be aged 60 on his next birthday. Also, it is assumed that his taxable estate at death will be £250,000, all left directly to his children, so that capital transfer tax payable (there having been no tax on lifetime transfers) will be £114,750, leaving the net estate to successors of £135,250.

Example 1

5–04   It is assumed that the taxpayer is in robust health for his age, and has no difficulty in passing a medical examination so that an insurance company agrees to issue him with whole life assurance on normal terms. The taxpayer effects a whole life assurance with profits for £50,000 and meets the first annual premium of £3,250 out of his own resources. Simultaneously, and with the same or another insurance company, he pays £65,000 in order to secure an annuity on his life payable annually in arrear for his lifetime. The gross amount of annuity is £9,750 annually and the tax free capital content is £3,710 annually.

5–05   Immediately he has effected the insurance policy, the taxpayer assigns it to his children, and at the same time he assigns to them sufficient of the annuity to enable his children to pay all annual premiums of £3,250 under the life policy for the future, if they so desire. The consideration for these assignments is the taxpayer's natural love and affection for his children: as this is not " money or money's worth," the assignments do not bring the annuity or life policy within the scope of the chargeable event legislation for income tax purposes. The amount of the annuity assigned to the children is that purchased by £27,664 out of the total annuity purchase consideration of £65,000. This assigned annuity, after the deduction of basic rate income tax at 35 per cent. on the interest portion, will give the children £3,250 annually exactly. The children are well off in their own right, and may well find that they also pay higher rate income tax, and possibly the investment income surcharge, on the interest portion of the assigned annuity. The taxpayer decides however that since the intent behind the transaction is that ultimately the children should benefit handsomely, it is up to them to meet any income tax which becomes payable on the assigned annuity apart from basic rate tax.

5–06   The taxpayer thus retains that annuity purchased by £37,336, and this amounts to £5,600 annually, the tax free capital content being £2,132. The taxpayer himself has such an income that the top portion of his income from investments is taxed at 50 per cent., plus the investment income surcharge of 15 per cent., making a total rate of 65 per cent. The total amount of investment capital he has realised to commence this scheme is £68,250, and assuming that this had been invested to yield 6 per cent., previously the income derived from

£68,250 was £4,095 which, after tax at 65 per cent., provided the taxpayer with £1,434 of spendable income. After the exercise just described has been completed, the taxpayer's income is improved roughly as follows:

	£
Taxable portion, retained annuity	3,468
Less: Income tax @ 65 per cent.	2,254
	1,214
Add: Tax-free portion, retained annuity	2,132
NET ANNUITY INCOME	3,346
Present net income from £68,250	1,434
NET INCOME INCREASE	£1,912

Thus the after-tax income derived from £68,250 increases by well in excess of 130 per cent. and of course the taxpayer is guaranteed this income for the remainder of his lifetime, since the retained annuity will not cease until his death.

5–07 Turning now to consider the consequences of this rearrangement of assets on the family's capital position, it is first necessary to contemplate the capital transfer tax position of the life policy. Its value on assignment to the children will be taken as the total of premiums paid to date, and on the facts as stated one annual premium of £3,250 has been paid, so this is the *quantum* of the transfer of value.[2] In addition, an annuity costing £27,664 has been assigned to the children, and this transaction clearly is a transfer of value. It will be assumed for illustration purposes that this transfer will in fact be valued for tax purposes at £27,664, although in practice the market value of the annuity[3] should be somewhat less than the annuity cost. The total value transferred by the taxpayer by his assignment of the life policy and of the annuity is £30,914, and assuming the taxpayer makes no other taxable transfers during that tax year, this also being his first taxable lifetime transfer, £2,000 will qualify for the transfers not exceeding £2,000 exemption.[4] Ignoring the exemption for gifts not exceeding £100 per donee, this leaves £28,914 of taxable value transferred, and £15,000 of this is taxed at the nil rate. Assuming that the children agree to pay the tax, it amounts to no more than £1,017, increasing to £1,131 if the tax is met by the father. Finally, when the father eventually dies, no capital transfer tax will be payable on the death benefit under the with profits whole life policy, since at that point of time no transfer of value takes

---

[2] F.A. 1975, Sched. 10, para. 11 (1).
[3] *Ibid.* s. 38 (1).
[4] § 3–12.

place, the life policy as an investment merely fructifying in the hands
of the children.

5–08   In the next table is shown the approximate revised capital positions
brought about as a result of this capital rearrangement, in the event of
the taxpayer dying either immediately after implementing the scheme,
or after having lived his approximate actuarial lifespan:

On death at age	60	75
	£	£
Original taxable estate	250,000	250,000
Less: Cost of annuity and first annual premium	68,250	68,250
REVISED TAXABLE ESTATE	181,750	181,750
Less: Capital transfer tax	89,115	89,115
Net estate after tax	92,635	92,635
Add: Policy claim value in estate of transferee(s)	52,000	82,000
NET AMOUNT TO SUCCESSOR	144,635	174,635
Net estate if no action	135,250	135,250
GAIN TO SUCCESSORS	£9,385	£39,385

5–09   It can be seen from this that even in the event of the taxpayer's
death very shortly after completing the scheme, successors in title
will be rather better off than had no action been taken. In fact, the
improvement shown above is over-stated slightly since capital transfer
tax of £1,131 or £1,017 has been ignored for simplicity, and stamp duty
on the assignment of the annuity (amounting to £554) also has been
left out of account. Obviously, of much more significance is the position
at around the actuarial life expectancy, when the capital position of
successors in title has been markedly improved: indeed, the claim
value of the insurance policy produces sufficient cash to meet all but
about £7,000 of the capital transfer tax liability. Other points to bear
in mind are:

   (1) By his age 75, the taxpayer has benefited personally by enjoying
       15 years' extra net income, calculated earlier as being £1,912
       annually. Hence, he has personally enjoyed almost £30,000 of
       extra value out of his original capital, as compared with the
       position had he taken no action. This statement does of course
       assume that the capital of £68,250 used to commence the scheme
       and the income derived therefrom would otherwise have remained
       constant in value over the period of 15 years.
   (2) The additional income just referred to would make it much

easier for the father to make regular or occasional gifts to his children and others during his lifetime, taking advantage of the various capital transfer tax exemptions. Although the tax-free element of the annuity, amounting to £2,132 annually, could not be regarded as income for the purpose of the normal expenditure from income exemption,[5] the father is not barred from taking advantage of the annual transfers not exceeding £2,000 exemption.

(3) If desired, the taxpayer could have commenced a whole life non-profit policy, instead of a with profits policy. In that case the gross annual premium would have been only £1,950, instead of £3,250, which would of course increase the taxpayer's improvement in spendable income for life by a further £1,300, making it £3,212. On this basis the return to the children under the life policy would at all times be £50,000, so that their own capital inheritance prospects would not have been improved by much more than a token amount. On the other hand, the income position of their father should have been very adequately secured for the remainder of his lifetime, even taking account of prospective future rates of inflation. A good compromise might perhaps be to effect two life policies, each for £25,000 sum assured, one non-profit and one with profits.

5–10 In the days of estate duty, it might well have been appropriate for the father to have retained the whole of the annuity in his own name, the policy being drawn up as a Married Women's Property Act or other trust for the benefit of his children. The father would then have met the life policy premiums each year, and the claim value of the policy at his death would probably have been estate duty free, since it would have been possible to take advantage of the old Finance Act 1968 normal expenditure from income exemption. However, under capital transfer tax the normal expenditure exemption is specifically precluded from applying in these circumstances, since it is not possible to include the capital content of the annuity as " income " for the purpose of the normal expenditure exemption.[6] Of course, if the taxpayer's overall income position is such that he could still meet the life policy premium as part of his normal expenditure, there is no problem. In the case of figures of the size used in the example, it must be very unlikely indeed that there could ever be any question of taking advantage of the normal expenditure exemption so as to secure freedom from capital transfer tax in respect of the annual premium payments. As noted earlier, it would still be open to the taxpayer to take advantage of the annual transfers not exceeding £2,000 exemption, but if the gross annual life assurance premium were £3,250, this would still lead to capital transfer

---

[5] F.A. 1975, Sched. 6, para. 5 (3)—it is assumed that the annuity was purchased after November 12, 1974.
[6] F.A. 1975, Sched. 6, para. 5 (2), 5 (3).

tax liabilities, as well as precluding the taxpayer from using the transfers not exceeding £2,000 exemption in other directions, or out of other assets.

5–11 The only real objection to using the advised technique of assigning the life policy and part of the annuity is that the taxpayer does retain rather less control and loses flexibility, as compared with the alternative of his retaining the whole of the annuity and personally paying the premiums to keep up the life policy under trust for his children. Most families are however, sufficiently close for the necessity of using the assignment technique not to be an insuperable drawback to implementing what, in the right circumstances, still remains a sensible financial transaction.

5–12 An alternative use of this combination of policies would be as primarily an income-improving exercise, as between husband and wife. There might be no children of the marriage, or no particular desire to benefit children at the first death. Assuming that the estate belonged to the husband, who in any event intended to leave his entire estate by his will to his wife, he could effect the combination of policies already referred to, having the insurance policy drawn up as a Married Women's Property Act trust for the absolute benefit of his wife. He would retain the whole of the annuity in his own name, and would meet the gross annual premium out of the annuity income. As each premium payment would be a transfer of value in favour of his wife, no capital transfer tax liability would arise.[7] At the husband's death, assuming that he predeceases the wife, the policy will fall in, returning the appropriate amount of capital. In the circumstances, the " appropriate amount " might well be £50,000 under a non-profit policy, since it would seem quite sensible to take the view that the widow could manage on rather less capital than was necessary when both spouses were alive, so that the scheme would have amounted to a conscious decision to spend £15,000 net of capital, in order to provide an increase to *after tax* income of around £3,200 annually. As the illustration was based on the husband being aged 60, assuming that he did survive to age 75, the net income return on the £15,000 of capital " spent " would have been highly satisfactory, representing an income return in excess of 20 per cent. for the remainder of the husband's lifetime and totalling some £48,000 in all.

5–13 It is vital, in considering this use of a whole life annuity linked to a whole life policy, to bear in mind the provisions of Finance Act 1975, s. 42. This reads as follows:

" (1) Where—
(a) a policy of life insurance is issued in respect of an insurance made on or after March 27, 1974 or is on or after that date varied or substituted for an earlier policy; and

---

[7] *Ibid.* Sched. 6, para. 1.

(b) at the time the insurance is made or at any earlier or later date an annuity on the life of the insured is purchased; and

(c) the benefit of the policy is vested in a person other than the person who purchased the annuity;

then, unless it is shown that the purchase of the annuity and the making of the insurance (or, as the case may be, the substitution or variation) were not associated operations, the person who purchased the annuity shall be treated as having made a transfer of value by a disposition made at the time the benefit of the policy became so vested (to the exclusion of any transfer of value which, apart from this section, he might have made as a result of the vesting or of the purchase and the vesting being associated operations).

(2) The value transferred by that transfer of value shall be equal to whichever of the following is less, namely,—

(a) the aggregate of—

(i) the value of the consideration given for the annuity; and

(ii) any premium paid or other consideration given under the policy on or before the transfer; and

(b) the value of the greatest benefit capable of being conferred at any time by the policy, calculated as if that time were the date of the transfer.

(3) The preceding provisions of this section shall apply, with the necessary modifications, where a contract for an annuity payable on a person's death is on or after March 27, 1974 made or varied or substituted for or replaced by such a contract or a policy of life insurance as they apply where a policy of life insurance is issued, varied or substituted as mentioned in subsection (1) above." [8]

5–14 It is understood that this measure is designed to prevent the use of a popular estate duty avoidance device, involving a combination of annuity and life policy, but which had a unique feature. The annuity and the life policy were both effected with the same insurance company which did not require any medical evidence before issuing the insurance policy. The insurance company was able to do this because the maximum sum assured it would grant under the life policy was usually 80 per cent. of the cost of the annuity. Because of the different taxation treatments of insurance company life and annuity funds, some insurance companies were able to issue this combination of policies, knowing that whenever the death of the taxpayer occurred, the insurance company was bound to show a net profit on the overall arrangement, after taxation. Although as is noted below, there seems no doubt that section 42 achieves its objective in making non-medical back-to-back arrangements unattractive to the taxpayer, it is important to consider whether or not the section has any relevance in other cases.

5–15 As applied under the equivalent estate duty legislation, whether or

---

[8] F.A. 1975, s. 42.

not section 42 is in point turns on whether the purchase of the annuity and the effecting of the life policy were associated operations, which is defined in Finance Act 1975, s. 44, as follows:

> " (1) In this Part of this Act ' associated operations ' means, subject to subsection (2) below, any two or more operations of any kind, being—
>
>> (a) operations which affect the same property, or one of which affects some property and the other or others of which affect property which represents, whether directly or indirectly, that property, or income arising from that property, or any property representing accumulations of any such income; or
>>
>> (b) any two operations of which one is effected with reference to the other, or with a view to enabling the other to be effected or facilitating its being effected, and any further operation having a like relation to any of those two, and so on;
>
> whether those operations are effected by the same person or different persons, and whether or not they are simultaneous; and ' operation ' includes an omission." [9]

5–16   The draftsman clearly did not intend very much to escape his net, and indeed the definition almost seems to give the Revenue unlimited powers to regard any combination of transactions, no matter how innocent, as potentially taxable transfers of value. In fact, it is understood that the official view of associated operations in relation to section 42 remains the same as in the days of estate duty. That is to say, the purchase of the annuity and the effecting of the life policy will not be regarded as associated operations if the life policy could have been effected by the taxpayer by itself, whether or not he had purchased the annuity. It is suggested however that it is important to take note of this official interpretation within the context of capital transfer tax legislation overall.

5–17   As has been noted earlier, if the insurance policy, instead of being assigned, is drawn up under trust, there can be capital transfer tax problems arising from the payment of the premiums since Finance Act 1975, Sched. 6, para. 5 specifically precludes the capital content of the annuity from being regarded as income for the purpose of the normal expenditure exemption. It should also be noted that paragraph 5 (2) contains an anti-avoidance measure which is designed to prevent any advantage where premiums are met by the taxpayer out of an annuity effected on his own life, the purchase of the annuity and the effecting of the life policy being associated operations. This appears to operate side by side with section 42 in appropriate cases—a classic example of taking a sledgehammer to crack a nut.

---

[9] F.A. 1975, s. 44 (1).

5–18   Bearing in mind the plethora of anti-avoidance measures aimed specifically at preventing what the legislature regards as abuse of insurance policies so as to avoid capital transfer tax, it is suggested that the taxpayer should tread very warily indeed. The fact is that the purchase of an annuity and the effecting of a life policy, as a back-to-back scheme, manifestly are associated operations, and if the Revenue's stated benign attitude towards these matters changed, taxpayers could find themselves faced with unexpected and perhaps substantial demands for capital transfer tax.

Example 2

5–19   It is felt that there is a fairly simple " copper-bottoming " device which can be implemented if desired, so as to avoid any possibility of a back-to-back arrangement effected with the benefit of full medical evidence attracting undue capital transfer tax. It will be recalled that in Example 1 the taxpayer spent £65,000 on an annuity which was in fact split into at least two smaller annuities. That annuity purchased with £27,664 he assigned to his children, retaining for his own benefit that annuity purchased by £37,336. Instead of spending the full £65,000 on an annuity immediately, the taxpayer could use the £37,336 so as to generate a guaranteed income in another way. The suggested method is to purchase a number of short-dated gilt-edged stocks, maturing within the next few years, the maturity value being earmarked as spending money in part and for deferred annuity purchase as to the remainder.

5–20   Suppose the taxpayer spent the cash so as to buy gilts as follows:

Stock	Cost £	Price	Nominal Stock Purchased £
Cash	2,000 *		
Treasury 3% 1977	4,000	94½	4,232
Treasury 3½% 1976–79	2,000	87⅜	2,288
Treasury 3½% 1977–80	2,000	85⅞	2,328
Treasury 3½% 1979–81	27,336	84	32,542
	£37,336		

* For year 1976–77 £2,000 of the £37,336 is held back and used as spending money.

5–21   These purchases are based on the price of gilts on July 16, 1976, and obviously the exact portfolio in any one case would depend on the state of the short gilt market on the day of purchase. The intention however is to concentrate as far as possible on stocks with a low interest rate, since these will have a greater element of capital appreciation to maturity than stocks of comparable maturity late but with a higher coupon, and any capital gain on a gilt held for at least 12 months is tax free.[10]

5–22   The intention will be to hold the gilts until maturity in every case, regarding the whole of the net income from the portfolio plus the capital sums received at maturity of the various stocks as spending money. The only exception is that none of the maturing 1981 stock will be spending money. The whole of the maturity value of the 1981 stock will be used *to purchase an annuity.* Assuming still a marginal income tax rate of 65 per cent., the following table shows what income amounts will be derived from the portfolio

Year	Gross Taxable Interest	Net Taxable Interest	Tax-free Capital	Total Net Income
	£	£	£	£
1976	1,427	499	2,000 *	2,499
1977	1,427	499	2,116	2,615
1978	1,300	455	2,116	2,571
1979	1,300	455	2,228	2,683
1980	1,220	427	2,328	2,755
1981	1,138	398	—	398

* For year 1976–77 £2,000 of the £37,336 is held back and used as spending money.

5–23   It should be noted that the gilts will mature at differing dates within the calendar years shown, so that the income will arrive irregularly but the table shows the rough averaged position year by year. The overall income position for the five years is similar to what the tax-payer would have received had he used the £37,336 to purchase an immediate annuity for his own benefit, although over the five years the income from the gilt portfolio is some £3,200 in total less than had the annuity been purchased. The taxpayer will use the 1981 stock maturity value so as to buy an annuity for life, naturally for his own benefit. Since the annuity will be purchased at age 65 rather than age 60 the rate secured should be significantly better than would have applied had the £37,336 been used for annuity purchase at age 60, and this should compensate for the fact that somewhat less than £37,336 will be available at age 65. Based on rates current in 1976, the annuity purchased by £32,542 would give the taxpayer an income after tax of £3,360 which compares favourably with the net income of £3,346 he would otherwise have enjoyed from retaining in his own name an annuity purchased for £37,334 at his age 60.

5–24   What is the point of this somewhat tortuous exercise? It is for the taxpayer with capital available for the purpose to be able to secure an enhanced income for his lifetime and to ease the burden of capital

[10] F.A. 1971, Sched. 10, para. 4.

transfer tax with no risks of falling foul of the anti-avoidance net. The potential mischief of section 42 is that apparently the Revenue, by invoking its provisions, could bring about a chaotic, not to say farcical tax position. In the circumstances of Example 1, section 42 would enable the Revenue to claim that the *quantum* of value transferred by assignment of the life policy to the children was no less than the policy death benefit of £50,000. Assuming that the transferor paid the tax in those circumstances (it would hardly be realistic to expect the children to do so) the net effect of the exercise, assuming death to occur within the first policy year, would be to *reduce* the overall net capital to successors by about £10,000 instead of the illustrated increase of £9,385. Even this calculation ignores the tax which might otherwise be payable in respect of the transfer of the life policy to the children [11]; such tax would be leviable in addition to that payable by virtue of the transferor being treated as having made a £50,000 transfer of value. Allowing for the accrual of bonuses to the policy, it would be the fifth year at earliest before the break-even position was reached. It is known that current Revenue indications are that they would not intend to invoke section 42 where the insurance policy is effected subject to full medical evidence of health, since in those circumstances the more or less simultaneous purchase of the annuity will not be regarded as " associated " with the life policy. The problem is that this benign attitude hardly fits in with the letter of what is a very specific anti-avoidance provision, let alone with the spirit in which section 42 was enacted.

5–25   Whereas some advisers may well take the view that there will be no problem if the life policy is effected subject to full medical underwriting, and particularly so if the two contracts are effected with different insurance companies, the alternative method shown at Example 2 would appear to put the matter beyond all dispute. It could hardly be contended that the purchase of an annuity five years after an insurance policy had been effected subject to medical evidence, and then assigned to persons other than the annuity purchaser, fell within the capital transfer tax definition of " associated operations."

5–26   A simpler alternative might be merely to leave the cash of £37,336 on deposit for one or two years, and then to buy the annuity. This might be acceptable in many cases, and indeed if the transferor is not concerned too much about income it would not be necessary even to earmark cash for this purpose at all. The exercise then becomes strictly one of estate preservation, the illustrated benefits becoming even greater because the initial reduction in the father's estate would be restricted to the cost of the smaller assigned annuity, £27,664, plus the first annual premium of £3,250.

5–27   One final yet perhaps vital point remains to be considered. Section 42 is intended to inhibit the general use of combinations of annuity and

---

[11] *i.e.* any tax chargeable by virtue of F.A. 1975; Sched. 10, para. 11 (1) (*a*).

whole life policy, where their use might give rise to an undue tax advantage. There seems no doubt that the section is effective to prevent such combinations producing a capital transfer tax saving in cases where the taxpayer is unacceptable for life assurance on the grounds of ill health. Thus, assume the same facts as in Example 1 except that the taxpayer is uninsurable. As has been noted earlier, if the same contracts were effected and the same procedure followed, the value transferred by assignment of the annuity would, by virtue of section 42 (2) (*b*), be £50,000 *plus* the value of the assigned annuity *plus* the value of the life policy at the time of assignment. The last of these three items is unlikely in practice to present any real problem, as it would be quite possible for the life policy to be commenced on a monthly premium basis, the assignment taking place immediately after payment of the first such premium. However, the first two items would result in a substantial immediate tax payment such as to make the family significantly worse off than had no action been taken.

5–28   Section 42 achieves its apparent objective of preventing back-to-back arrangements on a non-medical basis, yet also remains hanging as a Damoclean sword over the medically fit taxpayer. It is hardly satisfactory to rely on the Revenue's statement concerning when it will not invoke " associated operations," since it is manifest that the effecting of the two contracts close together are indeed " associated " irrespective of the taxpayer's state of health. The method for overcoming the potential mischief of section 42 is as follows. In order for the section to apply, it is necessary that two conditions are met. The first is that an annuity is purchased on the life of the insured person; the second is that the life policy is vested in a person other than the person *who purchased* the annuity. If therefore the person who buys the annuity is the same as is entitled after assignment to the benefit of the policy, no problem arises. This position would be achieved in the example given if the father made a cash gift to his children of £27,664 which gift they then voluntarily use to buy an annuity on their father's life. The annuity will be treated for tax purposes exactly as if the father had bought it on his own life, and there will incidentally be a saving of stamp duty since no assignment of annuity will be necessary. If the father defers for some reasonable period buying an annuity to protect his own income (perhaps by using the short gilts technique already described) the whole operation is taken outside the scope of section 42. Indeed, in the final analysis it is only by proceeding as suggested in this paragraph that it is possible to eliminate all risk of any charge to capital transfer tax beyond that payable on the £27,664 annuity purchase price and on the value of the first life assurance premium.

5–29   Unfortunately, it would not produce any great benefit if the technique outlined in the last paragraph were adapted to the circumstances of a medically unfit taxpayer. The life policy for £50,000 could then only be issued upon condition that a total of £65,000 was spent on annuities on the same life, so it would be imperative to buy both annuities simultaneously with effecting the life policy. The larger annuity purchased for £37,336 would be retained by the taxpayer and the act of assigning the life policy to the children would be bound to result in a deemed transfer of value of £50,000. An interesting thought here is that in these circumstances it might be quite practicable for the children to insure the life of their father on a life of another basis. Insurable interest would be established by the section 42 potential capital transfer tax, the transferor having indicated that any tax liability must fall on the children. If this were done, section 42 is *almost* circumvented but not quite. Although it is true that the benefit of the insurance policy would then be vested *ab initio* in " the person who purchased the annuity "—in this case, the children—this is only true with regard to £27,664 of the annuity consideration. The larger annuity costing £37,336, as part of the same transaction, is purchased by the father on his own life, so for the purpose of the section 42 charging provisions he becomes " the person who purchased the annuity." The total amount transferred by the father for section 42 purposes therefore becomes £27,664 (cash gift to children to buy the premium funding annuity) *plus* £50,000 (the claim value of the life policy immediately it is effected).

Short term annuities

5–30   Annuities payable for a short term of years can be the foundation for the taxpayer to rearrange a proportion of his capital so as to enjoy a secure income after tax comparing very favourably indeed with that available through other investment media. The principle here is that capital is used to purchase an annuity payable for a restricted term of years, part of the annuity income being used to build up a capital fund which becomes available for reinvestment at the end of the annuity income period.

5–30A   Consider a taxpayer aged 50 who has retired from business early, and is largely dependent on income from invested capital to meet living expenses. He has £100,000 of investment capital, which yields an average income of 6 per cent. gross. This gives him £6,000 gross investment income each year, and in addition he is entitled to a pension of £3,000 annually. After allowances and allowable interest, the net effect is that the top £3,000 of his taxable income suffers income tax at an average rate of 60 per cent. He therefore pays £1,800 of income tax on this top £3,000 of income, which is thus worth *£1,200* in terms of net spendable income—hardly an adequate income return on capital of £50,000.

The taxpayer decides to arrange one half of his investment capital into a combination of annuity and life assurance contracts. First, he uses £46,325 to buy an annuity payable half yearly in arrear for a term of nine years only. The gross annuity is £8,952, and the tax free capital element is £5,315. The taxable or interest content of the annuity is £3,637, and this will suffer income tax at an average overall rate of 60 per cent. (basic rate income tax being deducted at source by the paying insurance company): hence, the £3,637 is worth £1,455 spendable, after income tax of £2,182. The tax-free capital element is £5,315, so that the average net spendable income for nine years is £6,770. The second contract is an endowment insurance with profits for a period of 10 years, secured by a gross annual premium of £3,675. This policy has an expected minimum maturity value at the end of 10 years of £50,000. It is anticipated therefore that when the policy matures, it will return to the taxpayer the £50,000 of investment capital which he has committed to this scheme. The gross annual premium for the endowment policy is £3,675, but it is assumed that £1,000 annually of this premium qualifies for life assurance relief, worth £175. Hence, the net annual premium is reduced to £3,500. Deducting the net endowment premium of £3,500 from the net income for nine years of £6,770, it is seen that the taxpayer now has a net spendable income of £3,270, compared with the net spendable income of £1,200 before the rearrangement. His net income after tax therefore increases by in excess of £2,000 annually, representing an after-tax increase of about 170 per cent. of income derived from the £50,000.

–30B In terms of cash flow, the enhanced income begins to be available six months after the scheme has commenced, and ceases six months before the insurance policy matures, and if there is any objection to this, the term of the annuity can be varied. For example, it could be paid for 9½ years six-monthly in arrear, or it could be paid for 10 years, six-monthly in advance. The annuity received would then be somewhat less than the illustrated figures, but practice shows that in the majority of cases, taxpayers are quite happy to settle for an annuity payable as illustrated. The endowment assurance which matures after 10 years returns the original £50,000 investment, and the taxpayer's financial position can again be reviewed at that stage. He will then be aged 60, and it may well be appropriate for the exercise to be repeated when similar benefits would be generated for a further span of nine or 10 years.

30C In the case of an exercise of this kind, the taxpayer will usually regard it as fairly important that the return of capital at the end of 10 years should be as nearly guaranteed as possible. It would therefore normally be recommended that the endowment policy should be a conventional with profits contract effected with a major traditional life office. Policies linked to units of variable value, such as units in equity or property funds, would not normally be appropriate for this kind of exercise. The endowment assurance would be issued subject to normal medical underwriting, and should the death of the taxpayer occur within 10 years from inception, the appropriate death benefit would be paid out to his estate. This would be the minimum sum assured of £33,500 plus bonuses accrued to the date of death. Since the first year's bonus normally attaches immediately the first annual premium has been paid, this means that the minimum capital return to the estate (payable if death occurred within the first policy year) would be £35,000.

If the taxpayer were concerned that there could be a maximum reduction of about £15,000 in his estate, the annuity could be guaranteed to be payable for a minimum term of five years, or could be capital protected. Either of these solutions would result in a somewhat lower gross annuity payment, and in any event neither a guaranteed nor a capital protected annuity would ensure that there would be no shortfall of capital in the estate should the taxpayer die within the second half of the 10 year period. The solution to protect the estate capital therefore would be to effect a decreasing term assurance on the life of the taxpayer for a sum assured commencing at £15,000 and reducing by £1,500 annually. The cost of this would be relatively modest (it should not exceed £110 payable for six years only) and it will always be up to the individual taxpayer to decide whether in his own circumstances it is prudent to protect the estate capital position. If the decision to protect is taken, the best net result will normally be obtained by deciding to pay for decreasing term assurance, rather than through accepting the reduced income from a guaranteed or capital protected annuity—neither of which would in any event protect the position during the latter part of the 10-year term.

BOND-LINKED SCHEMES

5–31 The life assurance industry has arrogated for its own purposes a new definition of the word "bond." It is now generally accepted as a convenient word for defining a single premium or annual premium life assurance contract which is primarily an investment, the value of the investment being expressed in terms of units in various types of investment funds. This section is concerned with the use of single premium life assurance policies as a medium for funding regular annual payments, and the word "bond" must be understood to mean an insurance policy of this kind.

5–32 Although it is possible to use a single premium bond as the medium for funding annual premium policies designed to mitigate capital transfer tax, their use is much more common as part of an income exercise. Taking the example of the taxpayer considered in the preceding section dealing with short-term annuities, a single premium bond might be considered as an alternative funding medium to the annuity. Unfortunately, the single premium bond suffers from certain disadvantages compared with the annuity. The disadvantages are of uncertainty, first as to the exact investment return which the bond will provide, and secondly as to the exact tax liability which will attach to the bond. This tax liability will be dependent on two factors: the first is the overall investment value derived from the bond, and the second is the policyholder's exact personal taxation position from year to year.

5-33 Under legislation introduced in 1968,[12] and subsequently refined, mainly in 1975,[12] the profit element derived from a single premium bond is subjected to higher rates of income tax and to the investment income surcharge. The exact tax liability is calculated by reference to the taxpayer's income during the year that a chargeable event occurs, which may be at any time within the duration of the bond contract. When the contract is terminated by surrender of the bond or by death of the life assured a final calculation of tax liability takes place. The detail of the legislation is considered elsewhere,[13] and for present purposes it is sufficient to note that if a single premium bond is effected, the policyholder is permitted to encash each year up to 5 per cent. of the amount of a single premium investment, without incurring any liability to taxation *at that time*. The liability (if any) is in effect postponed until termination of the contract. If the taxpayer makes an encashment equivalent to more than 5 per cent. annually of the single premium, the excess over 5 per cent. is charged to higher rates of income tax and the investment income surcharge during the year of encashment. At termination of the contract a final calculation takes place and depending on a combination of the investment success of the bond and the taxpayer's personal tax position in the year of termination, there may and may not be a further tax liability. Also there is the possibility, depending on the exact circumstances, that the taxpayer would be entitled to a return of income tax previously paid, although if circumstances are such as to warrant this, the taxpayer is likely to have enjoyed very rough justice indeed for his temerity in effecting the single premium bond. This is not any matter for surprise, bearing in mind the objective behind the relevant 1968 and 1975 legislation, which is quite simply to prevent those with high incomes from deriving what are regarded as undue income tax advantages from investment into single premium bonds.

Suppose the same circumstances as are mentioned in the previous section, concerned with the short-term annuity funding technique. The taxpayer in this case however decides that instead of using £46,325 in order to buy a short-term annuity, he will spend out the same amount on the purchase of a single premium bond. Further capital of £3,675, as before, is used to pay the first premium for a 10-year endowment assurance with profits, and this increases the total capital outlay to £50,000.

5-34 In the earlier example, it was shown that the taxpayer could expect

---

[12] Taxes Act 1970, ss. 394, 395 and F.A. 1975, Sched. 2, **Pt. IV.**
[13] §§ 4-42—4-59.

to enjoy net spendable income of £3,270 for a period of nine years, as well as meeting the *net* annual premium of £3,500 to keep up the endowment policy. Suppose therefore that he decided to withdraw from the single premium bond on each policy anniversary cash of £6,770. If there were no income tax liability on the regular annual encashments, his net position would be exactly the same as if he had effected the short-term annuity. In practice, there undoubtedly would be an income tax liability in respect of each encashment of £6,770, since under the 1975 legislation, the taxpayer is permitted to encash each year only up to one-twentieth of the single premium without incurring any immediate tax liability. In other words, he could withdraw from the bond each year up to £2,316 without tax liability: any annual excess encashment over and above £2,316 will be subject to taxation. If therefore he does encash £6,770 annually, each year there will be an " excess value " of £4,454, subject to higher rates of income tax and to investment income surcharge.

5–35   On the assumptions that the insurance company deducts 5 per cent. of the single premium before investing the balance into units, and that the units purchased appreciate in value at a level annual rate of $7\frac{1}{2}$ per cent., the return under the bond would be as follows:

End of Year	Value of Bond	Encashment	Excess value	Remaining value of Bond
	£	£	£	£
1	47,308	6,770	4,454	40,538
2	43,578	6,770	4,454	36,808
3	39,508	6,770	4,454	32,798
4	35,257	6,770	4,454	28,487
5	30,623	6,770	4,454	23,853
6	25,641	6,770	4,454	18,871
7	20,286	6,770	4,454	13,516
8	14,529	6,770	4,454	7,759
9	8,340	8,340	6,024	NIL

5–36   At the end of the final year, the taxpayer would receive rather more than the sum of £6,770 encashed in earlier years. On this basis then, assuming that there were no income tax liability related to the encashments, the taxpayer would be marginally better off than had he effected the short-term annuity. In practice, he would be far worse off, because of the liability to taxation. For eight years, the taxpayer would have the amount of £4,454 treated as if it were the highest slice of his investment income; in the ninth year, he would be entitled to a substantial deduction from his total income for that year of assessment, and as a result would undoubtedly pay only basic rate income tax in that year. The saving of taxation in the final year would be of the order of £1,000, but as against this, in the eight previous years a total of £35,632 would have been subject to taxation (higher rate income tax plus investment income surcharge) at a minimum average rate of 35 per cent., making a total tax bill of £12,471. After allowing for the tax saving of about £1,000 in the final year, it can be seen that this method of funding will have cost the taxpayer approximately £11,500 of additional taxation, as compared with the short-term annuity funding method.

5–37   The particular tax liabilities which have been indicated are approximate calculations, based on the data set out earlier—*i.e.* assuming that after having made the £50,000 investment, the taxpayer is left with gross income of £6,000. If his income were higher than this, the indicated tax liabilities would be greater, and conversely if taxable income were lower, so would be the tax liabilities. However, it must be borne in mind that if taxable income is lower than has been illustrated, there would be a smaller income tax liability on the taxable portion of the short-term annuity, so that the net income return thereunder would be greater. There is no doubt that in such circumstances a back-to-back funding arrangement based on a single premium bond is highly inefficient from the tax aspect, and certainly should not be recommended bearing in mind that the much safer alternative of the short-term annuity is available.

5–38   The other unsatisfactory aspect of single premium bonds is that generally the investment return to be expected is very uncertain. Most bonds are linked to the performance of funds of equities or commercial property portfolios and unit prices are liable to wide fluctuations. It has been all too common in the past for taxpayers to embark on the type of single premium bond exercise which has been outlined, only to find that well before the end of the ninth year, there is simply no investment value left in the bond. This has arisen because the performance predictions made when the bond was effected have not been achieved.[14] Unfortunately, the commissions paid by insurance companies for the introduction of new business make it far more financially attractive for an intermediary to sell his client a single premium bond, than to sell him a short-term annuity. There will always be unscrupulous intermediaries whose scale of values will be balanced much more heavily in favour of their own pockets than in favour of their client's.

5–39   Objections concerning investment uncertainty can be overcome to a large extent, if not entirely, by making use of a bond where the growth rate is guaranteed, or alternatively where the underlying investment is in gilt-edged securities and other fixed interest investments. However, even given reasonable certainty as to the ability of the underlying investment to appreciate at $7\frac{1}{2}$ per cent., or whatever rate is assumed, the taxation consequences outlined in this section will still exist, so it remains very difficult indeed to see any justification for recommending a single premium bond based back-to-back arrangement for a higher rate taxpayer.

---

[14] See § 4–57.

CHAPTER 6

ANNUITIES

6–01   An annuity is an annual payment, which may be fixed or variable, with a duration usually but not always determined by reference to a human life or human lives. Provision is often found in the case of will trusts for annuities to be paid to family servants or others, but we are concerned here with the commercial annuity contracts which will probably form an important part of the business of any life assurance company. For estate planning purposes it is necessary to consider primarily purchased life annuities, but it should be noted that one of the most common types of annuity will be pension payments emanating from insurance company pension funds, or from private pension funds. A passing nod should also be made in the direction of the annuity certain, which is a commitment to make an annual payment for a fixed term of years without reference to any human life; this type of annuity is most commonly encountered in the case of certain types of capital payment school fees schemes, where the annuity payer's liability might commence immediately or might be deferred for a number of years.

Purchased life annuities

6–02   An annuity purchased from the taxpayer's own funds from an insurance company in the ordinary course of a business of granting annuities on human life is treated as containing a capital element (usually referred to as the " capital content ") which is not regarded as taxable income.[1] The tax-free portion of any purchased life annuity is determined by reference to official actuarial tables, and varies with the age of the annuitant—*i.e.* the person on whose life the annuity depends. The capital content increases with each extra year of age attained of the annuitant. Purchased life annuity treatment will not be granted in the case of annuities purchased with the funds provided pursuant to a direction in a will or settlement, whether the direction is to purchase an annuity or merely to pay an annuity out of income and/or capital of the will or settlement.[2] Also, purchased life annuity treatment is not available where the annuity is purchased in recognition of past employment, and this will include any annuity directly purchased under a sponsored superannuation scheme.[3] Thus, the acid test is whether or not the taxpayer who purchased the annuity had absolute personal dominion over the purchase consideration, and could of his own free will have used the funds for another purpose.

---

[1] Taxes Act 1970, s. 230 (1).
[2] *Ibid.* s. 230 (7).
[3] *Ibid.*

Example

6-03   Whilst it may appear trite to state that perhaps the greatest attraction of a purchased life annuity is that the annuitant can never outlive his income, experience shows that the significance of this fact is often ignored.

6-04   Consider the case of a taxpayer aged 70 with a pension income of £3,000 and £5,000 of investment income from a portfolio worth £100,000 yielding on average 5 per cent. gross. Assuming he is a married man, his annual income tax liability will be £3,250, leaving him with a net spendable income of *£4,750*. If he raised £30,000 from his portfolio and applied that to purchase an annuity payable half-yearly in arrear for life, he could expect to receive a guaranteed gross income of £6,000 annually, the tax-free capital content being £2,450, the balance of £3,550 being taxable as investment income. He would also have £3,500 of continuing investment income from his retained £70,000 portfolio, so that his gross taxable income would increase to £10,050. Income tax liability on this would be £4,740, leaving £5,310 after tax and in addition he would have the annual tax-free annuity content of £2,450, leaving him with a net annual spendable income of *£7,760*. As a result of buying the annuity therefore, the taxpayer has increased his net spendable income by £7,760 less £4,750, being a net improvement of *£3,010*. The rearrangement of 30 per cent. of the investment portfolio into an immediate annuity therefore increases net spendable income by 63 per cent.

6-05   Naturally, the price which has to be paid for achieving such a substantial increase in net income is the loss of capital: this will often be regarded as perfectly acceptable after potential capital transfer tax is taken into account. Suppose the taxpayer above referred to possessed other assets, including the matrimonial home or a share therein worth £50,000, and that by the terms of his will the entire gross estate of £150,000 is left to his widow. At the death of the taxpayer if he is predeceased by his wife, or alternatively at her death if she is the survivor, the minimum amount of capital transfer tax payable will be £54,750, reducing the net estate to successors to *£95,250*. After the expenditure of £30,000 on the purchase of an annuity, the gross taxable estate is reduced to £120,000, the minimum capital transfer tax bill becomes £38,250, and the net estate to successors becomes *£81,750*. The net capital cost of buying an annuity for £30,000 is therefore seen to be *£13,500*. This net amount will be recouped by the taxpayer by way of increased spendable income if he survives for only four-and-a-half years from the time of buying the annuity; this is probably the way that the taxpayer should be advised to weigh up the attractions and drawbacks of annuity purchase, regarded solely as a commercial proposition. Of course, many other matters may also have to be taken into account, depending on the complexity of the taxpayer's family and general financial affairs, but it can be seen that in principle annuity purchase has much to commend it in days of apparently ever-increasing costs, which tend to concern the elderly more than younger generations not weaned on the old traditions of strict public and private financial rectitude.

Variants of the basic annuity

6–06   The two problems most commonly raised by prospective annuity purchasers, and their advisers, are " what about the loss of capital? " and " how about inflation? " There is no doubt that the answers can be a little disconcerting, but the fact is that an annuity is designed for a specific purpose, and is by no means a panacea for the solution of all financial ills.

(i) What about capital?

As was indicated above, the purchase of a whole life annuity inevitably means a diminution of capital. This diminution may however be mitigated, at least in the event of death in an early year, by the purchase of a *capital protected* annuity. Under this type of contract, the insurance company guarantees that the total amount it will pay out will never be less than the annuity cost. Thus, if an annuity of £2,000 per annum is purchased for £20,000, and the annuitant dies after having received only three years' instalments totalling £6,000, the insurance company will return £14,000 to his estate.

Another type of contract which can have a similar effect is a *guaranteed* annuity, where the insurance company will guarantee to continue paying annuity instalments for a minimum period of say five or 10 years, irrespective of the annuitant's death.

A further possibility is the purchase of a *short-term* annuity, with part of the annuity income being utilised to build up a capital sum intended ultimately to replace part or even all of the original annuity cost. An explanation of such an arrangement is to be found at § 5–30.

6–07   (ii) How about inflation?

No adviser can honestly claim that there is a complete answer to this problem. In the case of the example noted above, it was shown that the rearrangement of 30 per cent. of the taxpayer's investment capital could be expected to give him an immediate income increase of about 63 per cent. If such an annuity were purchased in 1976, and inflation in the United Kingdom subsisted at around the future annual rate of 13 per cent. which is generally predicted at the time this book goes to press, within five years the taxpayer's income in real terms would have reverted to its 1976 level. Undoubtedly, he would at that time probably be better off than most of his peers who did not have capital in the first place, but if at the age of 75 the taxpayer was still hale and hearty he might well be regretting not having postponed the purchase of his annuity for a few more years. This is a syndrome which all advisers must expect to encounter. In practice most taxpayers in the circumstances mentioned having all of the facts explained to them will opt to buy the annuity at age 70 rather than to postpone purchase, first because of the very understandable urge to enjoy an immediate boost to income, and second for the somewhat ignoble reason that most such persons take the view that the longer they postpone the purchase, the more likely it is that the insurance company, rather than the annuitant, will enjoy the better side of the deal.

6–08   Insurance companies have from time to time introduced *equity-linked* and *property-linked* annuities. The hope behind such contracts is that the price of units to which the initial annuity is linked will progressively increase, so that the annuitant's income will be gradually enhanced. The actual performance of such unit-linked annuities over the past few years hardly suggests that the objective of protecting income against inflation has been achieved: indeed, many purchasers of such annuities find in 1976 that their gross annuity entitlement is significantly lower than when they effected the annuity three or four years ago. If some kind of unit link is felt desirable, there seems little doubt that the relatively stable price movement of property-linked units in recent years is grounds for preferring a property as opposed to an equity link. However, unit-linked annuities generally offer an initial annuity level which is significantly below that available at the particular time through a conventional fixed interest annuity, so that there has to be an upward movement in the unit price before the annuitant even has an income comparable with what he would have enjoyed *ab initio* from a conventional annuity contract.

6–09   For some years before unit-linked annuities were concocted, certain of the more forward looking insurance companies had been offering *escalating* annuities. This is an annuity which will be guaranteed to increase in level by say 3 per cent. or 5 per cent. annually. Even 10 years ago, such a regular increase in income was meaningful, but with inflation expected to average at least 13 per cent. annually until the early 1980s, escalation at 3 per cent. or 5 per cent. annually is little more than a drop in the ocean. As with unit-linked annuities, escalating annuities usually commence from a much lower base than is available from a conventional fixed interest annuity.

Further variants considered

6–10   There are two other major tyes of annuity which require mention:

(i) Deferred annuity.

A deferred annuity is one where the liability for payment will not arise until a predetermined future time. Thus, pension annuities under section 226-approved annuity contracts (considered later in this chapter) are invariably deferred annuities, and a *deferred annuity certain* is often the kernel of a school fees scheme. That part of a guaranteed income bond which returned the investor's cash after the income period was, in the days before the Finance Act 1975 worsened the taxation position, a deferred annuity with an option to take a commuted cash sum.

(ii) Joint life and last survivor.
This is an annuity which will usually be dependent upon two human lives, although in theory any number is possible. Its most common and most obvious application is in the case of husband and wife who wish to provide an increased income until the death of the survivor. It is usual for provision to be included for the annuity to reduce by one-third or one-half at the death of the first annuitant. Such annuities may be arranged as a single bond or a double bond. If the single bond basis is selected the capital content (computed by reference to the actuarial life expectancy of both lives) is calculated and is fixed at inception. In the case of the two bond basis, there will be provided a combination of immediate annuity (probably on the male life which is usually the older of the two) and a *reversionary* annuity, which is one which will only become payable at all if the second life survives the first life. The cost of this reversionary annuity will usually only be a small proportion of the overall annuity purchase consideration, and when and if the reversionary annuity becomes payable, the capital content will at that point of time be recalculated, applying the appropriate factor to the purchase price of the reversionary annuity. This means that when the first life drops, there will often be a quite drastic reduction in the non-taxable element of a joint life and last survivor annuity.

6–11   In the days of estate duty, joint life and last survivor annuities were commonly arranged on the two bond basis, since there could be a distinct estate duty advantage to the wife purchasing the reversionary annuity element out of her own resources, even if those resources were given to her by her husband. It frequently occurred as a shock to the widow to discover that following her husband's death, she sustained a significantly higher income tax liability because the capital content of the annuity was drastically reduced. However, there is not under capital transfer tax the same incentive to choose the two bond arrangement so that there is probably now a much greater case for selecting the single bond basis with the fixed capital content.

Retirement annuity contract

6–12   A retirement annuity contract approved by the Board of Inland Revenue under the Taxes Act 1970, s. 226 can, and very often should, be one of the most important factors in the financial matrix of those eligible to effect such contracts. Policies of this kind are usually known as self-employed deferred annuities, and this expression does sum up very neatly the essence of what is involved. Within limits which are considered below, a person eligible to effect a self-employed deferred annuity can make annual or irregular tax-relieved contributions to build up a personal pension fund, part of which fund may upon retirement be taken as non-taxable cash. Although section 226 approval may be given to trust schemes established for the benefit of groups of individuals engaged in or connected with a particular occupation (for example, employees of a professional partnership)[4] it is much more common for single contracts to be effected by individual taxpayers, so that another popular name for a self-employed deferred annuity is an " individual retirement annuity."

6–13 Those eligible for an individual retirement annuity are all persons in receipt of " net relevant earnings " from any trade, profession, vocation, office or employment.[5] In general terms, this means that those with earnings normally taxed under Schedule D will be eligible, and employees subject to Schedule E also will be eligible, either if their employment does not provide an approved pension scheme, or if they are not members of such scheme. In the case of employees or directors who have pensionable employment, and also non-pensionable income from another source, the non-pensionable other source income will be " net relevant earnings " for section 226 approval purposes. Thus, an employed person who also has significant income from consultancy work can quite legitimately build up two separate pension funds, quite irrespective of any state pension entitlement. The only specific exclusion from net relevant earnings is remuneration received as a controlling director of an investment company: " controlling director " for this purpose means a director of a company controlled by the directors who directly or indirectly owns or controls more than 5 per cent. of the ordinary share capital of the company.[6]

6–14 Where eligible premiums are paid, full relief from income tax is granted within the approved limits.[7] The limitations on qualifying premiums which were set when the self-employed deferred annuity was first introduced by the Finance Act 1956 have in recent years been increased progressively, and with effect from tax year 1977–78 the maximum contribution which would normally be relieved is the lesser of £3,000 or 15 per cent. of " net relevant earnings."[8] These limits are increased in the case of those taxpayers born before 1913 in accordance with the following table[9]:

Taxpayer born in	*Limits*
1914 or 1915	£3,200 or 16%
1912 or 1913	£3,400 or 17%
1910 or 1911	£3,600 or 18%
1908 or 1909	£3,800 or 19%
1907 or earlier	£4,000 or 20%

[4] Taxes Act 1970, s. 226 (5).
[6] *Ibid.*
[8] *Ibid.* s. 227 (1A).
[5] *Ibid.* s. 226 (9).
[7] *Ibid.* s. 227 (1).
[9] *Ibid.* s. 228 (4).

These increased limits will not however be available to an individual who is already in receipt of a pension from earlier fulltime employment, or who has a right thereto at some future time.[10] In cases where there are two or more sources of income, one of which is pensionable, " net relevant earnings " are reduced by 15 per cent. of the pensionable emoluments, or by the higher percentage applicable to those born before 1913.[11]

6–15 The Finance Act 1971 imported section 226A into the Taxes Act 1970, with the intention of enlarging the range of benefits which the self-employed could provide, so as to bring section 226-approved annuities more in line with the benefits commonly available under sponsored superannuation schemes generally.

Section 226A permits the payment of premiums not exceeding the lesser of 5 per cent. of net relevant earnings or £1,000, into a contract having the main objective of providing an annuity for the wife, husband, or dependant(s) of the individual or intended to provide a lump sum on the death of the individual before he attains the age of 75, such sum being payable to his personal representatives. If the taxpayer opts to make provision of this kind, the premium which he pays will be deducted in assessing the limit of premium which he otherwise can contribute to a section 226 annuity.[12]

6–16 Premiums paid will usually be a deduction for purposes of income tax for the tax year in which they are paid. In cases where a tax assessment relating to any year becomes final and conclusive after October 5 of that year, the individual may pay a premium within six months after the date of the final assessment, and provided he makes an election within the six months, the premium will be treated as relating to the year of assessment in question.[13] It should also be noted that if the premium paid in any year exceeds the relevant percentage limitations, any excess can be carried forward and relieved against tax in future years.[14]

6–17 The contract may provide for the policyholder to commute part of his annuity for a lump sum, which must not exceed three times the annual amount of the remaining part of the annuity.[15] Thus, if after extracting a cash sum of £12,000 the annuitant was left with a minimum pension of £4,000, this would be permissible. The pension income itself is taxed as earned income, and normally would have to commence at any age between 60 and 75, although the Revenue has discretion to vary these limits,[16] and certainly will do so in the case of occupations with traditional earlier retirement ages—*e.g.* deep sea

---

[10] *Ibid.* s. 228 (5).
[11] *Ibid.* s. 228 (1).
[12] *Ibid.* s. 227 (1A).
[13] *Ibid.* s. 227 (3).
[14] *Ibid.* s. 227 (2).
[15] *Ibid.* s. 226 (2) proviso.
[16] *Ibid.* s. 226 (3) (*c*).

divers. In the event of premature death of the taxpayer, the return must be restricted either to a return of premiums paid plus reasonable interest or bonuses (in practice, appreciation to the value of units in the unit-linked contracts is allowed) or to an annuity payable to the widow or widower of the individual, which annuity must not exceed that which otherwise would have been payable to the policyholder.[17] Of course, there may also become payable an annuity and/or lump sum to the estate under the terms of a collateral section 226A annuity on the life of the same individual. Any annuity which becomes payable to a widow, widower or dependant is free of capital transfer tax, notwithstanding that under the terms of the particular contract the deceased might have been able to exercise an option for a return of premiums to his estate: the existence of such an option is not regarded for the purpose of the Finance Act 1975, section 23 (2) as a general power of disposal.[18]

Finally, the premiums received by the insurance company, relating as they do to pension business, are invested through a fund which is exempt from income tax and capital gains tax.[19]

Illustration of benefits

6–18   So as to prevent abuse of section 226 annuity contracts it is provided that no annuity shall be capable in whole or in part of surrender, commutation or assignment[20]: the only exception to this is that if the annuity is payable for a term certain, the contract may include provision for the annuity to be assignable by will.[21] When the financial benefits ultimately available under an individual retirement annuity are considered, it will be understood why there is a need for this requirement to prevent abuse of the system.

6–19   As with interest payments which qualify for relief from income tax, the availability of individual retirement annuity tax relief is proportionately more beneficial to the higher-paid. A person with net relevant earnings of £6,000 and normal family and mortgage commitments who contributes £1,000 gross would be relieved from income tax at the basic rate, and if this is 35 per cent., the true net cost of his contribution is *£650*. On the other hand, a person earning £30,000 also with normal family and mortgage commitments would almost certainly be relieved from income tax at the top rate on earned income, and if that rate is 83 per cent., the net cost to him of contributing a premium of £1,000 is *£170*. It therefore costs the lower-paid individual almost four times as much in crude terms to make the same contribution of £1,000: the disparity in terms of proportion of net income after tax paid by each individual is even more striking.

---

[17] *Ibid.* s. 226 (2).
[18] F.A. 1975, Sched. 7, para. 2.
[19] See § 1–07.
[20] T.A. 1970, s. 226 (2).
[21] *Ibid.* s. 226 (3) (*e*).

6–20   Suppose that an individual aged 35 decides to start contributing £1,000 annually, and that he maintains this contribution for 30 years, when he retires and commences to enjoy his individual retirement annuity contract benefits. Bearing in mind that the insurance company pension fund is tax free, it is probably reasonable to assume that the value of his contributions has increased on average over the 30 years' term at 10 per cent. The value of the fund at the age of 65 would be £163,000. Assuming an annuity rate of 15 per cent., this could be used to provide a gross annuity of £24,450. Alternatively, the taxpayer could take a tax-free lump sum of £50,000, with a reduced annuity, purchased with the balance of £113,000, of £16,950.

6–21   As can be seen, the tax-free return of cash at age 65 could well amount to nearly twice the gross premium contributions over the preceding 30 years, and the policyholder would still enjoy a very substantial pension income for the remainder of his lifetime. The benefits would have been engendered at a net cost to the basic rate tax payer of £19,500; the net cost to the top-rate tax payer over the 30 years would be just £5,100. Of course, the top-rate tax payer would be in the position to contribute up to £3,000 annually, and enjoy appropriately greater benefits.

Annuities and chargeable events

6–22   As applies in the case of policies of assurance, life annuity contracts can give rise to a liability to income tax on the happening of a chargeable event.[22] Furthermore, in the case of contracts made after March 26, 1974, the happening of a chargeable event can result in a liability to basic rate income tax as well as to higher rate income tax and the investment income surcharge.[23]

6–23   To the uninitiated, it might appear somewhat perverse that life annuities, being essentially contracts intended to protect income, should be capable of falling within a special charge to income tax, particularly when there is specific legislation designed to ensure that a proportion of all purchased life annuities is exempt from income tax. The reason for including life annuities within the chargeable event provisions is that they were being increasingly used as a medium for tax avoidance, principally in the area of guaranteed income bonds; this subject is considered in detail later in the chapter. Thus, no chargeable event will occur unless a purchased life annuity is surrendered or assigned in whole or in part, and in the vast majority of all cases there is never any prospect of any such event occurring. In the case of contracts effected on or after December 10, 1974, death also can be a chargeable event, being treated as a surrender in whole of the rights conferred by the contract, but in the case of a purchased life

---

[22] *Ibid.* s. 393 (1).
[23] *Ibid.* s. 397 and F.A. 1975, Sched. 2, para. 17.

annuity effected in the normal way of business with the genuine intent of supplementing income, this need not cause concern since the cash return under a capital protected annuity, or the cash alternative under a guaranteed annuity, will never be sufficiently large to attract an income tax charge.[24]

6–24   A chargeable event occurs in relation to any contract for a life annuity on the surrender or assignment for value of the whole of the contract. In the case of partial surrender of assignment, the " excess aggregate value " charging provisions of the Finance Act 1975 operate, as in the case of life policies.[25] Broadly, this means that it is possible for partial surrenders or assignments to take place, up to the annual limit of 5 per cent. of the cost of the annuity, without there being any immediate taxation liability. As with life policies, the occurrence of a terminal charge (death; surrender in whole; or assignment in whole) is the occasion for a final " mopping up " calculation which takes account of any previous partial surrenders or assignments. Also as with life policies, with effect from December 10, 1974, it is no longer possible to avoid the chargeable event provisions by the " double assignment technique." This means that if a taxpayer effects an annuity and then assigns it the annuity subsequently being assigned back to him, he can no longer subsequently deal with the policy with exemption from the chargeable event provisions. Also as with life policies, any assignment between spouses living together, or effected by way of security for or on the discharge of a debt, is not a chargeable event.

6–25   On the happening of a chargeable event there is treated as a gain then arising:

(i) If the event is the surrender in whole of the rights conferred by the contract, the excess (if any) of the amount then payable *plus* any sum or other benefit of a capital nature paid or conferred before the happening of the chargeable event **over** the consideration paid for the annuity *less* the capital content of any instalments of annuity already paid, *plus* the total of excess values, if any, which have previously arisen.[26] Where a capital sum is payable on death and the contract was made on or after December 10, 1974, death is treated as a surrender.

(ii) If the event is an assignment, what is chargeable is the excess (if any) of the consideration *plus* any capital payments received under the contract before the happening of the chargeable event (or of any previously assigned share) **over** the same amounts as are specified at (i) above.[27]

Finally, in the event of the occurrence of " excess aggregate value " in any policy year, there will be a chargeable gain.

---

[24] See § 6–27.   [25] See § 4–47.
[26] T.A. 1970, s. 397.   [27] *Ibid.*

6–26   In summary, these apparently complicated provisions for calculating the chargeable gain are simple. Where the event is death, assignment or surrender in whole, what is chargeable at that time is any surplus of all *capital* payments received under the contract over the purchase consideration less capital contents, if any. In the case of an excess aggregate value charge, what is chargeable is any surplus of payments received over the then total of " credits," each credit being 5 per cent. per annum of the purchase consideration. The annual " totting up " of 5 per cent. credits is dated from the time of purchase of the annuity, or from the policy year in which there last occurred a chargeable excess.

6–27   It was mentioned above that the practical effect of these charging provisions is to preclude any liability, in the case of " normal " purchased life annuities where no attempt is made so to manipulate them as to provide an undue taxation advantage. For example, consider the case of a capital protected annuity purchased for £100,000 and paying an annuity of £20,000 annually, of which £7,100 is tax free. Suppose that the annuitant dies after two full years' instalments have been paid. The return to his estate is £60,000 and from this must be deducted the purchase consideration of £100,000 *less* the total (£14,200) of capital contents of the annuity instalments already paid: this gives a net amount of £85,800, and the calculation results in a negative figure of £25,800. Hence there would be no tax charge, since application of this formula does not result in an excess. The real point of this legislation is to impose a tax charge where the annuitant accepts the cash option under a guaranteed income bond or similar contract, as is considered below.

Guaranteed income bonds

6–28   The guaranteed income bond was a method whereby substantial income benefits could be generated for high-rate tax payers, by taking advantage of the relatively sheltered tax treatment of insurance company annuity funds, and of purchased life annuities in the hands of annuitants. The typical guaranteed income bond consisted of two separate contracts:

  (i) A temporary immediate annuity, designed to provide a relatively lightly taxed income for a period of typically five or 10 years.

  (ii) A deferred annuity with a cash option. Ostensibly, this annuity was intended primarily to give the taxpayer the opportunity of continuing to enjoy a high income at expiry of the five or 10 years period of contract (i) above: in practice, the intention invariably was that the annuitant would exercise the cash option. The amount of that option would normally and conveniently be the sum of the considerations paid for contracts (i) and (ii) together.

6-29   Specific insurance companies were able from time to time to invite the public to make substantial subscriptions towards these guaranteed income bonds. Depending on the investment state of the general annuity fund from time to time, individual insurance companies were able, using these specially subscribed funds, to make substantial purchases of government stock, in the knowledge that because of the balance of investment income in the general annuity fund, no income tax would ever have to be paid on the interest received. They were thus able to pass the benefit of this freedom from taxation on to individual policyholders, who in turn (because of purchased life annuity treatment) were only lightly taxed on the income received. The net effect was that guaranteed income bonds were exceedingly attractive to basic rate income tax payers, although on the whole the higher the individual policyholder's top rate of income tax, the less attractive they were since the taking of the cash option under contract (ii) was a chargeable event giving rise to liability to higher rate income tax and the investment income surcharge, on the top slicing basis. The basic rate income tax payer was not inhibited by considerations of a tax penalty from taking the commuted cash value of his deferred annuity contract. Therefore, a basic rate income tax payer was in effect enabled to enjoy an after-tax income for say five or 10 years of in excess of 10 per cent. (being the net annual instalment of the temporary annuity). At the time this type of guaranteed income bond was popular, a tax free return in excess of 10 per cent. was noticeably better than could be obtained elsewhere by a basic rate income tax payer, so that inevitably the insurance companies were starting to attract funds which traditionally would have been placed with building societies or simply left on deposit with the bank.

6-30   It was partly because of the distortion in the traditional savings market referred to at the end of the last paragraph that the Finance Act 1975 introduced a charge to basic rate income tax on the profit element arising under life annuity contracts. In the case of chargeable events in connection with any life annuity contract made after March 26, 1975, the gain is chargeable to tax under Case VI of Schedule D. As, in a typical case, the cash option under a 10-year deferred annuity would be in excess of twice the annuity consideration, this provision in effect sounded the death knell for the old type of guaranteed income bond. One of its main attractions was the ability to receive back after say 10 years the combined cost of the two (immediate temporary and deferred) annuities, possibly tax free, but the effect of bringing the gain into a basic rate income tax charge would in most cases be to impose a tax liability equivalent to at least 20 per cent. of the initial consideration for the combined annuities. This liability would of course be significantly greater if the policyholder were in any event subject to the higher rates of income tax.

6–31   Purveyors of guaranteed income bonds have now been forced to alter the contractual basis. The current favourite arrangement is to link the bond to the life fund (as opposed to the general annuity fund) and to generate the " income " element through the regular encashment of bonuses. In cases where the income thus provided exceeds 5 per cent. of the capital cost of the bond, there is a chargeable excess aggregate value in each policy year,[28] but this will result in a nil liability to a basic rate taxpayer. The basic endowment policy itself may be a non-qualifying policy,[29] so that maturity after say five or 10 years also is a chargeable event: once more this holds out no danger so far as the basic rate income tax payer is concerned. Because the taxation treatment of the life fund is generally less favourable than is the tax treatment of the general annuity fund, the net yields available under the endowment-based version of the guaranteed income bond are much less favourable than applied when the bonds were linked to the annuity fund.

Loan to purchase life annuity

6–32   One potentially important application of the purchased life annuity within the field of overall estate planning occurs in the case of what are popularly known as " house and income " plans. This entails the making of a loan advance by an insurance company, secured against the collateral of an elderly taxpayer's private residence. The borrower is then required to apply most if not all of the sum borrowed to the purchase of an annuity from the insurance company which has made the loan advance. The loan is usually repayable at death of the annuitant, and it is usually envisaged that the cash required to repay the loan will be produced from the deceased's estate through the sale of his private residence; the insurance company secures its interest by means of a legal charge. This can be a very useful method of enabling an elderly taxpayer to enjoy during his own lifetime the benefit of the equity in his own house, which equity he may well have spent the best part of a lifetime in acquiring. Such a scheme is basically good business for the insurance company, which receives captive life annuity business as well as being able to lend money out from its general annuity fund at a good rate of interest, well secured. The security aspect is the only real weakness from the point of view of the insurance company, if only because on the winding up of an estate there are always liable to be problems of title or related to claims against the estate which could mean undue prolongment of the loan being repaid. House and income plans will generally commend themselves to widows, widowers, or married couples without children or whose children are already reasonably independent financially.

---

[28] See § 4–47.
[29] Either because it matures within less than 10 years, or because it does not provide death benefit equal to at least 75 per cent. of all premiums.

Insurance companies who are prepared to accept this type of business will usually grant a joint loan to husband and wife, coupled with a joint life and last survivor annuity. As a general rule of thumb, it is felt that in days of high inflation schemes of this kind should not be contemplated at less than age 70. The table which follows gives a rough assessment of the type of income which might be provided from an advance of £10,000 to a taxpayer entering the scheme five years either side of the suggested minimum age of 70:

AGE OF TAXPAYER	65	75
	£	£
Interest on loan @ 12%	1,200	1,200
Less: Taxable portion of annuity	1,295	1,340
	(95)	(140)
Deduct: Income tax at 35%	33	49
	(62)	(91)
Add: Tax-free portion of annuity	705	1,198
NET INCOME FROM SCHEME	£643	£1,107

The income tax position in relation to these contracts can probably best be explained by the following extract from *Hansard* of November 3, 1975:

" Life Annuities (Loans)

Mr. Graham asked the Chancellor of the Exchequer whether he will make a statement about the position, under the new rules introduced by the Finance Act 1975 for the tax treatment of loans taken in connection with life annuities, of schemes of the house and income type.

Mr. Robert Sheldon: Yes. The ' House and Incomes ' schemes operated by some life offices enable an elderly person owning his own home to increase his income by obtaining a loan from the life office on the security of his property and apply the money to the purchase of an annuity from the life office. In appropriate circumstances income can later be increased by taking an additional loan with which to buy a further annuity.

When the rules under which tax relief is allowable on interest paid were amended in the Finance Act 1974 a specific provision—paragraph 24 of Schedule 1 to the Act—was incorporated to ensure that interest payable on loans up to a maximum of £25,000 under this type of scheme would qualify for tax relief.

It has now emerged that where a second or later loan is taken in connection with an arrangement of this kind which was effected after 26th March, 1974, the combined effects of paragraphs 16 and 17 of Schedule 2 to the Finance Act 1975 is to impose a tax charge, based on the amount of that loan, as though there had been a surrender of rights under the original annuity contract. This result was not intended, and where it occurred it would largely defeat the purpose of paragraph 24.

The Government therefore propose to include in the next Finance Bill a short provision to rectify the position in those cases where the conditions for tax relief under paragraph 24 are satisfied. In the meantime the Inland Revenue will, by concession, refrain from raising a tax charge in any case of this kind which may arise."

This undertaking was duly implemented by the Finance Act 1976, s. 35.

CHAPTER 7

CLOSE COMPANIES

7–01   THE role of life assurance in funding capital transfer tax liabilities has been examined. One of the most important practical applications of building up such funds is in dealing with transmission of the ownership of successful businesses from one generation to the next. An interest in a successful and therefore valuable business may take the form of a formal or informal partnership; this introduces special capital transfer tax and other taxation problems which are considered elsewhere. Manufacturing and service industries are much more likely to be organised in the form of a company, and it should be noted that a sizeable proportion of the work force in this country is employed by small, privately owned (and hence closely controlled) companies.

7–02   It is manifest that the transmission of a valuable block of shares in a private company, other than between spouses, can give rise to very serious liquidity problems. The tax payable on an *inter vivos* transfer worth £150,000 is just over £30,000, and although this liability is high, it is modest when compared with the liability on the same shares transferred on or within three years of death, when the tax payable jumps to just under £55,000. It is stressed that these figures are minima: if the transferor *inter vivos* has made previous taxable transfers the liability will be higher, and assuming (as is highly probable) that the estate at death comprises other valuable assets in addition to £150,000-worth of shares, the effective rate of tax will be greater and the liability will exceed £55,000.

7–03   Given the difference of around £25,000 in the liability, comparing an *inter vivos* with a testamentary disposition of the same assets, there is obviously a very strong case in favour of disposing of as many as possible of the shares during the shareholder's lifetime. In most cases, this fine theory will be incapable of execution, for the simple reason that persons whose main asset comprises close company shares are unlikely to have ready access to £30,000. Even if such an amount of cash were readily available, most close company shareholders would undoubtedly prefer, if at all practicable, to put the cash into the business, rather than spending it on making a bountiful gesture in favour of the next generation.

7–04   In circumstances such as these, it can be seen that the taxpayer has Hobson's choice for all practical purposes. He is almost bound to accept the near-impossibility of making *inter vivos* transfers of shares on a meaningful scale, and must hope that at his ultimate death some method will be found to enable the burden to be met. Although this does mean accepting that the low scale of tax applicable to life-time transfers will not be available, prudent planning through life assurance can go a long way towards ameliorating the taxpayer's natural dislike of being forced to accept tax at the higher of the two scales.

Funding by the company

7–05   Staying for the moment with the figures used above, let us assume a taxpayer, aged 55 and in good health, who is the managing director of a successful close company, and whose shareholding is indeed estimated to be worth £150,000 at probate value, with a probable minimum capital transfer tax liability (allowing for aggregation of his other assets) of £60,000. Because the business is a successful one, the probability is that the probate value of the shares will steadily increase with successive years of profitable trading, and it is desired therefore that any arrangement for funding the tax liability should make some allowance for this. Probably the most suitable contract in this case will be an equity-linked whole life assurance where there is a good probability that the death benefit payable under the policy will progressively increase.

7–06   The company decides to insure the director's life, and immediately after effecting the policy declares that it holds the policy as trustee for a class of beneficiaries comprising the director's wife, children and grandchildren, the trust terms being such as to give the director's two children (to whom he wishes to pass his shares) interests in possession in the trust fund. The gross annual premium payable by the company is £2,000, and since the managing director has a life service contract with his company, the expectation is that the company will in practice keep up the payment of the £2,000 premium annually until the managing director's eventual death or until the premium payment falling due after his eighty-third birthday, when under the terms of the policy premiums in any event cease. The initial and minimum death benefit under the policy is £47,500 and assuming that the equity units allocated to the policy each time a premium is paid increase in value on average at 3 per cent. annually, the size of the trust fund if the director should die at age 80 would be £63,600.

7–07   Provision by the company of this " benefit in kind " will be assessed as a Schedule E benefit, so that the director will have to pay tax on the amount of the annual premium.[1] Let us take it that at the present time his remuneration, all earned, is £12,000. His additional income tax assessment, because of the £2,000 annual premium payment, will be £1,350. If the company wishes to ensure that the managing director's take home pay, after tax, is no less than applied prior to the insurance policy having been effected, it will have to pay

---

[1] Taxes Act 1970, s. 220.

him an additional £5,000 (which will be worth an extra £1,350 to the director, after income tax). The extra £5,000 should, without too much difficulty, be allowed as an expenditure item in calculating the company's income tax liability,[2] so that the net cost to the company will be £2,400 annually. In addition, it must bear the £2,000 annual premium out of its taxed profits, so that the net annual drain on company profits amounts to £4,400. In exchange for this, the company does know that it has taken a vital step towards ensuring its own survival, since the insurance trust fund ultimately will provide the right cash in the right hands at the right time to discharge capital transfer tax payable when a large block of shares in the company passes to the next generation. It should be noted that payment of the premium by the company will not result in a capital transfer tax apportionment by virtue of the director's shareholding, as he is assessed to income tax on the premium.[3]

This is certainly not the most tax-efficient method of passing a successful business from generation to generation. It does however have the merits of simplicity, and of providing a perfectly legitimate way for the company to make additional financial recompense towards its managing director, without the director himself feeling that he is unnecessarily extracting profits from the company.

7–08 It is stressed that the figures quoted, as throughout this book, are purely for illustration purposes and very much hypothetical. It is manifest that this approach is most likely to be found attractive, and to succeed in practice, in the case of the smaller close company. If the shares to be protected are worth £500,000, the minimum tax liabilities are £224,000 on a lifetime transfer, and £265,000 on a transfer within three years of death. Although even liabilities on this scale *could* in the right circumstances be contained through insurance, the probability is that it will be necessary to look towards other methods of mitigation. The capital transfer tax liability on a shareholding worth £500,000 could relatively easy be funded, using the method just described, if the controlling director is aged 30, and it should not present too great a problem up to about age 40. Beyond that however, the costs involved become prohibitive—*not* in terms of the straight cost of providing the required level of life cover, but in terms of the net annual cost to the company after allowing for the very high additional personal income tax liability which would be generated in most cases.

7–09 It should also be emphasised that in this chapter the writer has deliberately ignored the very valuable benefits which can be achieved through taking maximum advantage of capital transfer tax exemptions and reliefs, in particular the ability for each of two spouses to give away assets worth up to £2,000 each year, without incurring liability.

---

2 *Ibid.* ss. 250, 130.　　　　　　　　　　3 F.A. 1975, s. 39 (2) (*a*).

This obviously must form part of the mitigation process in planning any estate, and it will be obvious to any professional adviser how the use of life assurance, as described in this chapter, might well fit into an overall plan.

7–10   Separate consideration is given below to life cover through an approved pension plan, and this certainly can have its attractions. It should be noted however that there are strict limits on the level of life cover (broadly, it cannot exceed four times annual salary) which can be provided through an approved scheme. In addition, the great drawback to this type of provision is that in practice the director has to face the choice of the payments into an approved scheme providing *either* permanent life assurance cover *or* a pension when he retires coupled with temporary life cover—he cannot have it both ways. Since the tax advantages, and indeed the ultimate pension entitlement, of an approved pension scheme are highly attractive, it is the author's view that in the majority of cases pension provision should be regarded as an entirely separate subject from capital transfer tax planning. If the director does indeed want to draw his pension age 65 or 70, he must face up to the fact that under an approved scheme his potential tax-free life assurance protection will vanish when he starts to draw his pension, and of course it will vanish at precisely the time when it otherwise would be most valuable to him.

7–11   Before the coming into effect of the code of approval for occupational pension schemes in accordance with Chapter II, Part II of the Finance Act 1970, as amended by the Finance Acts 1971 and 1973, there was little by way of financial benefit which could be provided by a close company to a " controlling director " without adverse taxation consequences. The definition of " controlling director " was a director of a company, wherein the directors had a controlling interest, who was the owner of, or able to control, more than 5 per cent. of the ordinary share capital of the company. To all intents and purposes therefore, any director owning more than 5 per cent. of the shares in a family company was precluded from taking any financial benefit, apart from remuneration and usual business expenses. The Finance Act 1973 heralded a much more favourable financial climate for such directors. Under the pre-1971 *pensions* legislation, it was not possible for a controlling director to become a member of his company's approved pension scheme. Thus, he was denied the benefit of the taxation advantages stemming from membership of an approved pension scheme, which may be summarised as:

(i) any contribution made by the scheme member personally is allowed to be deducted as an expense in assessing tax under Schedule E;

(ii) any contribution paid by the company is a deduction against trading profits for corporation tax purposes;

(iii) the pension fund itself is exempt from income tax and capital gains tax;

(iv) the pension, when paid, is taxed as earned income;

(v) provision can be made to pay a pension to the member's widow, children or dependants; and

(vi) significant life assurance cover can be provided, covering death in service, which benefit would normally be payable to the deceased's widow, children or dependants *free of capital transfer tax.*

–12 After 1973, the position of a controlling director is generally *pari passu* with that of any employee of the company. The obvious inference to be drawn is that what was widely considered to be an injustice has been removed in that a man is no longer denied the benefits of approved pension scheme membership, merely because he owns shares in a company as well as working for it. However, it is necessary to probe a little deeper in order to reveal the total potential value to a close company shareholder of approved pension scheme membership.

–13 Two preliminary points must be made. First, all references which will be made are based on the Finance Act 1970 legislation, as amended and implemented by the Finance Acts 1971 and 1973, which in effect means that there may be some difference in approval requirements and conditions if it is desired to extend new membership to or the benefits provided by, an existing approved pension scheme in force before April 5, 1973. Secondly, it cannot be stressed too strongly that for the benefits of an approved pension scheme to be enjoyed, it is essential that the occupational pension scheme in question be approved by the Board of Inland Revenue. Practically, this means that all future schemes (commonly referred to as " new code " approved schemes so as to distinguish them from " old " schemes approved under Chap. II, Pt. IX of the Taxes Act 1970) must be submitted to the Superannuation Funds Office for approval. In the writer's experience, approval is currently unlikely to be withheld from any arrangement following the suggestions set out in this chapter. Also, it is to be recognised that in a book of this kind it is expedient to take no note of what for simplicity can best be described as " special situations." By this is meant a recognition that the Revenue currently tends to be generous in exercising its discretion under section 20 of the Finance Act 1970; indeed it is no exaggeration to state that the discretion tends to be generous to a fault. This observation is made so as to reassure those with significant shareholdings in close companies, and their advisers, that they should not decide against investigating what might be achieved through an exempt approved scheme merely on some such grounds as that the company is involved in a cyclical business, hence subject to wide variations in profitability.

Estimate of potential income tax savings

7–14   Before examining the annuity and life assurance benefits which can be provided through an exempt approved scheme, it is interesting to contemplate the *maximum* taxation benefits which might accrue.

7–15   Consider a close company with trading profits for corporation tax purposes of £100,000. The tax payable on this trading profit would be £52,000, leaving a net profit after tax of £48,000. Under section 94 of and Schedule 16 to the Finance Act 1972, it may well be necessary for the company to pay out by way of dividend 50 per cent. of its trading profit, after taxation, of £48,000. Therefore the company may decide to distribute £24,000 and assuming that this goes wholly to four shareholding directors, each of whom has remuneration of £17,500 from the company but no other income, the total income tax payable by the four directors on that £24,000 will be at least £17,420. The overall position therefore is that on trading profits of £100,000, the total taxation is £69,420, leaving a total net amount, mainly in the hands of the company but with a tiny proportion in the hands of the directors, of £30,580.

7–16   Suppose now that the company implements an approved pension scheme, and decides to make total contributions of £30,000 (most of which is, in practice, used to build up benefits specifically for the four directors). The taxable profit for corporation tax purposes is reduced to £70,000, and the corporation tax on this is £36,400, leaving a net amount of £33,600. Even if the company is obliged to distribute one half of this, when the income tax borne by the directors would be £12,470, the total tax liability on trading profits of £100,000 is reduced from £69,420 to £48,870, being a tax saving of £20,550. It can be seen that the net cost to the company and its directors of making pension contributions totalling £30,000 is just £9,450, and in exchange for this there will ultimately be secured benefits attributable to the full gross contribution of £30,000.

7–17   In practice, it may be in some cases that the reduction by £30,000 of trading profits subject to corporation tax will result in a significant additional saving. As profits for tax purposes have been reduced to £70,000, it may be easier for the company to secure the Revenue's agreement that there should be no apportionment of income to the shareholders under section 94. In the event of such a happy outcome, the total amount of tax paid would be only the corporation tax of £36,400, as compared with the earlier illustrated figure of £69,420, being a tax saving amounting to no less than £33,040, or £3,040 more than the gross pension contribution of £30,000.

7–18   Naturally, it is not to be assumed by companies and their advisers that the mere implementation of an approved pension scheme is a magic formula for achieving an improvement in the apportionment position. Whether or not an apportionment is appropriate will invariably depend on all of the circumstances surrounding the company's trading results and proven needs to retain profits for future expansion of business activities. Nevertheless, if there is a smaller cake to be divided after all allowable outgoings, including pension contributions, this is bound to strengthen the negotiating hand of the company and its accountants.

Legislative background

–19   As the whole question of pensions is, to the average practitioner, shrouded in mystery, it will be as well to note here the essential legislation.

–20   Section 19 of the Finance Act 1970 sets out conditions, all of which must be satisfied, in order for Revenue approval to be given to " any retirement benefits scheme." The conditions are set out in subsection (2), as follows:

" (2) The said conditions are—
    (*a*) that the scheme is bona fide established for the sole purpose of providing relevant benefits in respect of service as an employee (as defined in this Chapter), being benefits payable to, or to the widow, children or dependants or personal representatives of, the employee,
    (*b*) that the scheme is recognised by the employer and employees to whom it relates, and that every employee who is, or has a right to be, a member of the scheme has been given written particulars of all essential features of the scheme which concern him,
    (*c*) that there is a person resident in the United Kingdom who will be responsible for the discharge of all duties imposed on the administrator of the scheme under this Chapter,
    (*d*) that the employer is a contributor to the scheme,
    (*e*) that the scheme is established in connection with some trade or undertaking carried on in the United Kingdom by a person resident in the United Kingdom,
    (*f*) [repealed by F.A. 1973],
    (*g*) that in no circumstances, whether during the subsistence of the scheme or later, can any amount be paid by way of repayment of an employee's contributions under the scheme." [4]

The legislation goes on to define the general limits of benefits, and restrictions on their application, as follows:

" (2A) Subject to subsection (1) above, the Board shall approve a retirement benefits scheme for the purposes of this Chapter if

[4] F.A. 1970, s. 19 (2).

the scheme satisfies all of the conditions in this subsection, that is—

    (*a*) that any benefit for an employee is a pension on retirement at a specified age not earlier than 60 (or, if the employee is a woman, 55) and not later than 70, which does not exceed one-sixtieth of the employee's final remuneration for each year of service up to a maximum of 40,

    (*b*) that any benefit for any widow of an employee is a pension payable on his death after retirement such that the amount payable to the widow by way of pension does not exceed two-thirds of any pension or pensions payable to the employee,

    (*c*) that no other benefits are payable under the scheme,

    (*d*) that no pension is capable in whole or in part of surrender, commutation or assignment, except so far as the scheme allows an employee on retirement to obtain, by commutation of his pension, a lump sum or sums not exceeding in all three-eightieths of his final remuneration for each year of service up to a maximum of 40." [5]

7–21   In order to take care of special circumstances, the Revenue is given discretion by the Finance Act 1970, s. 20 (1), to approve a retirement benefits scheme which does not satisfy one or more of the prescribed conditions. Section 20 (2) states:

" (2) The Board may in particular approve by virtue of this section a scheme—

    (*a*) which exceeds the limits imposed by the prescribed conditions as respects benefits for less than 40 years' service, or

    (*b*) which exceeds the limits imposed by the prescribed conditions as respects benefits payable on the death of the employee, and in particular which provides a pension for the employee's widow, or

    (*c*) which provides for the return in certain contingencies of employees' contributions, or

    (*d*) which relates to a trade or undertaking carried on only partly in the United Kingdom, and by a person not resident in the United Kingdom." [6]

7–22   Perhaps the most important case where it is known that the Revenue will exercise its discretion favourably is in the case of controlling directors of close companies who, prior to the Finance Act 1973, were unable to participate in an approved pension scheme. Take the case of a director who was born in 1910, joined the family company in 1935 having already inherited more than 5 per cent. of the equity, and who

---

[5] F.A. 1970, s. 19 (2A).
[6] F.A. 1970, s. 20 (2).

is managing director in 1976. He has a service contract with the company whereby he is expected to retire at age 70—*i.e.* in 1980. Strictly speaking, it would appear that if the company wanted to give its managing director a decent pension, it could be severely circumscribed as to *quantum* by the fact that the director would have only nine years' service between 1971 and retirement in 1980. In practice, the Revenue will normally approve a scheme whereby the company can provide a pension based on two-thirds of final remuneration (defined as the average annual remuneration of the last three years' service),[7] and of course the whole of the cost of this pension provision, once the scheme has been approved, would have to be met out of trading profits over a relatively short period of time. This can clearly result in substantial amounts of trading revenue being paid directly to the insurance company underwriting the pension scheme, rather than the amounts of pension contribution being subjected to corporation tax, with the amount net of that tax possibly being subject to an apportionment resulting in a substantial income tax liability to the managing director.

7–23 Because of the provision allowing commutation of so much of a pension as to provide the scheme member with a lump sum not exceeding three-eightieths of final remuneration for each year of service up to a maximum of 40, it is known that some companies have been advised that they should enter into pension schemes, designed mainly if not solely to provide lump sums at retirement, rather than a true pension. For example, a managing director currently earning £20,000 annually, and due to retire four years hence, might be advised to encourage his company to seek approval for a pension scheme ostensibly to provide him with a pension within the maximum permitted limit in his case of £13,333, but where the intention is that at pension age, most or all of the pension will simply be commuted so as to give him a tax-free lump sum of £30,000. Considering that this lump sum would have been provided out of company profits which had been relieved for corporation tax, there must be some doubt as to whether such ploys are advisable. It was after all the fear of approved pension schemes being utilised to avoid taxation on a large scale which was responsible in the first place for controlling directors being debarred from occupational pension scheme membership. It would be a great pity if abuse by the few of the relief for controlling directors introduced by the Finance Act 1973 were to lead to the whole range of benefits which can arise from an approved retirement benefit scheme being again withdrawn. Whilst it is often difficult to draw the line between what constitutes proper and fair use of relieving provisions, and what constitutes abuse in the sense of clearly being outside the spirit of what Parliament intended, there

---

[7] F.A. 1970, s. 26.

seems little doubt that the concessions to controlling directors introduced by the Finance Act 1973 were certainly not intended primarily
to enable those directors to drive a coach and horses through the close
company apportionment provisions of the Finance Act 1972, s. 94.

Illustration of practical application

7-24   As has been noted, the Revenue tends to be generous, not to say
imaginative, in giving discretionary approval under the Finance Act
1970, s. 20 to retirement benefits schemes which are outside the usual
prescribed conditions. Therefore, it would be quite impossible, as well
as undesirable, in a book intended mainly to give guidance to
practitioners, to attempt to suggest all of the ways in which the
sensible use of a new code approved scheme could improve the financial
wellbeing of companies and their controlling directors. One illustration
of a practical application now in common use should suffice to show
what can be achieved through using a little ingenuity.

7-25   Consider the case of a controlling director aged 60 who has a
pressing capital transfer tax problem. It is estimated conservatively
that the amount of capital transfer tax payable at his death, in
relation to his shares in his close company, is £80,000. Whilst he is
aware of the probable postponement of capital transfer tax which
could be achieved if his wife, who is his junior by eight years, were
given a life interest in his estate, nevertheless he is realistic enough
to recognise that this at best would have the effect of postponing the
day of reckoning. In any event, it is the director's wish that his son,
who already is showing promise as a junior director of the company,
should for preference inherit his father's shareholding directly at the
death of the father. It would certainly be easier to justify transmitting
the shares directly from father to son if some method could be found
of ensuring that if the father does predecease the mother, adequate
financial provision has been made for the widow.

7-26   As is common with closely controlled companies, the managing
director has a life service agreement; a copy of the agreement will
have to be supplied to the Superannuation Funds Office. It is plain
that if the managing director is legally bound to work for the company
throughout his lifetime, it would be nonsensical for the company to
seek approval for his membership of a normal approved scheme,
designed to provide him with a pension on retirement at no later than
age 70. However, approval should be forthcoming for the company to
contribute the cost of *whole life assurance* intended to provide the
following combination of benefits:

  (i) a maximum sum assured payable on death equivalent to four
      times salary; and
  (ii) a pension payable to the managing director's widow, in the
      event of his death in service, equivalent to two-thirds of the

maximum pension that could normally have been provided for the director on retirement at age 70.

7–27   Under (ii) above the Revenue currently takes the view that the maximum pension which could have been provided to the director personally, at age 70, is two-thirds of final remuneration, provided that his age at commencement of service was under 60. Therefore, the maximum widow's pension which will be payable is four-ninths of final remuneration, which in this case would give the widow a pension of £8,889. Bearing in mind that the wife is aged only 52, a substantial cash sum would be needed to provide her pension, should her husband's death occur shortly after entry into the scheme. Therefore, it may well be necessary for the sum assured by the whole life policy to be equivalent to approximately ten times the managing director's salary of £20,000. Then, in the event of an early death, £200,000 would be paid out to the scheme trustees, and they would utilise £80,000 of this in order to pay out the death benefit, in accordance with the terms of the scheme trust, leaving £120,000 available to buy an annuity so as to provide the widow with a pension for life of £8,889.

7–28   It will be appreciated that since there are bound to be unknown variable factors (*e.g.* the exact level of final remuneration when death occurs, and the cost of securing an annuity to pay the widow's pension) the cash sum payable at death could well show a surplus, after meeting the trustees' commitments. Here, it is worth commenting that provision for a widow's pension may be made even though the director, at the time of commencement of the scheme, is not married. Should this facility be incorporated, and the director be unmarried at his death, there could be a very substantial surplus available, after paying out the maximum permissible death benefit of four times final remuneration. Other factors contributing towards a potential surplus are the difficulty of estimating the rate at which bonuses might accrue to a with profits policy, the possibility that the director's remuneration as he grows older and frailer might reduce, or the fact of deaths occurring in the " wrong " order so that although there is a prospective widow when the plans commence, there is alas no widow to enjoy a pension, when the managing director eventually dies. In the event of there being a surplus, the approved course is for that surplus to be paid back to the employing company, when it will be regarded for tax purposes as a trading receipt. In the right circumstances, this can mean that payment of premiums to keep up the whole life policy could turn out to be a lucrative investment, bearing in mind that all premiums are relieved for corporation tax purposes. However, the return of a substantial cash sum to the company in this manner would no doubt have the effect of increasing the probate value of the deceased's shares, for capital transfer tax purposes. One of the features of a Revenue approved retirement benefit scheme is that once approval has been received, the position is very flexible. In particular, there should be no undue complication in the event that the director leaves the company or retires (possibly for reasons of poor health) notwithstanding his lifetime service agreement. The whole life policy would be converted to a paid up contract, or surrendered, probably with a view to providing a pension (part of which could be commuted for cash) at age 70, or a reduced lump sum in the event of prior death. In the case of the director withdrawing from service after his fiftieth birthday, the more likely course is that the policy would be forthwith surrendered, and the cash proceeds used to provide a range of benefits similar to those which would have been available, had the original Revenue approval been to a more conventional approved scheme, specifically designed to provide benefit at age 70 together with the usual permitted benefits for a widow or dependant.

7-29   Reverting to the case under consideration, the cost of providing £200,000 of whole life assurance with profits for the managing director currently aged 60 would be approximately £11,000. The net cost to the company, after corporation tax relief at 52 per cent., would be £5,280 each year. As part of the approval procedure, the Revenue would have approved pension scheme rules which would incorporate a discretionary or other trust to receive the benefit of the four times final remuneration part of the death benefit.[8] Through this trust, it will be possible for the trustees to pay out the full £80,000 death benefit, or whatever the actual amount is based on final remuneration, directly to the son, who will thus be in funds to meet the capital transfer tax liability in respect of his inheritance of his deceased father's shares in the company. Further, the widow will receive a substantial pension for the remainder of her lifetime, so that reasonable financial equity as amongst the various family members will have been achieved.

Importance of Revenue attitude

7-30   For the arrangement just described to achieve the optimum capital transfer tax position (that is, complete freedom from taxation on the £80,000 death in service benefit) it is necessary to obtain Inland Revenue approval to the pension scheme. As was noted earlier, Revenue approval to an arrangement of the kind described will be forthcoming, if at all, because of the Board exercising its right of discretionary approval under the Finance Act 1970, s. 20. Whereas it is mandatory for the Board to approve any scheme falling within the criteria noted at section 19 (2A) of the Finance Act 1970, there is no such compulsion in circumstances, such as those described in the foregoing section of this chapter, where it is improbable that the director concerned will ever in fact draw a pension.

7-31   Prior to February 28, 1977, it was Revenue practice to approve

---

[8] See Appendix III.

an arrangement of the kind just described, whereby at death of the director the four times salary death benefit of £80,000 would be payable by the pension scheme trustees in such a way as not to attract capital transfer tax. Presumably because of undue emphasis which was given to this method of financial planning, it was decided that as from the date indicated approval would only be given to arrangements whereby under the terms of the trust deed, any death in service benefit arising after age 75 is payable to the deceased's spouse or estate. Although it is always possible that there will be a further change of Revenue practice in this matter, it seems unlikely that this will occur, so it is necessary to consider the practical effect brought about by the death benefit having to be paid out to the estate. Fortunately, it seems that in very many cases the financial planning damage caused will be of containable dimensions.

7–32 Reverting to the facts assumed at §§ 7–25, 7–26 it was assumed that a capital transfer tax liability of £80,000 levied by reference to close company shares would be more or less exactly matched by a tax free death benefit of £80,000, paid by pension fund trustees to the son. On the assumption that Revenue approval to the scheme will only be forthcoming on the basis that the trustees must pay the £80,000 to the deceased's estate on death after the age of 74, it is reasonable to assume that under the terms of his will the £80,000 will finish up in the hands of his widow, still wholly intact since dispositions in favour of a deceased's spouse are tax exempt. The position within the family then becomes that the son has to find £80,000 of capital transfer tax, whereas his mother has £80,000 of cash. It must be presumed that the widow's full co-operation would normally be available to ensure that the family business does not founder through an unsupportable capital transfer tax burden. The widow, of course, will in any event have been well provided for financially, since she will receive a substantial pension for life.

7–33 The simplest method of dealing with the £80,000 would be for the mother to make an outright gift of that amount to her son, he being liable for the capital transfer tax. This should not exceed £8,825, assuming that the mother survives for at least three years from the time of the gift, has made no previous taxable *inter vivos* transfers of value, and has failed to absorb her current and preceding tax year £2,000 annual exemptions. On this basis then there still remains every possible justification for implementing the Revenue approved pension scheme, since the son receives the close company shares, plus sufficient cash almost to discharge the whole of the tax liability. In most cases, sensible planning should enable the position to be further improved.

7–34 It is probable that the son will be able to opt to pay the tax in eight annual or 16 half-yearly instalments.[9] This would obviously be

---

[9] F.A. 1975, Sched. 4, paras. 13, 14.

a considerable benefit to him, particularly as interest is only chargeable on the outstanding tax if an instalment is not paid when it falls due.[10] The mother therefore could make eight regular annual gifts to her son, equivalent to the amount of tax (£10,000) payable by him each year. Assuming that no other taxable transfers had been made by the mother, it would thus be possible to absorb nine annual £2,000 exemptions, so that the tax payable by the son on the gifts from his mother would be reduced to that eligible in respect of taxable transfers amounting to £62,000. On this basis, total capital transfer tax payable by the son would amount to no more than £6,025, and he would have the benefit of spreading his own tax liability over eight years, with little or no actual liability in the earlier years. From the widow's point of view, this also is a very sensible procedure, as she can derive the benefit of income from the invested balance of the £80,000 over a period of seven years, plus possibly some useful tax free capital appreciation, assuming that the balance is invested into short or medium dated gilts.

---

[10] *Ibid.* Sched. 4, para. 16.

CHAPTER 8

PARTNERSHIPS

8–01 ALL too often, the most intractable financial problem encountered by professional advisers concerns their own partnership. At any time, the partners may be faced collectively or individually with problems arising out of the provision of partnership capital; the re-structuring of a partnership because of incoming partners or early retirement of one partner or more; moral or legal obligations arising out of the death or permanent disablement of a partner; and the payment of capital taxes at a partner's death or retirement. Many of these problems can be tackled through the use of life assurance: indeed, it is no exaggeration to state that in very many cases a good insurance-based plan can cope with all of the financial planning problems with which a typical medium-sized partnership is likely to contend. Emphasis is made on *medium-sized* partnerships for one very good practical reason. Experience shows that the suggestions to be made in this chapter (apart from those dealing with partnership funding, which is a separate consideration) are rarely if ever adopted by large partnerships—*i.e.* those with more than about 10 partners. Ten seems to be the maximum number of partners who are capable of agreement amongst themselves on such a complex and emotional issue as deciding to cope with financial problems through an insurance scheme. It is vital that there is unanimity amongst all the partners, and experience shows that there is rule of nature to the effect that 10 partners will perhaps agree one time out of three, whereas 20 partners will not reach agreement one time out of a hundred.

8–02 It is now generally accepted in commercial life, particularly in the professions, that the main criterion for inviting a new member to join a partnership should be ability. It is rumoured that even some firms of stockbrokers are beginning to recognise the pre-eminent importance of this quality in a partner. This general acceptance of the recruitment of new partners on a merit basis means that many of the traditional methods of introducing new funds into a business, and of paying out retiring partners or the estates of deceased partners, have ceased to be valid. Consequently, it is very often an easy matter these days to amend existing partnership agreements so as to allow for the smoothest of transitions when new partners are taken on, or old partners retire or die. The method used is for all partners to accept that partnership goodwill (often its most valuable asset) *and* working capital always belongs to the partners as a whole from time to time. No retiring partner or estate of a deceased partner therefore has any entitlement to a payment in respect of a goodwill or partnership working capital share. Similarly, no incoming partner is expected to find a substantial cash sum, or make arrangements to fund such a sum, in order to purchase his partnership interest. One great advantage to this modern type of partnership agreement is that, since it is clearly an arm's length commercial transaction, there should be no question of any capital transfer tax liability if a partner retires or dies.[1] Similarly, it is considered that such an arrangement may be successful to obviate any question of a disposal for capital gains tax purposes on the happening of either of these events. Since it is germane to the partnership arrangement that just as an incoming partner makes no payment, so an outgoing partner receives no payment, it appears that there is in fact no question of the disposal of an asset for consideration such as is required to induce a capital gains tax liability.[2]

8–03   It can be seen that a partnership deed with carefully drafted clauses giving effect to the kind of arrangement just described can avoid many of the financial problems which in the past have been associated with every change, for whatever reason, in the make-up of a partnership. However, if further clauses are inserted which make provision for an insurance arrangement, two further advantages can be expected. First, it becomes that much easier to demonstrate, if this is ever necessary for Revenue purposes, that the whole partnership deal was an arm's length commercial arrangement. Secondly, the individual partners are encouraged to make that type of financial provision, for their own retirement and for their families' protection, which is absolutely essential for a professional man but which experience shows is surprisingly overlooked in far too many cases.

8–04   Typically, the financial provision which a partner will need to make will be:

(1) Protection of his income, in the event of long term or permanent disability.

(2) Provision of a decent pension for himself, and probably for his widow.

(3) Provision of a cash sum, capital transfer tax free or at worst lightly-taxed, for his widow and/or dependants. This need can be divided into two parts: the need for family income benefit in the event of the partner's early death; and secondly, provision of a lump sum for the protection of his widow no matter at what age his death occurs.

8–05   It seems proper that the partners as a whole should agree on what range of benefit they would ideally like to see provided for all partners. Participation in the agreed range of benefits would then be made

---

[1] *Att.-Gen.* v. *Rolli* (1936) 15 A.T.C. 523; and F.A. 1975, s. 20 (4).
[2] F.A. 1965, ss. 22 (3) and 45 (7).

a condition of partnership membership, and the total annual cost of the insurance provision then would fall as a first charge against partnership profits. This procedure is recommended since it has the effect that in broad terms the younger partners help to subsidise the effective cost of the insurance package on the lives of the older partners. It is generally accepted as being equitable that this should be the case, and indeed where an existing partnership agreement is being altered along the lines suggested, it is most reasonable that older partners should insist on a *quid pro quo* for their agreement to altering existing arrangements. Generally speaking, where an existing partnership is altered, there is an element of financial sacrifice on the part of the older partners, and it is very reasonable that the younger partners should agree to bear a larger part of the cost of insurance provision.

8–06 In the case of an insurance package of the kind here contemplated, normally it will be felt equitable that a partner who for health reasons is unacceptable at tabular rates for life assurance, should have the increased premiums which have to be paid in order to secure the agreed level of benefit met as part of the first charge. As is noted later, however, it is not considered that there is generally speaking any case for the partnership consenting to make a contribution towards higher premiums imposed for health reasons, where life assurance is used for convenience as a method of funding partnership capital requirements.

Explanation of " first charge " technique

8–07 Consider a partnership where it is desired to make optimum provision for the continued existence of the firm whilst producing a range of insurance benefits which are considered to be consistent with that aim. There are two senior partners of similar age, each of whom has a 20 per cent. interest in the partnership. In addition, there are six younger partners, all broadly of the same age, and each of these younger partners is entitled to an equal share in the remaining 60 per cent. of profit. The cost of an agreed insurance package for the younger partners averages £666·67 annually in the case of each life; the cost of the agreed cover for the two senior partners is £1,500 annually. The total cost of the insurance scheme therefore is £7,000 annually, and it is agreed that this should be paid out on the first charge basis. For the purpose of this illustration, it is assumed that taxable profits are running at £100,000 annually. Also, it is assumed that each older partner (referred to as the " A " partners) has no allowance for income tax purposes apart from the married allowance. In the case of the younger partners (referred to as the " B " partners) it is assumed that each is married with two children aged less than 11, and pays £1,500 annually of allowable mortgage interest. Finally, it is assumed that no partner has any income apart from that derived from the partnership.

The collective net income position before any action is taken is as follows:

	Share of Income £	Income Tax £	Spendable Income £
" A " partners	40,000	21,820	18,180
" B " partners	60,000	16,560	43,440
TOTAL	£100,000	£38,380	£61,620

8–08   Suppose now that each individual partner was simply left to meet the cost of the insurance on his own life. The " A " partners would therefore pay £1,500 annually out of taxed income, and each " B " partner would pay £667 annually. The collective net position would then become:

	Share of Income £	Tax plus Premiums £	Spendable Income £
" A " partners	40,000	24,294	15,706
" B " partners	60,000	19,860	40,140
TOTAL	£100,000	£44,154	£55,846

Overall then, the eight partners sustain a combined reduction in net income of £5,774, in order to pay insurance premiums totalling £7,000 gross. All premiums paid will qualify fully for assurance relief which, whilst basic rate income tax is 35 per cent., is worth a total of £1,225, thus reducing the net cost to all partners by £1,225, making a net figure of £5,775. The £1 which has been " lost " in the preceding calculation is accounted for by a rounding adjustment.

8–09   Assume now that it is decided the £7,000 of premiums, instead of being met by the individual partners out of taxed income, will be paid by the partnership. There are two main fiscal consequences. The first is that although the premiums are no longer physically paid over to the insurance company by the individual lives assured, life assurance relief will continue to be granted as if the individual partners were in fact paying their own premiums for the cover on their own lives. Secondly, the total payment of £7,000 becomes a charge against partnership profits which is not, however, allowed as a deduction for income tax purposes. Each partner's income tax assessment therefore will be adjusted for this item, and all of the eight partners will be assessed to income tax on one-eighth of £7,000, which is £875. Hence, the two older partners will pay income tax on a sum which is considerably less than the £1,500 of premium paid on his life. The six younger partners on the other hand will also be assessed on an extra £875, which is in excess of the gross premiums of £667 paid annually on their lives.

The revised collective net income positions of the partners will now be as follows:

	Net Income Received	Adjustment for Premiums	Income for Tax Purposes	Income Tax	Net Spendable Income *
	£	£	£	£	£
" A " partners	36,800	1,750	38,550	20,206	16,594
" B " partners	56,200	5,250	61,450	16,752	39,448
	£93,000	£7,000	£100,000	£36,958	£56,042

* Throughout these calculations, "spendable income" in the case of the " B " partners is shown before payment of allowable mortgage interest of £1,500 each.

8–10   The next table of figures gives a comparison of the net positions of the " A " and " B " partners, on the alternative bases of the £7,000 premiums being met as a personal charge out of taxed income, or being met as a first charge against partnership income:

	" A " partners		" B " partners	
	£	£	£	£
Partners' present net income	18,180	18,180	43,440	43,440
Net income—no first charge	15,706	—	40,140	—
Net income—adopting first charge	—	16,594	—	39,448
NET INCOME REDUCTION	£2,474	£1,586	£3,300	£3,992

8–11   In summary then, the net cost to the " A " partners, instead of being £2,474, becomes £1,586, a collective improvement in their net position of £888, which means that the net cost to each " A " partner of his insurance provision is 35·89 per cent. less than would have been the case had the first charge basis not been adopted. In the case of the " B " partners, there is a collective increase from £3,300 to £3,992 in the cost of their insurance benefits. Each of the " B " partners therefore pays 20·97 per cent. more than if the first charge basis had not been adopted.

8–12   It can readily be seen that in the case of very many partnerships, the first charge method of funding insurance costs will be entirely equitable. In the case of the example, the additional cost for each " B " partner is but £115 annually, whereas each " A " partner has his costs reduced by £444 annually. It will be clear from the more detailed worked example what level of benefit might be provided in exchange for insurance costs of roughly the level indicated, and the overall partnership insurance package can be seen as a wholly sensible financial package which is extremely tax-efficient within the context of the generally onerous tax position of partnerships.

8–13   A cautionary note should be sounded here. It might well be decided that it would be proper for a partnership to make provision for each partner to receive, through insurance, a cash sum of, say, £15,000 or £20,000 on attainment of normal retirement age of 60 or 65. In such circumstances, because each partner becomes entitled to a useful cash sum at normal retirement age, it may be that the Revenue would feel that it had a case for arguing that when retirement occurred, there was some disposal of goodwill for purposes both of capital gains tax and of capital transfer tax. In practice, it is considered that the possibility of there being a successful assessment in such circumstances is remote, bearing in mind the *Rolli* case already referred to, and taking into account the fact that in practice each retiring partner would have built up his capital sum *out of his own income.* Any possible taxable element of bounty would have arisen (particularly between the "A" and "B" partners) at the time the partnership agreement was established or renegotiated.

Working Example

8–14   What type and level of benefit should a good partnership insurance scheme provide? There is no optimum answer; partnerships are as diverse as the individuals who make them up and the solution for any partnership will always take account of the individual partners' needs as well as those of the partnership. There is little doubt that one ideal partnership arrangement would be of the kind described at the beginning of this chapter where partnership goodwill and working capital belongs to the partners as a whole. If agreement to operate on this basis can be reached, the inclusion in the partnership deed of a requirement for all partners' lives to be insured on a pre-determined basis can mean that the financial future of the partnership and of the partners is as secure as could ever be expected in a less than perfect world. However, a good range of benefits might be as follows:

Permanent health insurance

8–15   Considerable disruption can be caused to the smooth working of a partnership if one partner becomes permanently disabled, through injury or disease, and ceases to be capable of making his contribution. If this happens, depending upon the seriousness of the complaint and the degree of permanence, the partnership may well have no alternative other than to recruit a replacement partner. In such unfortunate circumstances, the continuing members of the old partnership may well feel strong moral obligations to provide the maximum possible financial support for the disabled partner, and his family. This in turn could place an intolerable financial burden on the partnership. A very simple way to deal with this problem is for each partner's life to be insured so that in the event of his becoming unable to attend to business matters, an insurance company will agree to pay out a fixed weekly or monthly benefit until the partner's health is restored, or until an agreed retirement age of 60 or 65, whichever event happens the sooner.

Family income benefit

8–16   This kind of protection would be relevant to the case of married partners, especially those with children. In the event of the death of a partner, an insurance company will pay to his widow or to trustees for his family (depending on how the policy has been arranged) an agreed annual sum for the remainder of a period of years agreed at the outset of the policy. For example, the policy might be one where the insurance company agrees to pay out £4,000 annually for the balance of a term of 20 years from inception of the policy, if the death of the insured life occurs within the 20 years.

Endowment assurance

8–17   Notwithstanding the ability of partners to build up a tax-free capital sum at retirement age, and a pension, through a section 226-approved annuity, it may well be felt that the partnership has at least a moral obligation to encourage all partners to build up a useful cash sum outside of the partnership. This can be justified on many grounds, not the least of which is the general desirability that partners, once they reach retirement age, be encouraged to have nothing further to do with the business of the partnership, rather than being retained in a consultancy or similar capacity. This *may* be desirable in certain circumstances, but on the whole it is preferable that once retirement age is reached, a complete break from the partnership is made. It will be easier for this to be achieved if it is known that after retirement partners will be independent financially, and a valuable contribution towards achieving this can be brought about through endowment assurance.

Whole life assurance

8–18   The three categories of insurance mentioned above will all terminate by retirement age, yet the general utility of insurance cover increases with age. It is undesirable that, after retirement, a partner should find that he is bereft of all insurance, if only as a method of funding capital transfer tax, or leaving legacies for his family at his death.

8–19   As part of a process of reorganisation, involving the admission of two new younger partners, a partnership decides to commence an insurance scheme, and details of the partners' ages plus the range of agreed benefits are as on the accompanying table.

Premium for:	Partner's age next birthday							
	31 £	33 £	35 £	37 £	39 £	41 £	53 £	55 £
£5,000 whole life [a]	121·17	127·61	134·63	142·82	151·59	161·54	244·02	262·74
£5,000 endowment to age 65 [a]	157·54	167·97	180·26	194·30	210·09	228·81	469·25	560·51
Permanent health insurance [b]	129·70	139·00	149·20	160·75	173·65	188·20	341·50	388·00
Family income benefit [c]	74·00	85·50	100·00	119·50	144·00	175·00	—	—
Total cost	£482·41	£520·08	£564·09	£617·37	£679·33	£753·55	£1,054·77	£1,211·25

Overall cost = £5,882·85

[a] The whole life and endowment assurances are on a with profits basis.
[b] The agreed level of cover is £150 per week to continue until age 65, payment of the benefit commencing after 13 weeks of disablement.
[c] The family income benefit is £5,000 per annum payable for the balance of 20 years. The two senior partners in this case have agreed that their own family circumstances make it equitable that the cover should not be provided in their case.

8–20   As will be clear from the earlier explanation, if the premiums for this package, which total £5,882·85 annually, are paid by the partnership as a non-allowable first charge against profits, the cost of the whole package will bear proportionately more on the younger partners. However, as part of the negotiations leading up to implementation of the partnership insurance scheme, it may well be that the senior partners have agreed to give up certain pre-existing rights, including specific shares of goodwill and of partnership capital. Whilst implementation of the agreement may technically result in disposals, particularly by the senior partners, for capital gains tax purposes and transfers of value for capital transfer tax purposes, the *quantum* of charge may be little or nil, depending on the availability of exemptions. For the future, assuming it has been agreed that goodwill and working capital belong to the partnership as a whole, there should be no capital gains tax or capital transfer tax payable either at the death or retirement of an existing partner, or on the admission of new partners.

PARTNERSHIP FUNDING

8–21   It will often be necessary for a partnership to raise capital so as to sustain its business. The main reasons this need is likely to be felt are for expansion; to acquire new partnership premises; to ease amalgamation with another partnership in the same profession; or, especially in times of high inflation, merely to give the partnership a sounder financial base.

8–22   It is usually possible to find a commercial source which is prepared to lend money to partnerships for the development of the business: indeed there is still a smattering of insurance companies which set aside a very small proportion of the investment content of their life fund to lend out for this purpose. Such a partnership loan will normally be repayable over a period of between 10 and 25 years. The method of repayment is often a matter of indifference to the lender, provided that it has some security, or at the very least, covenants for repayment from the individual partners. The most common method of repayment will be through a sinking fund, and very often the most satisfactory form of sinking fund can be created using insurance policies effected on the lives of the partners.

8–23   Consider a firm of 30 partners, which decides to raise £150,000 of working capital. It finds a suitable lender, and the loan is made on terms including interest payable at a fixed rate, with repayment falling due at the end of 15 years, repayment to be secured through policies of assurance effected on the lives of 10 partners. (It should be noted that although insurance policies are effected on the lives of 10 partners only, all 30 partners will of course have to join in the basic loan agreement. As is explained below, repayment of the loan will however be secured by covenants from the 10 insured partners.)

8–24   It is fundamental to creation of the sinking fund that the *proceeds* of the insurance policies be available for that purpose. Provided that the lender is satisfied that the insured lives have given adequate covenants to this effect, the lender will not usually be concerned as to how the policies are owned beneficially—the lender's rights are fully protected provided the individual partners concerned covenant firstly that repayment of each partner's agreed proportion of the loan is a first charge against the maturing policy proceeds, and secondly to keep up premium payments. How then should the insurance policies be owned, and the premiums funded? Considerable taxation consequences flow from the decision taken by the partnership on this matter.

8–25   First, approximate figures. Assuming that there is a suitable range of 10 lives, aged between 30 and 45, each life could be insured for 15 years on an endowment with profits basis and for an initial sum assured of £11,000. The gross annual premium would be approximately £800 on each life. It would be expected that the maturity value of each policy would be at least £15,000, making the most cautious of estimates with regard to the allocation of future bonuses. The total gross annual premium on all policies is £8,000, and this has to be kept up for 15 years, so that the total premium expenditure will be £120,000. The main tax considerations are:

Income tax

8–26   On the assumption that the payment of premiums can qualify for life assurance relief, experience shows that it would be unusual if every premium of roughly £800, paid to keep up policies on the lives of each of 10 partners, failed fully to qualify for income tax relief within the one-sixth of income limitation. Assuming an average basic rate of income tax over the full 15 years of no more than 30 per cent., total income tax relief available annually to the 10 partners works out at £1,200. Over 15 years, the total amount of relief potentially available therefore is *£18,000.*

Capital gains tax

8–27   If, at maturity of the policies, the conditions of section 28 (2) of the Finance Act 1965 are satisfied, no capital gains tax will be payable on the maturing proceeds. It was mentioned earlier that the total gross premium expenditure over 15 years will be £120,000, and that the maturity proceeds will total at least £150,000. In practice, they would be expected to be £170,000 or more. Capital gains tax, if exigible on the maturing policy proceeds, presumably would be at 30 per cent.[3] and it is levied on the difference between the total of gross premiums paid, and the maturity proceeds.[4] The expected chargeable gain under the

---

[3] F.A. 1965, s. 20 (3).
[4] *Ibid.* s. 28 and Sched. 4.

policies thus is between £30,000 and £50,000: capital gains tax at stake therefore is between *£9,000* and *£15,000*.

8–28   It will be seen that based on conservative assumptions the total net benefit secured from the policies will vary between surprisingly wide limits, depending on whether or not income tax relief on premiums is enjoyed on the one hand, and capital gains tax on the policy proceeds is payable on the other. The minimum amount of taxation involved is £27,000 (*i.e.* the sum of prospective life assurance relief *plus* the prospective minimum capital gains tax bill) which amounts to more than one-sixth of £150,000, or almost one-quarter of the total premium expenditure over the full 15 years. It is obviously worth while devoting a lot of thought to ensuring that the most favourable tax position is achieved, and it does appear that this is possible, whilst preserving equity amongst the partners as a whole. Before considering this question in detail, mention should first be made of the actual manner of funding the life assurance premiums.

8–29   It is suggested that the most equitable method will be for the partnership itself annually to pay the total of premiums physically over to the insurance company. This is partly a matter of administrative convenience, but is considered also to be proper from the point of view of psychological acceptance by *all* partners concerning the essential equity of the whole arrangement. The 10 individual partners will be entitled to claim life assurance relief provided that the policies are retained in their beneficial ownership.[5] Now it will usually be the intention at the end of the loan period that the full £150,000, or the assets representing it, will become a partnership capital entitlement, to be shared equally amongst all those who were members of the partnership at the time the loan was negotiated. Assuming that all 30 partners share equally, the effect at the end of the term is that each partner will become entitled to a capital share of £5,000. It is suggested that, in the case of the 10 partners whose lives are insured, with premiums funded centrally, each partner concerned should have a special memorandum account, which will debit each year against his capital entitlement the amount of premium. The memorandum account will be cleared at maturity of the policies, or in the event of an insured partner earlier leaving the partnership. The actual premiums paid by the partnership will be assessed against the individuals concerned as Schedule D remuneration, assuming that the policies remain the personal property of the 10 lives assured. Turning now to the question of how the policies are to be owned, there seem to be two possibilities:

Policies owned by partnership

8–30   It would be possible for the individuals to assign the policies so that they became a partnership asset. Alternatively, the partnership could

---

[5] Taxes Act 1970, s. 19.

propose for the policies in the first instance, which would be issued to the partnership as grantee. In either eventuality, it is felt that capital gains tax could be payable at maturity of the policies.

8–31 If the policies were first effected by the individual lives assured and then assigned, the ultimate maturity would be a capital gains tax disposal, since the ultimate owner would not be the original beneficial owner, and further would be deemed to have acquired the policies for valuable consideration.[6] It is necessary for both limbs of the charging subsection to be satisfied before there can be a capital gains tax liability. In the circumstances of the partnership arrangement, what does need to be considered carefully is whether the second limb (requiring that the ultimate owner should have acquired the policy for money or money's worth) is satisfied.

8–32 The real problem which emerges is that, in the case of a partnership, there are bound to be changes in the structure within a period of 15 years. New partners will be brought in, some will retire, perhaps prematurely, and some will die. Each time there is a change in the number or constitution of partners, technically a fresh partnership is created, and capital gains tax liability arises.[7] In theory, each partner's share has to be valued immediately before the change, and capital gains tax is paid at that time on any increase in his partnership share value, either since the time of the last preceding partnership alteration, or since April 6, 1965. Hence, whether the partnership proposes initially for insurance policies, or has them assigned to it by individual partners, the probability is that by the time the policies mature, they will not technically be in the hands of the original beneficial owner, even if the partnership originally proposed. This is the explanation for the near certainty that the first limb of the charging section will be satisfied.

8–33 By pursuing a similar line of thought, it is clear that if there is a new partnership every time a change occurs, the assets held by the new partnership must have been acquired for a consideration in money or money's worth. True the consideration will in fact be the transfer to the new partnership of the assets and goodwill of the old, and the assumption by the new partnership of the debts of the old. Nevertheless, it is known that the Revenue takes the view that under these circumstances, the new partnership is deemed for tax purposes to have acquired all the assets of the old partnership for valuable consideration. Even so, it can be argued that freedom from capital gains tax *should* exist in relation to the proceeds of any one policy where the individual partner whose life is insured remains a partner throughout the term of the policy. This statement plainly requires to be explained. Although,

---

[6] F.A. 1965, s. 28 (2).
[7] It is assumed that the " ideal " partnership arrangement described earlier in this chapter will alas not apply.

as has just been stated, any change in the partners technically dissolves one partnership and gives rise to a new partnership, there is a strong case for claiming that any insured partner who has remained with the firm throughout the term of the loan is, at maturity of the policy of his life, in the position of being the original beneficial owner. The fact that over the term of the loan his interest in the partnership has varied (and in most cases it will presumably have tended to increase over the endowment term) may have some effect on the *quantum* of freedom from capital gains tax. Suppose that partner A has his life insured for £11,000 plus profits, at a time when he is entitled to 5 per cent. of partnership profits. The policy matures after 15 years for £15,000, and total annual premiums paid amount to £8,000, so that there is a crude gain of £7,000. By the time the policy matures after 15 years, the number of partners has risen from 15 to 20, but the interest of A has increased from 5 per cent. to 7 per cent. The line of reasoning is that since A was entitled over the full period of 15 years to at least 5 per cent. of partnership profits, the policy on his life, even though it was a partnership asset throughout, was for A's personal benefit to the same extent that the maturity value of the policy (£15,000) bears to the loan of £150,000.

Over the endowment term, A's interest in the partnership has increased from 5 per cent. to 7 per cent., so that his direct interest in the loan has increased from £7,500 to £10,500. Therefore, should not the same proportion of the £7,000 profit under the policy as £7,500 bears to £10,500 be capital gains tax free? If so, £5,000 of the £7,000 would be capital gains tax free, and tax would only be chargeable on the surplus of £2,000.

8–34 This reasoning appears to be consistent with the Finance Act 1965, s. 45 (7), which has the effect of treating any partnership dealings in chargeable assets, for capital gains tax purposes, as if they were dealings by the individual partners rather than by the firm as such. Because of this, it is necessary to regard each partner as owning the appropriate fractional share of each partnership asset. In the case of the example, A at the beginning of the period owns 5 per cent. of the partnership, and at the end he owns 7 per cent. Amongst the assets is the benefit of the £150,000 loan which ultimately is paid off at maturity of the endowment policy. It is true that on a strict interpretation of section 45 (7), A could be deemed *ab initio* to have had the appropriate fractional interest (*i.e.* initially 5 per cent.) in all 10 policies, but equally it would seem reasonable in the circumstances to attribute or hypothecate to A, for Revenue purposes, beneficial ownership of the whole of the policy on his own life at the point in time that the policy is effected. The alternative is to concede that at all material times A was entitled to 5 per cent. at least of the value of all 10 policies, so that to the extent of that proportion of the maturity proceeds of all policies, A should be entitled to the section 28 (2) exemption. It would appear simpler, more logical and perfectly equitable rather to concede in these circumstances that the appropriate portion (in the example five-sevenths) of the policy on the life of A is capital gains tax exempt.

So far as income tax is concerned, as the premiums will have been paid by the partnership, and not by the individuals whose lives are insured, no tax relief will be available.

Individual partners own policies

8–35 In this case, it is indisputable that the insurance policies will be free from capital gains tax at maturity, and that premiums will qualify for life assurance relief. It has been suggested that so far as capital gains tax is concerned, it could be argued that the existence of a covenant in effect charging the policy proceeds to repay the partnership loan might take the policies out with the capital gains tax exemption. However, notwithstanding the covenant, there is no question but that the policies are owned at all times by the individuals, who have the legal right to call for the policies, and to demand that the insurance company deal with the particular policy in any way (including surrender). The existence of the covenant for repayment of the loan does not in any way act as a legal assignment [8] of the policy or of any part of its benefit. The individual lives assured therefore remain beneficial owners of the policies.

8–36 It might be argued that for the policies to be retained by the individuals is inequitable, since any surplus above £15,000 of maturity value per policy will belong as of right to the individuals, and not to the partnership. If necessary, this presumably could be dealt with by requiring the individuals to enter into an undertaking to pay any surplus over £15,000 to the partnership. This on the other hand can be seen as unfair so far as the individuals are concerned. It must be remembered that repayment of the policy loans through insurance policies generally makes sense in commercial terms. That is to say, the return at maturity of the policies can reasonably be expected to justify itself, when regarded as the end product of a 15 year investment programme. Any partner who chose to do so would be quite at liberty to effect a with profits endowment policy out of his own resources for his own benefit, and the fact that agreeing to participate in a partnership funding arrangement, using insurance, throws up a small additional benefit at the end of the day for some partners to the exclusion of others is hardly inequitable.

8–37 There is in fact a fairly simple solution to dealing with the question of equity as amongst the partners, should it be considered that an attempt should be made to remove any feeling (however unwarranted

[8] The Policies of Assurance Act 1867.

this may be) of unfairness. The answer is that *all* partners whose lives can be insured on reasonable terms would be required to effect endowment assurances, basically to be for their own benefit. It may be considered that the most equitable way of spreading the cost then would be to adopt the first charge technique, so that the totality of premiums would be treated as a non-allowable partnership expense, to be apportioned across the board for tax purposes, rather than each individual's premium being returned separately as a taxable benefit.

8-38 Although this might remove feelings of unfairness from the minds of certain partners, there is much to commend it as a general practice. It will be recalled that the illustration in this section has been based on the assumption of a loan of £150,000 needed for the purpose of funding partnership requirements. As the business develops the chances are that further funds will be required from time to time— and it may well be that expansion will justify a further *tranche* of borrowing well before the agreed 15 years' period of the original £150,000 loan has expired. The existence at such time of a further group of partners with endowment assurances readily available to be used as collateral security for repayment of a fresh loan could be most helpful. Each new incoming partner, assuming that his life is insurable, would be required to effect an endowment assurance on his life, so that there should always be a pool of insured partners with readily available collateral. Equity as amongst the partners is seen to have been preserved, and the partnership itself benefits through the existence of a pool of uncommitted endowment policies available to help the partnership secure alterations to its rolling credit requirements.

8-39 One practical point to note is that if it is decided that all insurable partners should carry endowment assurance, it would be sensible to ensure that maturity dates of uncommitted policies should run in groups of partners. Thus, in the example, the £150,000 loan is to be repaid after 15 years. If there happened to be a further dozen insurable partners who do not already have policies committed for repayment of the £150,000 facility, the recommendation might be that six of the partners should effect 18 year endowment assurances, six should effect 21 year endowment assurances, and the next six incoming partners admitted to the scheme should effect 24 year endowment assurances.

8-40 Constant reference has been made to the insurability of the partners. In any group of professional men of this kind, the probability is that one or more partner will be uninsurable for health reasons, and where the first charge against partnership profits technique is used to pay premiums, it is clear that there should be no apportionment of a slice of the charge against uninsurable partners' own tax liabilities. In cases where the life is acceptable for insurance subject to an additional premium, there is little doubt that in the case of a general partnership life assurance scheme, any enhanced premium charged for health reasons should be brought in as a part of the first charge, so that the extra cost will be spread right across all partners participating in the scheme. In cases where the sole reason for effecting endowment assurance is partnership funding as described in this section however, it is considered that a partner whose health position warrants an increased premium should bear that increased premium himself, if he wishes to participate in the scheme. Generally, there will be a pool of lives available for insurance at first-class premium rates, and bearing in mind that at the end of the funding period, when the policies mature, the individual partners will usually receive a tax-free capital surplus, there seems no reason why a partner in poor health should expect his co-partners to contribute towards that ultimate benefit in his own case. As in all partnership matters, however, the final decision will of course be taken by reference to the particular circumstances of each partnership.

Sinking fund policy

8–41   Another method of repaying a loan taken for partnership purposes might be for the partnership to effect a sinking fund policy. This is one where, in the case of our example, the insurance company would agree to pay £150,000 exactly at the expiry of the loan term. It is a fact that the minds of certain partners would automatically turn to a sinking fund or capital redemption policy of this kind, in order to service such a debt as a partnership loan. There are two main arguments against this:

(1) Because repayment at the end of 15 years would be a mere contractual liability, there would be no element of life assurance involved. Because of this, there could be no question of premiums paid qualifying for income tax relief[9]—even assuming that it was possible to secure a sinking fund policy based on an annual premium, most insurance companies preferring to transact this category of business on a single premium basis only. The profit element taken at maturity of the sinking fund or capital redemption policy would not be subject to capital gains tax.[10]

(2) Capital redemption business of insurance companies is, by virtue of the Taxes Act 1970, s. 324, treated as a separate business from any other class of business carried on by the insurance company. This means that the taxation liabilities in an insurance company's capital redemption fund are usually more onerous than in its life or annuity funds. As a result of this,

[9] Taxes Act 1970, s. 19 (4) and Sched. 1.
[10] F.A. 1965, Sched. 7, para. 10 (1).

investment yields on sinking fund policies tend to be very much less attractive than those available through with profits endowment assurances. Typically, the yield to redemption on a sinking fund policy might be $4\frac{1}{2}$ per cent. compound, whereas the yield to redemption on a good with profits endowment assurance could be between 7 per cent. and 8 per cent.

CHAPTER 9

SCHOOL FEES

9–01   ALMOST without exception, the widely advertised schemes which offer to assist with school fees are based on the utilisation of some kind of life assurance or annuity policy. Frequently, a scheme will be based on some combination of insurance and annuity contract.

9–02   As with all practical applications of life assurance considered in this book, school fees planning amounts to no more than the careful management of what are usually limited financial resources. Most parents who decide on fee-paying education for their children meet the fees as they fall due out of current taxed income. This is the most inefficient method, if only because it can place undue strain on a family's finances, leading to all kinds of stress. Because life assurance provides some certitude of a reasonable investment return, as well as generating taxation advantages, its prominent position in the field of school fees planning is easy to understand. Subject to the *caveat* that the earlier action is taken the more pronounced is likely to be the benefit, there is little doubt that in this area of financial planning life assurance will continue to play a useful and prominent role.

9–03   Consideration of possible school fees plans in any particular case can be complicated by the blurring of the line between income and capital. As the payment of school fees is essentially a regularly recurring requirement, the payments tend to assume more the nature of income than of capital. On the other hand, the very level of school fees in modern times makes it increasingly difficult for parents or others to meet the cost out of current income. However, when no capital source is available the only practical funding method will be the building up of capital out of income. It is manifest that what must be avoided at all costs is the possibility that the fees themselves assume the nature of income of the child or his parents for tax purposes. Some types of infant settlement, for example, can give rise to this possibility, and in such cases the trustees must exercise every possible care to ensure that payments which are made out of capital, in pursuance of a power to advance for educational or other purposes, do not become taxable as if they were income.

FUNDING FROM CAPITAL

Commercial possibilities

9–04   Where a parent, grandparent or other benefactor is able to make capital available for the purpose, the funding of fees will usually be arranged through a contract of deferred annuity, or by utilising the capital to fund a series of endowment assurances with profits. In the former case, it is normal for the annuity in question to be effected by or assigned to trustees of a special educational trust. The trustees in due course will receive the annuity instalments, and will pay them over to the school in question. Most fee-paying schools are constituted as charities, so the school or the trustees will be able to reclaim any income tax which has been deducted at source on the interest portion of the annuity [1]; the return on capital thus will be significantly better than would apply in the case of an identical funding method not routed through an educational trust. Even so, the ultimate investment return on capital invested is unlikely to be attractive, and the return under such contracts tends not to be competitive compared with what can be achieved in other ways. The advantages of this method therefore can be seen as convenience, coupled with possible capital transfer tax advantages, as considered later in this chapter. These limited advantages may well be considered too high a price to pay for accepting the comparatively meagre return on capital which such schemes represent at certain levels of income tax.

9–05   In October 1976, when interest rates in the United Kingdom were standing at their highest-ever levels, a typical return under a school fees scheme based on the immediate investment of capital into deferred annuity contracts was as follows. The stated requirement, for a child who had just been born, was to fund school fees estimated at £1,000 annually from the child's age eight to 12 inclusive (a total of £5,000) followed by fees of £2,000 annually from the child's age 13 to 17 inclusive (a total of £10,000). The total fees to be funded therefore were £15,000, and the quoted cost of providing those fees was an immediate cash sum of £5,030. The fees guaranteed to be provided therefore amounted to almost three times the initial capital payment, which on the face of it is very attractive and no benefactor could be blamed for deciding in favour of this funding method. However, for purposes of comparison consider what might be achieved if the same fees are funded through a purchase of gilt-edged securities. Based on the price of gilts quoted in the Financial Times on October 14, 1976, a capital sum of £8,375 would be required to generate capital sums totalling £15,000 at the maturity of various gilt edged stocks, spread out over the ensuing 17 years. The purchases required were as follows:

---

[1] Taxes Act 1970, s. 360.

	Stock Price	Nominal Stock Purchased	Cost	Running Yield
		£	£	£
Funding 5½% 1982–84	70	2,000	1,400	110
Treasury 8½% 1984–86	75	1,000	750	85
Funding 6½% 1985–87	60½	2,000	1,210	130
Transport 3% 1978–88	44¾	2,000	885	60
Treasury 8¼% 1987–90	64½	2,000	1,290	165
Funding 5¾% 1987–91	48⅛	4,000	1,925	230
Funding 6% 1993	45¾	2,000	915	120
		£15,000	£8,375	£900

For simplicity, dealing expenses and the effect of buying stocks cum-dividend have been ignored: those factors do not significantly affect the argument.

9–06　　The initial income generated through this gilt-edged portfolio was £900 annually gross, although this would reduce to £790 gross after maturity of the Funding 5½ per cent. 1982–84, with a further reduction after maturity in June 1986 of the Treasury 8½ per cent. 1984–86 stock. After that, the income would still further reduce with the maturity of the later-dated stocks. Consider if the income of the portfolio until 1986 were used to maintain an endowment assurance with profits maturing in 1993—*i.e.* at the child's age 17. For this purpose, the income generated by the portfolio until 1986 *only* would be utilised, and an endowment assurance with profits for a term of 17 years therefore would be effected on the life of the parent, assumed to be aged 40 next birthday. The gross annual premium assumed is £622 annually, which is arrived at by taking the gross portfolio income until 1986 of £790, deducting basic rate income tax at 35 per cent. and grossing up the result to allow for income tax relief of 17·5 per cent. on the net income of £513·50.

Assuming that the premium is kept up for 10 years, and the policy then converted to a paid-up contract, the minimum estimated tax-free maturity value in 1993 is £14,400, or roughly £6,000 more than the £8,375 cost of the gilt portfolio. On this basis then, school fees of £15,000 are generated; the capital originally invested *plus at least £6,000* is returned at the child's age 17; and the parent enjoys the benefit of the residual income from the gilt portfolio after 1986.

It should also be noted that if the parent is subject to income tax at 50 per cent. on the income from the gilts, the gross life assurance premium which could be met for 10 years from the income is reduced to £478, and the tax-free return of capital in 1983 becomes £11,000. At a 60 per cent. rate of income tax, the self-funded tax-free return of capital reduces to £8,900, which is still in excess of the initial capital commitment.

9–07   So as to give a fair comparison of the result available using a deferred annuity, it is necessary to assume that simultaneously with putting up £5,030 to secure the school fees, the benefactor would have provided further cash of £3,345, making a total available pool of £8,375. Assuming that the balance of £3,345 were used to purchase Funding 6 per cent. 1993 at the price ruling on October 14, 1976, the tax-free capital available at maturity of the stock would be £7,311. The overall return therefore is more than £7,000 inferior to that available using the alternative endowment-based method, assuming the parent to be liable to standard rate income tax. The return is about £4,000 inferior assuming a 50 per cent. tax rate, and £1,750 assuming the tax rate to be 60 per cent.

9–08   It must be noted that the income received from the portfolio of gilts would arrive at irregular intervals. This should not be too much of an inconvenience as it is assumed that premiums for the endowment assurance would be paid monthly: nevertheless, the parent would probably need to explain the scheme to his bank manager so as to ensure that any short-term adverse cash flow did not result in embarrassment. Of more consequence from the cash flow angle is the fact that any coincidence between the maturity of any gilt and the need to pay a term's fees would be merely fortuitous. Thus, the fees due in September 1984, January, April and September 1985, and January and April 1986 are all to be funded from the £2,000 maturity proceeds of the Funding 5½ per cent. 1982–84 which will almost certainly be redeemed by the Bank of England on July 15, 1984. This gives a cash flow benefit and the opportunity to build up an unscheduled additional income, by having fees on deposit or with the building society until they are needed. It would be necessary to ensure that in any year when fees were required before the cash were to hand from a maturing gilt, the bank would advance the fees, and this could add slightly to the cost.

9–09   There is no doubt that the administration of the gilts/endowment assurance method is comparatively messy, but any competent insurance broker would be prepared to assume this responsibility on behalf of his client. The important conclusion to be drawn is that a ready-made school fees plan based on the purchase of deferred annuities does not of necessity represent the best value for money, merely because it is custom-made for the purpose. As the foregoing figures show quite conclusively, if the parent expects over the period of his child's minority to pay income tax at no more than about 50 per cent., he can expect to be significantly better off financially from adopting an endowment-based method. If on the other hand the probability is that his income tax liability will be much greater, the highest predictable return under the endowment method may well be inferior. Proper school fees counselling therefore amounts to far more than taking down from the shelf the first apparently attractive scheme which comes to hand. It is necessary to relate the available capital resources to the parent's immediate and expected future overall financial circumstances.

Capital transfer tax

9–10   The preceding paragraphs illustrate the need for care in selecting the commercial contract, or combination of contracts, which is best suited to individual circumstances. The conclusion drawn was that the optimum scheme for parents with prospective low future income tax liabilities is probably not also the best scheme where the parent's top slice of income is expected in the future to be taxed at an average rate exceeding about 60 per cent. It is necessary also to consider the capital transfer tax implications of school fees funding, and by the nature of the tax this is much more likely to be a practical problem where fees are funded from capital rather than from income.

9–11   The simplest position will be where a parent effects the capital-based scheme, either through an educational trust or by effecting contracts (probably including some combination of deferred annuity, endowment assurance and gilt edged security) in his own name. In the latter case, the contracts in question will remain the parent's own property, and will form part of his own estate for capital transfer tax purposes, should he die before maturity of all contracts forming part of the scheme. The same position will apply in the former case, provided that the parent retains the right, under the terms of the educational trust deed, to request the surrender of the policy and/or the return of his contribution at any time. All that needs to be considered therefore is whether the actual payment of school fees, either by the parent directly or by trustees of the educational trust, is a transfer of value for capital transfer tax purposes. The short answer is that there is no risk of a capital transfer tax liability under these circumstances, as any disposition made by a parent for the maintenance, education or training of his own child (or the child of his spouse) during the period ending not later than the year in which the child attains the age of 18, or after attaining that age ceases to undergo full-time education or training, is exempt from the tax.[2] This exemption also applies in favour of an illegitimate child of the person making the disposition, as well as in the case of any individual who stands *in loco parentis* to the child.[3]

9–12   In the case where capital to meet the cost of the school fees scheme is provided by a person other than a parent, the position is again

---

[2] Finance Act 1975, s. 46 (1).
[3] *Ibid.* s. 46 (2).

relatively straightforward. Where an educational trust is used, and the donor retains the right to a return of capital under the contract, there is no immediate diminution of the donor's estate, so no capital transfer tax is payable at that time. However, each time the trustees made a payment, this would rank as a chargeable transfer of value,[4] although the donor's various exemptions, including that for transfers not exceeding £2,000 annually, would be available to reduce or eliminate any actual liability. The same capital transfer tax consequences will ensue if the donor effects school fees funding policies in his own name, with a view to paying school fees as they fall due on an ad hoc basis.

9–13   In a case where the donor makes capital available to educational settlement trustees, and immediately forgoes any right to a return of capital, the payment made to the trustees will be a transfer of value and will be taxed accordingly.[5] This method does provide the " advantage " that the donor forthwith removes the payment from his estate for the purposes of capital transfer tax, but if he has already made significant taxable transfers, or is not in good health, it could well be much more sensible for him to retain the right of a payment back to his estate, with the intention of allowing school fees paid in the future to absorb the £2,000 annual capital transfer tax exemption.

Where the intending donor is a grandparent, it could be sensible for the grandfather and grandmother to divide the capital earmarked for school fees between them, and each to contribute one half. If they then relied on the £2,000 annual exemption, in order to avoid capital transfer tax on their generosity, fees totalling £4,000 annually could be paid without any tax liability.

9–14   Where the settlor, whether a parent or not, forgoes the right to request a return of capital under an educational trust scheme, this will create a binding trust for the maintenance, education, training and advancement of the child in question. Hence, if the policy is surrendered (for example because the child wins a scholarship place, or it is decided after all not to send him to a fee-paying school) the fund in question will, under the general law of trusts, have to be applied for the benefit of that child. Generally, on the creation of such a trust, there will be no capital transfer tax if the capital is being provided by the parent, but corresponding provision made by any other person (including a grandparent) will be a taxable transfer of value.

9–15   Most schemes involving an educational trust will provide for a return of capital in the event of the death of the donor, whether the child's parent or otherwise, before or during the schooling period. If the donor has not renounced the right to a return of capital, the value returned to his estate will be a taxable asset: furthermore, that value

---

[4] *Ibid.* s. 20 (2).
[5] *Ibid.*

will be dealt with in accordance with the terms of his will. In the case where the donor was the parent, and his will leaves the residuary estate to his widow, no capital transfer tax should be payable. In other cases, however, the donor should be advised to make specific provision under the terms of his will for dealing with any return of capital under the school fees scheme. It will usually be appropriate for the donor to direct under the terms of his will that any capital transfer tax payable in respect of the value of the school fees scheme should fall upon the rest of the estate, the whole of any return of school fees scheme capital being utilised to continue paying for the child's education.

9-16 Taking into account the possibility of future changes in the law, it will usually be difficult to justify advising the donor of school fees scheme capital that he should renounce the right to any return of capital. This after all is the only course which is *certain* to induce an immediate capital transfer tax liability (assuming the amount of capital involved is itself in excess of any available exemptions) and even though taxable transfers of up to £15,000 bear a nil rate of tax, the utilisation of any part of the £15,000 nil rate band will have an effect on all future taxable transfers made by the donor. It would appear to be preferable on general principles that donors should be encouraged to keep open as many options as possible, if only because it can never be certain where provision is made in advance that the school fees will actually be required. This approach is consistent with sensible capital transfer tax planning, since it postpones any liability until such time as the fees are actually paid, so there seems to be only one set of circumstances where the acceptance of an immediate capital transfer tax liability could be recommended. Those circumstances are where the donor is very elderly, or in poor health, so that death could well occur before completion of the education. In those circumstances, if the donor has a right to a return of capital, that capital will in the event fall into his estate and be taxable. It is probable in such circumstances that the better advice is for the donor to renounce any right to a capital return, since the chances then are that he will be able to take advantage of the lower rate of capital transfer tax applicable to transfers made more than three years before death.

FUNDING FROM INCOME

9-17 Undoubtedly the great majority of all plans for meeting future educational expenses have to be funded out of current income. The majority of parents who desire a fee-paying education for a child simply do not have capital resources available. Recent changes in tax legislation now make it very difficult, if not impossible, to produce the requisite capital through mortgaging or re-mortgaging the family house. In general, unless such a mortgage advance is taken up at the time the family residence is acquired, no income tax relief will be available on interest payments. The unavoidable annual servicing charge of such a scheme therefore would probably run at well in excess of 10 per cent. annually, and the capital-based school fees scheme would have to generate at least that return after tax before it started to make any positive contribution towards the problem.

9–18　　Where the only resource available to fund fees is income, it is obviously more important than ever that the last possible penny of value be extracted from whatever scheme is accepted. Life assurance has a vital role to play here, since a good with-profits endowment policy can be relied upon to produce a cash-free lump sum at a known future time; the cash received will represent a good investment return on premiums paid over the years; and the Treasury subsidy in the shape of life assurance relief can perhaps ensure that funding fees in this manner does not quite become the back-breaking straw financially.

There are probably as many income-based funding school fee schemes as there are insurance companies, but they will probably all be variations on one central theme. This theme is that the sensible way to tackle the problem is to spread the burden of fees over as long a period as possible. Ideally, therefore, plans for funding should be laid as soon as possible after the birth of the child. The more intrepid putative young parent will not hesitate to commence a funding scheme even before a child is born or contemplated. A good typical school fees scheme is as follows.

9–19　　Within the first year of the child's life, the father, aged 35 next birthday, decides to implement a school fees funding scheme, and agrees to make £1,000 gross annually available for this purpose. The child was born towards the beginning of a calendar year, and it is decided that fees should be made available in September of each of the years in which the child attains ages eight to 17 inclusive, a total of 10 years. A series of endowment assurances is effected on the life of the father, maturing at regular annual intervals of between 10 and 17 years. It is planned that the greater part of the fees will be met out of the maturing proceeds of the endowment policies, but as the shorter-dated policies mature, thus reducing the annual premium commitment, the annual premiums thus " saved " will be regarded as available to make a contribution towards schooling costs. At the child's ages eight and nine, 10-year endowment assurances will be surrendered in order to produce the fees, and this will not induce any income tax liability since all policies will be qualifying for income tax purposes, and the surrenders will not take place until more than three-quarters of the way through the term of the two policies in question.

9–20　　The schedule of payments in and out, and of potential tax relief, looks as follows:

Year	(1) Gross Premiums £	(2) Surrender/ Maturity Value £	(3) Cash Con- tribution £	(4) Total Fees— (2) + (3) £
8	1,000	1,000	—	1,000
9	900	1,200	100	1,300
10	800	1,460	200	1,660
11	700	1,720	300	2,020
12	600	1,950	400	2,350
13	500	2,210	500	2,710
14	400	2,480	600	3,080
15	300	2,770	700	3,470
16	200	3,070	800	3,870
17	100	3,400	900	4,300
	£5,500	£21,260	£4,500	£25,760
Years 1–7	£7,000			
	£12,500			
Tax relief @ 17·5%	£2,187			
	£10,313			

Even towards the end of 1976, when this manuscript was prepared, the schedule of school fees shown in column (2) might appear to amount to a generous over-provision in the case of any one child. However, the prudent parent will make as much provision as he possibly can to take account of future inflation, and bearing in mind that at the end of 1976 the cost of keeping a child in boarding at any of the leading public schools amounted to around £2,000 annually, it is in fact much more likely that for any one child destined for such a scholastic career the amounts shown in (4) will be closer to the mark, if not inadequate.

9–21 As can be seen from columns (1) and (2), this funding method is expected to produce a tax-free return under the endowment assurances of at least £21,260, in exchange for a maximum gross outlay of £12,500. This outlay could be reduced to £10,313, assuming that all premiums paid qualify fully for life assurance relief, and that the relief remains at 17·5 per cent. of qualifying premiums throughout. On the basis of the net of tax relief cost, the school fees provided amount to something more than twice the net premiums paid. The worst possible position would be that the fees shown in column (4), totalling £25,760 are provided, at a total cost of £17,000, this being the combined totals of the gross premiums shown in column (1) plus the additional parental contributions shown in column (3). Even on this basis, fees provided amount to slightly in excess of 50 per cent. more than the total gross cost.

9–22   As was noted above, most income-based school fees funding plans will be based on some variation of this kind of arrangement. One of its attractions is the total flexibility which is provided. If the insurances are effected in the name of the parent, there is no obligation on him to utilise any part of the maturing policy proceeds towards school fees, nor is he obliged to use any part of the policy moneys towards the maintenance of his children in any way. When the time comes to pay the fees, there is no question of capital transfer tax, all such payments being exempt where they are made in accordance with the principles mentioned at § 9–11. There would appear to be little if any point in having the insurance policies drawn up under trust for the benefit of the specific child, or of the parent's children generally, since there is no capital transfer tax advantage to doing this, yet the parent's hands would be immediately tied as he would be irrevocably committed to see that the policy moneys were disposed of in accordance with the trust, irrespective of whether or not the child or children went to a fee-paying school.

CHAPTER 10

POLICY TRUSTS AND CAPITAL TRANSFER TAX

10–01 In the chapter dealing with capital transfer tax, reference is made from time to time to insurance policies being issued under trust. In principle it is possible for a policy trust to be as simple or as complicated as is appropriate to the circumstances of particular estates. If it is desired to benefit only a spouse and/or children, it will usually be satisfactory to invoke the statutory trust provisions of section 11 of the Married Women's Property Act 1882; section 2 of the Married Women's Policies of Assurances (Scotland) Act 1880; or section 4 of the Law Reform (Husband & Wife) Act, (Northern Ireland) 1964. It should be noted that in the case of the Scottish Act, it is not possible for a wife to effect a policy on her own life for the benefit of her husband; the statutory trust facility is restricted to a husband insuring his life for the benefit of his wife. In cases where it is desired to benefit persons other than the spouse and children, it is necessary for the policy to be issued subject to an express trust. The most common case where this will be appropriate is if it is desired to include grandchildren within the class of potential beneficiaries, but it must be remembered that the statutory trusts are *only* applicable where the class of beneficiaries does not extend beyond spouse and children.[1] There is no difference in practice to the impact of capital transfer tax where the wording being considered is a statutory or express trust, but before considering the matter in detail various preliminary observations must be made.

10–02 The Finance Act 1975 contains a very specific valuation provision for life policies, as follows:

(1) Subject to the following provisions of this paragraph, in determining in connection with a transfer of value the value of a policy of insurance on a person's life or of a contract for an annuity payable on a person's death, the value shall be taken to be not less than—

(*a*) the total of the premiums or other consideration which, at any time before the transfer of value, has been paid under the policy or contract or any policy or contract for which it was directly or indirectly substituted; less

(*b*) any sum which, at any time before the transfer of value, has been paid under, or in consideration for the surrender of any right conferred by, the policy or contract or a policy or contract for which it was directly or indirectly substituted.

---

[1] *Re Clay's Policy of Assurance* [1937] 2 All E.R. 548.

140

(4) Where the policy is one under which—

    (*a*) the benefit secured is expressed in units the value of which is published and subject to fluctuation; and

    (*b*) the payment of each premium secures the allocation to the policy of a specified number of such units;

then, if the value, at the time of the transfer of value, of the units allocated to the policy on the payment of premiums is less than the aggregate of what the respective values of those units were at the time of allocation, the value to be taken under sub-paragraph (1) above as a minimum shall be reduced by the amount of the difference.[1a]

So that the value of a life policy for capital transfer tax purposes will rarely be less than the cumulative total of the premiums paid before the transfer of value occurs, less any sum which might have been paid out previously under the policy by way of surrender. In appropriate cases, the value of the life policy will exceed the total of premiums paid to date, because its market value is greater than that total. This will be most common where a with-profits life policy has been in force for a number of years, so that its surrender value is greater than the premiums paid, or where the policy is linked to units which fluctuate in value, and the units enjoy a favourable investment experience.

–03 The other important matter to note relates not to capital transfer tax, but to qualifying policy requirements. Under the 1975 legislation, no policy issued after April 1, 1976, is a qualifying policy unless it is certified as such by the Board of Inland Revenue, or it conforms with a form which is either a standard form certified as qualifying by the Board, or in a form which varies from such a certified standard in no respect other than by making additions thereto as are compatible with meeting the qualifying policy requirements.[2] Thus, the qualifying status of the policy could be placed in jeopardy if the writing into the policy of a form of trust wording were regarded as an unacceptable deviation from a standard certified form. The Revenue have agreed that where the " addition " to the standard form amounts to no more than incorporation into the policy by endorsement of a form of request addressed to the insurance company, plus a statement to the effect that the terms of the trust do not in any way affect the contract between the insurer and the person legally entitled to the policy, they will not require the letter of request to be attached to the policy for certification purposes. Thus, provided that the terms of the letter of request make it quite clear that the trustees are to hold what is in effect a standard form certified policy as the sole trust asset, there is no risk of the policy ceasing to be qualifying for income tax purposes.

[1a] F.A. 1975, Sched. 10, para. 11 (1), (4).
[2] F.A. 1975, Sched. 2, para. 1.

10–04   It should be emphasised here that it is certainly not the intention in this chapter to provide an exhaustive dissertation on settled property and capital transfer tax. The provisions of Schedule 5 to the Finance Act 1975, which govern this highly complex area of taxation are what this chapter is concerned with, but it is the function of more specialised books on the subject to deal with all of the ramifications arising out of Schedule 5, as amended by the Finance Act 1976 and in particular Schedule 14 thereto. It is proposed in this chapter merely to consider policy trust wordings of the kind most likely to be encountered in practice, and to comment on the relevant Schedule 5 charging provisions. It should however be noted here that as a general rule tax liability will arise by reference to an interest in possession in settled property,[3] and a life policy subject to a trust is settled property for this purpose. Generally, any person entitled to current income or to the use of the settled property is considered to have an interest in possession. In the case of a settlement of a current life policy there will usually be no income, and the test of liability will be applied by reference to who would have been entitled to the income, had there been any. These matters were considered in detail in various estate duty cases, and the interested reader should refer to *Re Midwoods Settlement* [4] and *Kilpatrick* v. *I.R.C.*[5]

Trust wordings considered

10–05   Throughout these examples, it is assumed A is a person whose life is insured, and the person who pays the premiums. Unlike the position which applied under estate duty, there would usually be no practical difference if the premiums were kept up by some person other than A. In the case of estate duty, liability was often calculated by reference to the value of " gifts of rights " secured during his lifetime by the person who paid the premium, but as has been noted elsewhere, under capital transfer tax, this cannot happen, since the tax is imposed in a different way from estate duty.

Policy for the benefit of B absolutely

10–06   B has an interest in possession so that if he should die before A, the value of the policy immediately before B's death will be a taxable asset in his estate.[6] B's interest in the policy will devolve in accordance with the terms of his will or intestacy. All too frequently policy beneficiaries omit to deal specifically with policy interests under their wills, as a result of which the interest is disposed of as part of the residuary estate, which would not necessarily have been the beneficiary's intention. Of course, the beneficiary will sometimes be unaware that A

---

[3] *Ibid.* Sched. 5, paras. 1, 3.
[4] [1968] Ch. 238.
[5] [1966] Ch. 730.
[6] *Ibid.* Sched. 5, para. 3 (1).

has effected a policy for B's benefit, and secret trusts of this type, usually not intended at all to be secret, are more frequently encountered in relation to interests under life policies than in the case of any other property.

Policy for B should B survive A, otherwise for C absolutely

–07 B has an interest in possession, see *Phipps* v. *Ackers* (1842) 9 Cl. & Fin. 583, which was the basis of the decision in the *Kilpatrick* case referred to *supra*—since he has a vested interest liable to be defeated if he should die before A.

(a) If B should predecease the life assured A, C becomes absolutely entitled so that capital transfer tax is payable. This would not be the case if C were the spouse of B, since the Finance Act 1975, s. 22 (3) will operate to make the transfer of value an exempt transfer, assuming that C is domiciled in the United Kingdom. C will now have an interest in possession, since the policy is now held for him absolutely.

(b) If C should die before A and B, no transfer of value will occur, since C has only a contingent interest at that point of time. However, if after the death of C, B should die before A, B's interest will come to an end and tax will be payable as at (a) above.

Policy for such of B, C, D (or any number of named beneficiaries) as A may by will or deed appoint: failing appointment for B absolutely

–08 (a) If A makes no appointment during his lifetime but does appoint by will excluding B entirely, that appointment will result in a transfer of value of the whole of the policy. The amount of tax chargeable will be calculated by reference to the individual capital transfer tax position of B, who would have had an interest in possession in the whole of the policy before the death.[7]

A fine point to be considered here is exactly what value is transferred under these circumstances. Because the transfer would come into operation by virtue of the will of A, the value transferred will be the whole of the policy proceeds and not merely the market value of the policy immediately before the death of A.[8]

(b) In the event of appointments to C or D being made by deed or by will, there will be a transfer of value if the person in whose favour the appointment is made had no interest in possession in that part of the policy which is appointed. Thus, if A appoints by revocable deed in favour of C absolutely, there is a transfer of value from B to C, the tax being calculated by reference to B's individual tax position.

(c) If B should die before any appointment has been made, he will

---

[7] *Ibid*. Sched. 5, para. 4 (2). [8] *Ibid*. Sched. 10, paras. 9 (2), 11 (2).

have an interest in possession and a chargeable transfer of the value of the policy will occur.

(d) If C or D should predecease the life assured with no appointment having been made, neither C nor D will have had any interest under the policy and there will be no liability to tax.

(e) If an appointment is made to B, giving him an absolute interest, all that has happened is that B's existing vested interest subject to defeasance has been enlarged into an absolute interest. B therefore was entitled to an interest in possession in the whole of the settled property for capital transfer taxes both before and after the appointment so that there is no transfer of value arising out of the appointment to him.[9]

(f) If a beneficiary entitled following an appointment in his favour dies during the lifetime of A, the deceased will have had a defeasible interest if the appointment in his favour were revocable, and that interest would form part of his estate for tax purposes. If there had been an irrevocable appointment in favour of the deceased, the position is as at (c) above.

Policy for such of A's unnamed children as may survive him or if none survive for the last of them to die

10–09   It is assumed that A had at least one child at his death. If he had no children at death the policy trusts would fail leaving a resulting trust for A so that the policy would revert to A's own estate, and would be taxable.

(a) Each time that a child is born to A there may be a reduction in the value of the interest in possession of existing children. It is unlikely however that any child will be considered to have an interest in possession unless he has attained his majority—see (c) below. If there is a reduction in the value of existing interests in possession, such reduction will be a transfer of value.

(b) If a minor child of A dies he will not have had an interest in possession so that no capital transfer tax is payable, since Schedule 5, paragraph 15 of the Finance Act 1975 will operate. If there is already one or more child who has attained his majority, there will still not be any tax charge since Schedule 5, paragraph 6 (8) will operate to prevent the occurrence of a taxable transfer of value.

(c) The position is rather more complex on the death of an adult beneficiary, other than the last to die. The beneficiary will have a beneficial interest in possession (unless the operation of Trustee Act 1925, s. 31 has been expressly excluded by the trust wording): this point was considered in *Re Jones Will Trusts, Soames* v. *Attorney-General*,[10] and the result is that there could be a transfer of value of that proportion of the value of the policy appropriate to the deceased's interest.

---

[9] *Ibid.* Sched. 5, para. 4 (3).   [10] [1947] Ch. 48.

(d) If the last surviving beneficiary dies before A, a transfer of value occurs of the whole of the value of the policy. If further children could in law be born to A, the policy will remain settled property. If A cannot have further children, the settlement will probably have come to an end in any case when that event occurred (if there were only one child of A) or after the death of the penultimate beneficiary if A was at that time incapable of having further children.

(e) It should be noted that where this wording is used, minor beneficiaries have contingent interests which for capital transfer tax purposes may amount to interests in possession once a beneficiary attains his majority. In cases where the trusts are such as to impose or imply a trust for accumulation of income during the lifetime of A, or for some other period, the position could be quite different—as in the following example.

Policy for B, C, D & E on attaining 25 (in equal shares if more than one) intermediate income being accumulated. If no beneficiary attains 25, for the last to die

10–10   (a) On the death of a beneficiary other than the last to die, there would be no charge to capital transfer tax if death occurs before age 25. If the death occurs after age 25, there will be a charge on the appropriate proportion of the value of the policy.

(b) In the event of the death of the last of the beneficiaries, the *quantum* of capital transfer tax liability will depend not only on whether the last beneficiary had attained age 25, but also on whether other beneficiaries who had died had attained that age.

(c) It should be noted that in the case of this wording, the policy is protected from the operation of the Finance Act 1975, Sched. 5, paras. 6–11. Indeed, the wording has been purposely chosen so as to take advantage of the exemption from the operation of paragraphs 6–12, which is afforded by Schedule 5, paragraph 15. The exemption from paragraph 12 is particularly significant, this being the paragraph which imposes a periodic charge to tax at 10-yearly intervals calculated by reference to the relevant anniversary, where there is no interest in possession in settled property. In the case of this specimen wording, there may and there may not be an interest in possession at the relevant anniversary, depending on the ages of the beneficiaries, but since the whole benefit of the policy is bound to vest by the time the youngest beneficiary has attained age 25, the paragraph 15 exemption applies.

10–11   Reference having been made to paragraph 15, it should be noted that the operation of the paragraph 15 exemption is restricted in scope by the Finance Act 1976, s. 106. The effect of section 106 is to make the paragraph 15 exemption available (in the case of settlements created after April 15, 1976) to one generation only of a particular family.

The section 106 changes would not in practice affect a pre-April 15, 1976, policy trust using the wording now being considered, as all of the beneficiaries are named and interests in possession in the whole of the trust fund are bound to have vested within 25 years from the policy being effected. In any event, the " one generation " restriction applicable to paragraph 15 will only apply in the case of pre-April 15, 1976, trusts if it is not possible for those trusts to be varied in order to fit in with the section 106 requirements. This matter is however drawn to the attention of readers as it does highlight a fundamental matter of principle.

10-12   It was observed at the beginning of this chapter that a policy trust can be as simple or as complex as circumstances dictate. In practice, the writer considers that it can be most unwise for life policies to be made the subject of trusts more complicated than such as would be created by the relatively simple wordings considered in this chapter. In nearly all cases, the reason for drawing up a life policy under trust is not only to create a tax-free fund when the death occurs, but also to provide estate beneficiaries with liquidity from which to discharge the tax payable on assets which are taxable by reference to the life assured's death. Therefore, it is generally vital that when that sad event occurs, entitlement to life assurance policy benefit is clear-cut and is *not*, for example, dependent on the exercise of discretionary powers vested in trustees. It is perfectly true that there may occasionally be special circumstances where it is imperative for policy trustees to be left with discretion as to the application of the policy claim value. This might be desirable for example where the settlor life assured was in some doubt as to the moral or other fitness of one or more of his children to benefit. In practice, these circumstances are rarely encountered and an estate owner who is prepared to commit himself to paying out a substantial annual life assurance premium will, in nearly all cases, have a very good idea as to who he does in fact wish to benefit.

10-13   Capital transfer tax as it affects settled property is exceedingly complex, and it is essential in the case of a settled life policy that the policy moneys should be shielded as far as possible from the charging provisions of Schedule 5. Thus, the writer can see absolutely no merit in a taxpayer insuring his life for £250,000, and having written into the policy a trust which gives no interest in possession, except at the discretion of trustees. In such a case, the taxpayer has created a new settlement squarely within the paragraph 5 charging provisions, and by the time any beneficiary receives any policy benefit the whole of the policy fund could already have been subjected to capital transfer tax.

10-14   The golden rule is that life policy trusts should follow as closely as possible the life assured's testamentary intentions, and in the vast majority of all cases this will amount to a simple trust for the spouse and/or children for life or absolutely, often with remainders over to born or unborn grandchildren. If this rule is followed, there is very little risk indeed of the position arising, after death of the life assured, where a large part of the policy claim value is dissipated by unnecessary capital transfer tax. Rather than devote many more pages to considering the capital transfer tax ramifications which can arise out of the use of exotic trust wordings (all of which can be worked out very easily by referring to any specialist book on capital transfer tax) it is proposed to terminate this section by considering three more relatively simple wordings of the type likely to be encountered in practice.

Policy for B for his lifetime, then for C and D in equal shares absolutely

10–15   This is the sort of wording which would be appropriate where A wishes to leave a life interest in his testamentary estate to B, who is not his lawful spouse.

   (a) In the event of B's death, there is a transfer of value of the whole of the trust fund.

   (b) If C or D predecease B, no capital transfer tax is payable, as the reversionary interests of C and D are specifically exempted as excluded property by the Finance Act 1975, s. 24 (3).

   It will not always be A's positive intention that the policy should inevitably enure for the benefit of others. He may only wish to benefit one or more other persons assuming that they survive him, or if he personally fails to survive to a particular date.

Whole life policy for B if B survives A, otherwise for A

10–16   (a) If A dies leaving B surviving no transfer of value occurs (B already having an interest in possession) and no capital transfer tax liability arises.

   (b) If B dies leaving A surviving the whole benefit of the policy reverts to A, and no capital transfer tax is payable because of the reverter to settlor exemption—Finance Act 1975, s. 22 (2). It here should be noted that if the level of premiums was such as to have attracted capital transfer tax during the lifetime of B, there is no provision enabling the tax to be recovered.

Endowment policy for the benefit of B if he is living at the death of A within the endowment term, otherwise for A

10–17   (a) If B dies during the lifetime of A before the maturity date of the policy, the reverter to settlor exemption again will apply.

Also, any capital transfer tax paid by A during the lifetime
of B will not be recoverable.

(b) If both A and B survive until maturity of the endowment
policy, the benefit reverts to the settlor and no tax is payable
because the Finance Act 1975, Sched. 5, para. 4 (5) will apply.

Scotland and Northern Ireland

10–18 This chapter has considered only the position under English law.
The position generally will be the same under the law in Northern
Ireland, although the law in that province does not necessarily
follow English law—for example, in regard to permitted periods of
accumulation. So far as Scotland is concerned, differences in the
general law and the non-application of the Trustee Act 1925 mean
that often the capital transfer tax consequences of a particular trust
wording will be quite different from the position under English law.
For example, in the case of a policy trust subject to the law of Scotland
containing a power of appointment, any beneficiary entitled in default
of appointment does not have an interest in possession for the purposes of capital transfer tax, which is the reverse of the position under
English law. The person so entitled has a radical right under Scottish
law, which does not have the same taxation consequences as does the
corresponding equitable interest under English law. This is a good
illustration of the general principle which has to be followed:
Scottish law is less likely than is the law in England to attribute positive rights to trust beneficiaries. This is perhaps best exemplified by
the need in Scotland to follow the doctrine of delivery (except in the
case of a statutory policy trust for wife and/or children) in order to
ensure that an intended beneficiary has any right at all prior to the
death of the life assured.

Pre-March 26, 1974, policies

10–19 Notwithstanding the disclaimer made in the preface to this book,
it is necessary here to make some brief comment on trust policies
which were implemented prior to the coming into effect of capital
transfer tax as from March 27, 1974.

10–20 The majority of such policies will be the subject of simple statutory
or express trusts, which do in practice give interests in possession.
The impact of capital transfer tax on policy trusts of this kind is
hardly likely to be adverse, and in many cases will be beneficial.
Whereas under estate duty the death of the life assured could have
given rise to a tax liability under the Finance Act 1894, s. 2 (1) (c),
this possibility no longer exists because the value transferred by
premiums paid after March 26, 1974, is in effect franked for capital
transfer tax purposes as each premium is paid. It should however be

remembered that in the case of policies with substantial premiums, benefits attributable to premiums paid before March 27, 1974, could attract a limited measure of tax liability, in the event of the death of the life assured within seven years of the time of payment of any premium. The same transitional provisions can apply if before March 27, 1974, the deceased had a beneficial interest in the settled property such as to give rise to an estate duty charge in accordance with the Finance Act 1894, s. 2 (1) (*b*) (i).

10-21   With regard to policy claim values subject to capital transfer tax by reference back to section 2 (1) (*c*) (premiums paid by way of gift) some form of relief may be available in the case of premiums paid under policies which were on foot prior to March 20, 1968. By virtue of the Finance Act 1975, s. 22 (7) such a policy where the death benefit does not exceed £25,000 remains as in the days of estate duty, taxable (if at all) as a separate estate. Further, in calculating the taxable *quantum*, the proportion of policy value attributable to premiums paid within seven years of the death continues to enjoy the benefit of the old estate duty "tapering relief." This will apply to that proportion of the policy claim value attributable to premiums paid in the fifth, sixth and seventh years prior to death. In the case of policies with excess of £25,000, a proportion of the claim value is treated as an estate by itself.

10-22   This curious position, which in practice is unique to life policies, is of interest as prolonging even under capital transfer tax the concept of non-aggregation introduced originally by the proviso to section 4 of the Finance Act 1894. However, the practical effect of these provisions will invariably be that the rate of tax payable on the non-aggregable portion of the policy claim value will be nil (since the effect of tapering relief will be to reduce the taxable *quantum* of the non-aggregable policy proceeds below the nil rate band of £15,000). Also, the amount of relief actually available in any one case where the policy is sufficiently large to derive any actual benefit from these transitional provisions will be very small indeed. Nevertheless, as many pre-March 20, 1968, policies will still be in being, an example is now given of how the benefit of a repealed estate duty principle which has been temporarily preserved under capital transfer tax ought to work in practice:

10-23   The deceased effected in February 1964 a policy on his own life for £150,000 plus profits. On his death in 1977, six days after payment of the 14th annual premium, the claim value of the policy is £225,000. The policy was effected as a trust for the deceased's wife and two children (all of whom survived him) in equal shares, and the tax position is:

Portion of £225,000 *prima facie* chargeable to tax: that secured by premiums paid in 1971, 1972, 1973 and 1974

$^4/_{14} \times$ £225,000 = £64,286

Deduct relief related to premiums paid in fifth, sixth and seventh years before death—

$(85\% + 70\% + 40\%) \times {}^4/_{14} \times$ £225,000 = £31,339

£32,947

Exempt part of chargeable portion (that part kept up by the deceased for his wife)—

$\frac{1}{3} \times$ £32,947 = £10,982

CHARGEABLE PORTION   £21,965

Part of £21,965 non-aggregable (policy trust effected before March 20, 1968)

$\dfrac{25,000}{225,000} \times$ £21,965 = £ 2,440

Thus, £2,440 is taxed as if it were an estate by itself, and the rate (as being less than £15,000) will be nil.

The balance of chargeable policy moneys (£21,965−£2,440 = £19,525) will be added in with the deceased's taxable estate and will bear capital transfer tax at the appropriate rate.

10–24   The point of this section is to draw attention to the need to review trust policies which were in existence as at March 26, 1974, in the light of capital transfer tax. In the great majority of all simple trust policies, no alteration to policy trust wordings will be necessary, although it may well be appropriate to reconsider carefully the role which a pre-March 1974 trust policy on a single life basis continues to play under capital transfer tax. It may be sensible for the policy to be converted to a paid-up contract, and substituted by a joint life policy where the death benefit will not be payable until the death of the survivor of the taxpayer and his/her spouse.

10–25   So as to circumvent the estate duty charging provisions on settled property which were introduced by the Finance Act 1969, many pre-March 1974 settled policies deliberately avoid giving interests in possession to those beneficiaries who it was in fact intended ultimately should derive the policy benefit. This was most commonly achieved by stipulating that during the lifetime of the life assured any notional income would be paid away to a charity. Although even this kind of wording may be innocuous for many years yet under capital transfer tax (since it avoids giving an interest in possession) it should be borne in mind that the effect may be to give rise to the periodic capital transfer tax liability charged by Schedule 5, paragraph 12, on property where there is no interest in possession. Any such charge would be relieved by reference to premiums paid within the 10 years preceding a periodical charge. It may therefore be possible in practice to keep such a policy on foot for many years without the appointment of an interest in possession before any liability to tax arises, or at least before the nil rate band of tax is exceeded. It must not however be overlooked that at such time as an interest in possession does come into existence, there will be a chargeable transfer of value,[11] and if the appointment of an interest in possession extends to the whole of the policy, the whole of the value at that time will be subject to capital transfer tax.

General points

Procedure for creating policy trusts

0–26   In the case of one of the statutory trusts, all that is required is a statement by the person effecting the policy that it is intended that the policy shall be for the benefit of spouse and/or children. Most insurance companies will upon request provide forms suitable for the creation of a statutory policy trust. It must be borne in mind though that in the absence of any contrary indication in the policy trust itself, trustees' powers will be restricted to those given by the Trustee Act 1925 and the law generally. This could be inhibiting in the case, for example, of a substantial policy which enures for minor children, the whole of the policy proceeds not being utilised to discharge capital transfer tax on the deceased's estate. It may be considered desirable therefore to write specific trustee powers into a policy issued subject to a statutory trust—for example so as to extend the trustees' investment powers beyond the limits of the Trustee Investment Acts 1961 and 1967.

0–27   In cases where it is desired to extend the class of beneficiaries beyond spouse and children, a special express trust declaration will have to be made. The procedure for setting up express policy trusts will differ from insurance company to insurance company, but the generally favoured method is for the person whose life is to be insured to effect the policy as sole trustee upon trusts stipulated in his letter of instruction. It is however essential that as soon as possible after the policy has been issued the sole trustee should retire in favour of others, or should appoint others to act with him. On the whole, it is preferable that the original trustee should retire, since otherwise there might be a case for arguing that the payment by the life assured of premiums after the first were payments made by him *qua* trustee so as to keep up or protect the trust property, thus giving the life assured trustee a lien over the policy claim value. In the days of estate duty this could

---

[11] *Ibid.* Sched. 5, para. 6 (2).

have led to unfortunate consequences when the policy became a claim, although it is not known that the Estate Duty Office ever took the point that in these circumstances the settlor life assured had a lien over the policy moneys, which amounted to the retention of an interest. Under capital transfer tax, there is the theoretical possibility that the personal representatives of a deceased settlor life assured who had remained a trustee would have a right, and even a duty, to claim back premiums after the first paid by the deceased in order to keep up the policy. If the relevant policy premiums had been outside the capital transfer tax exemptions, this might in turn lead to the estate being entitled to a refund of capital transfer tax paid within six years of the death. Clearly, this would all be prejudicial to the interests of the beneficiaries, and almost certainly not what the life assured had intended at all. Although it is true that such a lien is irrefutably established under English law only where the trustee maintains premiums to keep up the policy for the estate of a named deceased beneficiary (*Re Smith's Estate* [1937] Ch. 636) the fact is that the general principles of equity could result in the courts upholding that a lien existed in other circumstances, notwithstanding any specific disclaimer which might be written into the policy trust letter of instruction.

10–28   Another reason for recommending that the initial sole trustee should retire from the trusts is that this should ease the payment of the policy claim value at his death. Provided that the life assured is survived by properly appointed trustees of the policy, the claim value can be paid out to the trustees immediately upon proof of death of the life assured and of title to the policy. There is no need for the life office to withhold payment pending the grant of probate so that the policy moneys can be made available (provided that the policy trusts justify this) to help meet capital transfer tax on the deceased's free estate, which must be paid before probate can be granted. The life office could not pay out before probate were granted if the deceased were himself a trustee of the policy, unless the terms of the policy contract were such that the life office would be properly discharged by a receipt given say by any two out of three trustees.

Joint life policies

10–29   Where the policy is on a joint basis, either each proposer life assured can submit an individual trust declaration letter to the insurance company on identical terms, each letter being signed individually, or the two lives assured can be joint settlors, each of them signing one letter of request. It would not be advisable in England or Scotland to contemplate using the statutory trusts, since in each case the statutory protection is only available where a spouse effects a policy on his or her *own life*.

Death of life assured

10–30   Probably the point should be made that the comments in this chapter dealing with capital transfer tax consequences of different trust wordings will generally apply, irrespective of whether the policy is still on foot. In other words, where a policy is drawn up subject to trust, the happening of the death of the life or lives assured will not usually affect the legal construction of the trust or its tax consequences. The death of the life or lives assured is the occasion of the payment of the policy claim value, so at that point of time a non-income producing asset will be transmuted into cash, which is obviously capable of producing income if it is invested. However, the death of the life assured will often result in the termination of a trust by operation of law; for example, in a case where there are only adult beneficiaries, all of whom are absolutely entitled in exactly defined shares. However, the mere fact that the life assured dies and the life policy trustees receive a substantial cash payment to hold for the beneficiaries does not *per se* give rise to any tax liability. In the case just mentioned, the adult beneficiaries were *at all times* absolutely entitled to a proportion of the policy claim value, which is in effect " franked " for capital transfer tax each time a premium is paid.

Pension schemes

10–31   The capital transfer tax treatment of pension funds approved for income tax purposes is covered by the Finance Act 1975, Sched. 5, para. 16. The general principle is that any payment made to the estate of a deceased member of an income tax-exempt scheme is left out of account in determining the value of his estate immediately before his death. However, this would not be the position if the terms of the pension fund were such that the legal personal representatives of the deceased were entitled as of right to receive a payment.

Detailed consideration of pension fund trust wordings is outside the scope of this book, but practitioners will find that most questions can be answered by reference to Appendix III to this book, being an Inland Revenue press release of May 7, 1976, together with an Estate Duty Office practice note.

CHAPTER 11

THE USE OF LIFE ASSURANCE IN SETTLEMENTS

11-01   AN insurance policy does not generate taxable income; the proceeds
at maturity are generally free of capital gains tax; and in terms of
book-keeping and other records the administration involved in
possessing an insurance policy is minimal. For these reasons, an
insurance policy can be an attractive medium for trustee income
or capital investment. Before trustees can put themselves in the
position of effecting or accepting assignment of a single premium
policy, or acquiring a paid up or subsisting annual premium policy,
they will need to consider various technical aspects, such as the
existence of insurable interest; the particular settlement accumulation period, if any; and the usual need to maintain a proper balance
as between the interests of income and capital beneficiaries. Comment
on the first two of these topics is made later in this chapter, but
first consideration is given to some functions which life assurance
can fulfil for trust funds.

Income tax background

11-02   The first general principle to note is that in the case of infant settlements, any income which is applied for the benefit of the settlor's
own infant children remains the income of the settlor for tax
purposes.[1] Therefore, the only type of settlement which in general
tax planning terms can be recommended where it is intended to
benefit the settlor's infant children is one where there is a specific
power or direction to accumulate. This has the advantage that there
is no liability to the higher rates of income tax on the accumulations,
and of course in order to obtain this beneficial tax treatment it is
essential that the infant beneficiaries concerned have no more than
a contingent interest. There is undoubtedly a case for the creation
of new infant settlements of this kind, notwithstanding the introduction of capital transfer tax, since the potential savings of income
tax can still be substantial, and although the creation of a new
settlement will attract capital transfer tax, this will only be on the
lower lifetime scale provided that the settlor survives for at least
three years, and as long as the fund vests absolutely in the infant
beneficiaries by age 25, the vesting will not be a capital distribution
for purposes of capital transfer tax.[2] Also, in the case of myriad
pre-March 1974 discretionary settlements, " paragraph 15 " appoint-

---

[1] Taxes Act 1970, ss. 437–444.
[2] F.A. 1975, Sched. 5, para. 15 (2) (*a*). The fund also will be exempt from the
10-yearly periodic charge rule—*ibid*., para. 15 (2) (*b*).

154

ments whereby the appointed funds vest in infant beneficiaries by age 25 can result in substantial capital transfer savings.

1–03   The real practical problem which arises is that any payments made by the trustees to or on behalf of minor children, whilst there is accumulated income, will be treated as the settlor's for income tax purposes.[3] Therefore, whilst it still makes sense for funds to be held in trust for infant children with a view to appointment to or vesting in them no later than age 25, it can be difficult or impracticable for the trustees to make any payment on behalf of the children during their minorities, because of the income tax consequences. This problem can be overcome if, for example, a parent chooses to settle on his infant children a single premium insurance policy, or an annual premium policy the settlor having covenanted to keep up premiums, the effect being that a settlement is created for minor children with no risk of income being taxed as the settlor's—for the simple reason that if the sole trust asset is an insurance policy, there cannot be any income of the trust.

1–04   The next point to be made is that in the case of existing and new discretionary and other settlements, the legislation contained in the Taxes Act 1970, Pt. XVI, Chap. III presents all manner of pitfalls to trustees and beneficiaries where trust income arises and is dealt with, whether by way of accumulation or distribution, during the settlor's lifetime. The potential impact of much of this legislation can be reduced, or entirely eliminated, in the case of a settlement comprising solely a life policy. For example, if there is no accumulated income, there is no risk of the penal anti-avoidance section 451 ever having any effect. The section has the effect of grossing up and taxing as income of the settlor in the year of payment any capital sum (such as a loan) paid directly or indirectly to a settlor or his wife, to the extent of net income accumulations under the settlement not only in the year of payment but in any earlier year. There could obviously not be any section 451 problem if the settlement assets are incapable of generating income. There could be further advantages in the case of a settlement of this kind (including the settlor and/or the spouse as one of the discretionary objects) since under section 488, income of the trustees of such a settlement is deemed to remain the income of the settlor. As it is no longer futile under capital transfer tax, as it was under estate duty, to include the settlor and/or his spouse under a settlement—indeed the position is now just the reverse, since any reservation of benefit must reduce the *quantum* transferred for capital transfer tax purposes—there could be a strong tax planning case for the creation of new settlements of this kind.

1–05   One further point needs to be made again in relation to infant settlements. In recent years, an income tax provision was introduced

---

[3] Taxes Act 1970, s. 438 (2) (*b*).

whereby all income of minor children irrespective of whether it was derived from their parents, was aggregated with the parents' for income tax purposes.[4] The provision was repealed following the change of government in 1970,[5] but on the subsequent change in 1974, the Government then elected promised to reinstate the aggregation provisions. At the time of going to press, this has not happened, but if it did, there would be a very strong case for existing and new infant settlements to be invested partly or wholly into a non-income producing asset such as a life policy.

Capital transfer tax

11-06   Insurance can be used as a convenient and relatively certain method of investing trust funds against future capital transfer tax liabilities. Although the most obvious use is in the case of discretionary settlements which are subject to the 10-yearly periodic charge rule, there can be other uses. Consider the case of a settlement created in March 1974, just before the introduction of capital transfer tax, whereby income was to be accumulated for 21 years and the fund then to vest in the settlor's son if he be then living, at what would be his age 30. Assuming that in due course at age 30, the son's contingent interest becomes an absolute entitlement, capital transfer tax will be payable, and the trustees might think it prudent that they should devote part of the income accumulations commencing say in 1977 to meet the premiums on an 18 year endowment assurance with profits with a view to utilising the maturing policy proceeds to discharge capital transfer tax.

11-07   Although it is true that the maturity value of the endowment assurance would form a part of the capital of the trust fund and therefore would suffer capital transfer tax along with the other assets, the use of income accumulations in this manner should stand up on straight investment grounds, since a well chosen endowment policy with profits should provide a yield to redemption of at least 8 per cent. on premiums invested, which in days of economic turmoil could well turn out to be more successful than any other trustee investment. Funding capital transfer tax in this manner could be exceptionally prudent in cases where the trust assets comprise unmarketable securities such as close company shares or assets such as farmland which it is particularly desired to retain within the family.

Discretionary trusts

11-08   Consider a discretionary settlement created in April 1969. If no interest in possession is appointed, the trust fund will be subject to

---

[4] F.A. 1968, s. 15 (1) consolidated as T.A. 1970, s. 43 (1).
[5] F.A. 1971, s. 16 (1) (*a*).

capital transfer tax at 30 per cent. of the tax which would be payable if the whole capital were distributed, in April 1989 and thereafter at 10-yearly intervals.[6] Although there will frequently be a case for putting an end to the settlement or for creating interests in possession or trusts for accumulation and maintenance prior to April 1, 1980, when there would be a substantial reduction in the capital transfer tax which otherwise would be payable if any of those events were postponed beyond April 1, 1980,[7] it may be that it is the settlor's or trustees' wish to retain full discretionary powers over income and capital for as long as possible.

1–09 The difficulties of forecasting future investment performance, particularly if part of the fund comprises assets such as close company shares, are formidable. Nevertheless, the trustees are advised that in March 1989 the fund might be worth £250,000 with every prospect of it increasing to £350,000 by the time of the second 10-yearly charge in April 1999. On these assumptions, the capital transfer tax payable at the 1989 valuation would be £22,912, and in 1999, the tax payable would be £40,162. Some commentators argue that on the construction of the relevant legislation, the tax payable at the 1989 deemed capital distribution is a credit against the tax chargeable at the 1999 relevant anniversary.[8] Prudence however would seem to dictate that the trustees should contemplate having to find say £23,000 of tax in 1989 and £41,000 of tax in 1999.

1–10 The co-operation is enlisted of a 30-year-old beneficiary, and the trustees acquire on his life endowment assurances with profits which are effected in April 1977 for terms of 12 years and 22 years. The annual premium for the policy expected to mature in 1989 for £23,000 is £1,100; the premium for the policy which will mature in 1999 for an estimated amount of £41,000 is £765. The total cost of building up these funds intended to discharge capital transfer tax is £1,865 payable for 12 years, followed by £765 payable for a further 10 years, making an overall total of £30,030. In exchange for this outlay, it is expected that the combined maturity value of the two policies will be at least £64,000, and should the beneficiary die before the last annual premium under the 22 year endowment policy has been paid, the return on premiums invested up to the date of death would actually represent a better investment result. Trustees certainly should not overlook the fact that in the unfortunate event of the death of a beneficiary that proportion of endowment premiums which goes towards covering the mortality risk does mean that the investment return is enhanced rather than reduced, and in this respect life assurance has a unique attraction as an investment medium for trustees.

[6] F.A. 1975, Sched. 5, para. 12 (1), (6).
[7] *Ibid.* Sched. 5, para. 14.
[8] See *ibid.*, Sched. 5, para. 13.

11–11   The probability is that a discretionary settlement of the size here contemplated would have an annual net income, after basic rate tax and the investment income surcharge, of several times the initial gross annual endowment policy premiums of £1,865. For example, if the average yield on a trust fund of £200,000 is 7½ per cent. after expenses, the gross annual income is £15,000, which leaves £7,500 net of taxation. It is manifest that, assuming the trustees have the necessary explicit or implied powers to insure, the accumulation of under 30 per cent. of the net income by way of paying life assurance premiums to fund future capital transfer tax liabilities is exceedingly sensible forward planning.

11–12   It must be borne in mind that capital transfer tax payable under the periodic charging system is allowed as a credit against tax payable on a capital distribution of the fund made within 20 years of each periodic charge.[9] On the basis illustrated therefore, it would be possible to obtain a tax credit for the £41,000 of capital transfer tax assumed to be paid in 1999 if the whole of the trust fund were distributed before April 2019. Of course, a further periodic charge would have arisen in April 2009, and in principle that too could be funded through endowment assurance, either by the trustees effecting a 32 year endowment policy at the same time as those policies which mature in 1989 and 1999, or by a further policy being effected at any time up to and including April 1999. Tax payable in April 2009 would be added to that payable in 1999, in calculating the total tax credit available on any distribution from the fund made prior to April 2019.

11–13   Suppose that in principle it was the settlor's original wish in 1969 that the fund should be distributed at the discretion of the trustees in the year 2005, which would be 36 years after the time of the original settlement. He might have given the trustees a letter expressing his wish in this matter, the reasoning being that the settlor's youngest child would attain the age of 40 in 2005. The conventional advice following the introduction of capital transfer tax appears to be that interests in possession or trusts for accumulation and maintenance should be appointed prior to April 1, 1980. However, the appointment of interests in possession would clearly be against the original wishes of the settlor, and trusts for accumulation or maintenance would have to vest before the beneficiaries reach 25 to provide any real capital transfer tax advantage. Is it necessarily the best advice that the trustees' discretion over both income and capital should be removed before 1980, primarily because of fears about capital transfer tax? It is suggested that if arrangements are made to ensure that payment of the capital transfer tax periodic charge does not precipitate a liquidity crisis, the ability to retain total discretion until the year

---

[9] *Ibid.*

2005 could in fact be much more important in these circumstances than the fundamental altering of terms of the settlement to achieve a short-term tax advantage. However if the fund in question were to grow to £400,000 by 2005, when the whole of the fund is distributed, the capital transfer tax payable at that time is £163,875, but as a credit against this would be the tax totalling £64,000 paid on the periodic revaluations in 1989 and 1999. Therefore, the amount of tax payable on the distribution in 2005 would be almost exactly £100,000 (plus of course a certain amount of capital gains tax). The alternative to effecting endowment assurances in April 1977 to fund the periodic tax charges would presumably have been to accept an immediate capital transfer tax liability, by appointing the whole of the fund in such a way as to avoid future liability. If the fund was worth £200,000 in April 1977, the capital transfer tax payable on an immediate distribution would be 15 per cent. of £51,375 which is £7,706.[10]

1–14 There is a considerable gulf between an immediate tax liability of £7,706, and an ultimate prospective liability of £163,875. However, if the distribution of the whole fund is postponed until 2005, it is estimated that even after the payment of tax there will be some £300,000 available for distribution, as compared with an immediate net figure of about £192,000. Bearing in mind that the appointment of interests in 1977 could well result in the loss of the ability to accumulate income the probability is that over the family as a whole substantially more income tax would be paid in the later years than would apply if the discretionary trust were maintained intact until 2005. It is true that on the facts as stated, it would only be lawful for the trustees to continue income accumulations beyond 1990 in any event, if the stated accumulation period were the settlor's lifetime, and he survived beyond 1990.[11]

1–15 The fact is that in the case of many discretionary settlements, particularly those effected before March 27, 1974, there must be compelling reasons for maintaining the trust in its present or original form if at all possible. It will always be the trustees' duty to consider what is a proper discharge of their responsibilities without reference to the settlor's wishes. If however they feel within this principle that for the trust to subsist in its present form rather than for it to be varied is on balance likely to be in the long term interests of the beneficiaries, the future trustee capital transfer tax liabilities which such a decision entails should be provided for as a normal function of wise management. Whether or not life assurance has a part to play will depend on all the circumstances.

---

[10] *Ibid*. Sched. 5, para. 14 (2) (*c*).
[11] See Law of Property Act 1925, s. 164 and Perpetuities and Accumulations Act 1964, s. 13.

Income tax: provision of school fees

11–16   As has been noted *infra*, there are very many pitfalls awaiting those who wish to benefit infant children, particularly their own. In principle, it is inadvisable for an infant settlement intended to be used for the education or maintenance of the settlor's children to be capable of generating too much income during their minorities as the income either by statute [12] or on the basis of decided cases [13] in income tax law may be taxed as the settlor's own. This danger is removed if the sole trust asset is incapable of producing income, and as this is one potentially important application of certain kinds of insurance contract it is worth considering the possibilities in detail.

11–17   Take the case of a taxpayer wishing to provide school fees of £1,000 annually for his children commencing five years hence, followed by £2,000 annually for the ensuing eight years. He also wishes them to become entitled to a capital fund at age 21. He effects a single premium life assurance bond for an initial payment of £40,000 and pays the capital transfer tax which becomes immediately due as the policy is issued as a trust for his children, revocable only if they all die before the age of 25. The trustees have all the normal powers of reinvestment, but the intention is to retain the bond as the sole trust asset. The terms of the trust give the trustees powers to borrow, to surrender the policy in whole or in part, and to apply income or capital for or towards the education, maintenance and advancement of the infant children. At the appropriate times they surrender sufficient units allotted to the policy in order to meet school fees, and provided that the amounts surrendered do not exceed 5 per cent. of the single premium (which is £2,000) in any one policy year, no liability to higher rate tax or to the investment income surcharge will arise at the time of surrender. Any such liability is postponed until the final policy chargeable event. [14]

11–18   The cash sums received at each surrender of units are used to pay school fees, and as a matter of prudence the payments are made by the trustees directly to the schools concerned. Each such payment is clearly made out of the capital of the trust fund (which has no income in any event) so that there is no question of the arising of income which could be deemed to be the settlor's, or the children's (with consequent loss of the children's income tax allowance on the part of their father, the settlor). [15]

11–19   In the fullness of time the children attain age 21, when they become entitled to the capital of the trust fund. Suppose that at that time the single premium bond is worth £50,000, the earlier withdrawals having

---

[12] §§ 11–02—11–05.
[13] See *e.g. Brodie's Trustees* v. *I.R.C.* 17 T.C. 432 and *Cunard's Trustees* v. *I.R.C.* [1946] 1 All E.R. 159.
[14] F.A. 1975, Sched. 2, Pt. IV.
[15] T.A. 1970, s. 10 (5).

been at the rate of £1,000 annually for five years followed by £2,000 annually for eight years, totalling £21,000. The profit element overall is the difference between the initial single premium of £40,000 and £71,000, being £31,000. If the trustees surrendered the bond with a view to paying the net proceeds to the children, they would first have to make allowance for higher rate income tax and the investment income surcharge, calculated by reference to the tax position of the settlor in the year of surrender.[16] Much of the £50,000 therefore could be paid away in taxation. To avoid this complication and potential depletion of the trust fund, the trustees could decide to distribute the policy to the children *in specie*. The beneficiaries could then decide whether to keep the policy, and perhaps continue with immediately tax-free withdrawals at not exceeding £2,000 annually, or forthwith to surrender. Any tax liability on surrender would be calculated by reference to the children's own tax position[17] with the appropriate top-slicing relief[18] (*not* by reference to their father's tax position) and the probability is that no liability at all would arise.

11–20 As can be seen, this is an attractive way for the wealthy taxpayer to fund school fees economically. There should be no taxation liability after he has met the capital transfer tax incurred at the time of inception of the single premium bond, and this could be as little as £2,143 if he has not made any previous lifetime taxable transfer and has not utilised any part of the preceding tax year's £2,000 exemption. Income tax liability on the trust assets should be restricted to the insurance company's life fund rate, currently not exceeding $37 \cdot 5$ per cent.,[19] and if the method outlined above is followed no income tax will be payable when the trustees actually pay the school fees. Aggregation for income tax purposes thus is avoided, even though the trust fund is used to make payments on behalf of the settlor's infant children. Finally, after the trust fund has fulfilled its school fees role it can be distributed to the children before their age 25 with no capital transfer tax liability,[20] and can if appropriate be retained by them as a non-income producing asset capable of providing up to £2,000 annually tax-free until the eventual death of their father, assuming that the bond was effected on his life.

Insurable interest

11–21 Bearing in mind the principles considered in Chapter 1 it will be apparent that trustees could be faced with an insuperable problem if there is no beneficiary in whose life they have a pecuniary interest sufficient to fulfil the requirements of the Life Assurance Act 1774, ss. 1 and 3. The danger is that the insurance company could be justified in law in refusing payment under the policy if it is discovered sub-

[16] *Ibid.* ss. 395, 399.
[17] *Ibid.* s. 399 (1) (*a*).
[18] *Ibid.* s. 400.
[19] See §§ 1–04—1–07.
[20] F.A. 1975, Sched. 5, para. 15.

sequently to issuing the policy that it was voidable because of the absence of insurable interest. The trustees then could be liable personally for any loss sustained by the trust.

11–22   The problem will not arise in cases where it is decided to create a new trust by having a policy on the life of the settlor issued as a trust *ab initio* or where a policy on the life of the settlor is assigned to trustees. The settlor has an unlimited interest in his own life and insurable interest has only to be established at the time the contract of insurance is made.[21] Where however trustees of an existing settlement, particularly one with no interest in possession, wish to consider insurance, a real problem may exist. The difficulty is that although in practice it is unheard of for an insurance company to seek to repudiate a contract on the grounds of lack of insurable interest alone, it would undoubtedly be the duty of a liquidator to repudiate. Recent experience shows that it is all too easy for an apparently sound insurance company with substantial financial backing to overstretch itself, and even though the policyholder's position is largely protected financially now in the event of the insurer failing,[22] this would be of no avail if the contract itself could be avoided at law.

11–23   It will be appreciated that the mere inclusion in the trust document of a power to insure, whether or not the power refers by name or otherwise to specific lives, will be insufficient of itself to establish insurable interest. In cases where there is no interest in possession, the most sensible and practical way to overcome the problem is for the desired policy to be effected by a beneficiary on his own life, or similarly by the settlor if living and of a suitable age, and for the trustees to acquire the policy. If they do this by way of purchase, there should be no income tax or capital transfer tax repercussions but the policy would *prima facie* become subject to capital gains tax.[23] If on the other hand the policy is assigned voluntarily to the trustees, the assignment will rank as an addition to the settlement for tax purposes with the additional complication, should the assignment be made by a beneficiary, of introducing a further " settlor."[24] For income tax purposes however the beneficiary would become the settlor only to the extent of income originating from or provided by him,[25] which is hardly likely to be an inhibiting factor if the policy value at the time of assignment is low. It would in any event be recommended that the policy be assigned after the payment of a first monthly premium only so as to keep the value for capital transfer tax purposes to a minimum. The probability is that the value at assignment would be low enough to ensure that it fell within the assignor's £2,000 annual exemption.

---

[21] *Dalby* v. *India and London Life Assurance Co.* (1843–60) All E.R. 1040.
[22] Policyholders Protection Act 1975.
[23] F.A. 1965, s. 28.
[24] T.A. 1970, s. 454 (3).   [25] *Ibid.* s. 452.

11–24   It will often be the case that the settlor is still alive, but through old age or infirmity is uninsurable. In these circumstances the preferable course is for the policy to be acquired by the settlor from a beneficiary (or indeed an unconnected person) who has effected the policy on his own life. The acquisition will be for full consideration, which would not exceed the amount of the first monthly premium paid by the life assured at inception. Immediately after having purchased the policy for value, the settlor will assign it to the trustees as an addition to the settlement. Although dealing with a policy for money or money's worth can give rise to capital gains tax or to higher rate income tax liabilities there is no risk of either eventuality here. Capital gains tax cannot apply because the trustees' acquisition is not for value [26]; and the chargeable event for income tax purposes which occurs on the settlor's acquisition [27] gives rise to a nil assessment since the policy's value at that time cannot exceed the initial monthly premium. [28]

Power to insure

11–25   As with all uses to which trustee funds are put, the trustees must be satisfied that the application of trust moneys, whether income or capital, towards the payment of insurance premiums is permitted by an express, statutory or implied power. An express power to insure and to apply current income, accumulations or capital towards the payment of premiums would of course be conclusive. In a case where the settlor has himself settled the policy with directions to pay annual premiums out of trust assets there is clearly no problem. Further, if the direction is to pay premiums from income *Bassil* v. *Lister* (1851) 9 Hare 177 is authority for the trustees' ability to do this without regard to the rule against accumulations. It is probable that a special power to invest in assets which do not produce income can properly be construed as an implied power to insure, as can a power to invest in wasting assets.

11–26   There seems no doubt that trustees can never be under a *duty* to insure so as to protect the fund against prospective taxation liabilities, except perhaps where such a duty is implicit in an express power coupled with a direction to keep up premiums. The *power* to insure may however be found in the settlement investment clause, and problems of construction arise if the investment clause does not confer a specific special power to insure or to acquire non-income producing assets. It is sometimes argued that even a wide investment clause giving the trustees unfettered powers to invest as if they were absolute beneficial owners (a clause which is commonly encountered) does not imply a power to insure. The reasoning behind this assertion is the suggestion that the term " investment " means an asset which yields

---

[26] F.A. 1965, s. 28 (2).
[27] T.A. 1970, s. 394 (1) (*a*) (iv).   [28] *Ibid.* s. 395 (1) (*c*).

current income.[29] However, present rates of income tax often militate against investments which do yield an income, and the application of trustee funds to the acquisition of investments which do not yield income, such as reversions to leases or other property or the capital shares of a split level investment trust, is hardly likely to be outside the authority of a modern wide investment clause. This being the case, it is difficult to see how an insurance policy, acquired with a view to increasing the capital of a trust fund or to protecting the capital against depletion by taxation, can fail to fall into the same category, particularly in the case of discretionary trusts or others which give no right to current income.

11–27   Provided that the trustees follow the normal rules of prudence and maintain a reasonable balance between income and capital beneficiaries (where there are separate categories) they are unlikely to be faulted for devoting a proportion of the fund towards insurance. They may have to consider whether premiums should be met out of capital or income, but in principle if they have express or implied power to insure there must also be an implied power to pay premiums out of income accumulations or from capital. Payment out of accumulated income will automatically transmute the income into a capital asset, and this gives rise to consideration of how the policy can be kept up, if at all, once the period of accumulation allowed by law has expired. The longest period is likely to be 21 years or the lifetime of the settlor, if longer, whereas it would be lawful for a settlement to subsist for a much greater period with no interest in possession without infringing the rule against perpetuities. Since income which is invalidly accumulated is to be regarded as having been distributed to those entitled to the income, in cases where there is no interest in possession there is no effective Revenue sanction if the trustees decide not to distribute income after the accumulation period has expired. Hence, if the trustees continue to accumulate *all* income beyond the accumulation period, and pay insurance premiums out of that income, it is unlikely that there will be any repercussion, although the trustees would be well advised before taking such steps to be satisfied that no beneficiary is likely to ask the court to direct the trustees to distribute income. It is of particular importance that where the intention behind the policy is to protect or preserve the trust fund, but not to increase its value, there would seem to be no breach of trust if premiums are maintained out of income beyond the accumulation period. This statement follows the rule in *Re Gardiner* [1901] 1 Ch. 697 and seems to be authority for trustees to pay premiums from income outwith the accumulation period where the specific intent, as suggested earlier in this chapter, is to use the policy proceeds to discharge capital transfer tax.

---

[29] See *e.g. Re Wragg* [1919] 2 Ch. 58 and *Re Power* [1947] Ch. 572.

STATUTES

Life Assurance Act 1774

(as amended) (14 GEO. 3, C. 48)

An Act for regulating insurances upon lives, and for prohibiting all such insurances, except in cases where the persons insuring shall have an interest in the life or death of the persons insured.

2–01 WHEREAS it hath been found by experience, that the making of insurances on lives, or other events, wherein the assured shall have no interest, hath introduced a mischievous kind of gaming: for remedy whereof, be it enacted by the King's most Excellent Majesty, by and with the advice and consent of the Lords Spiritual and Temporal, and Commons, in this present Parliament assembled, and by the authority of the same, that from and after the passing of this Act, no insurance shall be made by any person or persons, bodies politic or corporate, on the life or lives of any person or persons, or on any other event or events whatsoever, wherein the person or persons, for whose use, benefit, or on whose account such policy or policies shall be made, shall have no interest, or by way of gaming or wagering; and that every assurance made contrary to the true intent and meaning hereof, shall be null and void, to all intents and purposes whatsoever.

2. And it shall not be lawful to make any policy or policies on the life or lives of any person or persons, or other event or events, without inserting in such policy or policies the person or persons' name or names interested therein, or for whose use, benefit, or on whose account, such policy is so made or underwrote.

3. And in all cases when the insured hath interest in such life or lives, event or events, no greater sum shall be recovered or received from the insurer or insurers than the amount or value of the interest of the insured in such life or lives, or other event or events.

4. Provided always, that nothing herein contained shall extend, or be construed to extend, to insurances *bona fide* made by any person or persons, on ships, goods, or merchandises; but every such insurance shall be as valid and effectual in the law, as if this Act had not been made.

Married Women's Policies of Assurance (Scotland) Act 1880

(43 & 44 VICT. C. 26)

Policy of assurance may be effected in trust for wife and children

2–02 **2.** A policy of assurance effected by any married man on his own life, and expressed upon the face of it to be for the benefit of his wife, or of his children, or of his wife and children, shall, together with all benefit thereof, be deemed a trust for the benefit of his wife for her separate use, or for the benefit of his children, or for the benefit of his wife and children; and such policy, immediately on its being so effected, shall vest in him and his legal representatives in trust for the purpose or purposes so expressed, or in any trustee nominated in the policy, or appointed by separate writing duly intimated to the assurance office, but in trust always as aforesaid, and shall not otherwise be subject to his control, or form part of his estate, or be liable to the diligence of his creditors, or be revocable as a donation, or reducible on any ground of excess or insolvency: And the receipt of such trustee for the sums secured by the policy, or for the value thereof, in whole or in part, shall be a sufficient and effectual discharge to the assurance office: Provided always, that if it shall be proved that the policy was effected and premiums thereon paid with intent to defraud creditors, or if the person upon whose life the policy is effected shall be made bankrupt within two years from the date of such policy, it shall be competent to the creditors to claim repayment of the premiums so paid from the trustee of the policy out of the proceeds thereof.

Note: This section has been extended to include adopted children (see the Adoption Act 1958, s. 14 (3)), and illegitimate children (see Family Law Reform Act 1969, s. 19 (1)).

Married Women's Property Act 1882

(45 & 46 VICT. C. 75)

Moneys payable under policy of assurance not to form part of estate of the insured

12–03 **11.** A married woman may effect a policy upon her own life or the life of her husband for her own benefit; and the same and all benefit thereof shall enure accordingly.

12–04 A policy of assurance effected by any man on his own life, and expressed to be for the benefit of his wife, or of his children, or of his wife and children, or any of them, or by any woman on her own life, and expressed to be for the benefit of her husband, or of her children, or of her husband and children, or any of them, shall create a trust in favour of the objects therein named, and the moneys payable under any such policy shall not, so long as any object of the trust remains unperformed, form part of the estate of the insured, or be subject to his or her debts: Provided, that if it shall be proved that the policy was effected and the premiums paid with intent to defraud the creditors of the insured, they shall be entitled to receive, out of the moneys payable under the policy, a sum equal to the premiums so paid. The insured may by the policy, or by any memorandum under his or her hand, appoint a trustee or trustees of the moneys payable under the policy, and from time to time appoint a new trustee or new trustees thereof, and may make provision for the appointment of a new trustee or new trustees thereof, and for the investment of the moneys payable under any such policy. In default of any such appointment of a trustee, such policy, immediately on its being effected, shall vest in the insured and his or her legal personal representatives, in trust for the purposes aforesaid. The receipt of a trustee or trustees duly appointed, or in default of any such appointment, or in default of notice to the insurance office, the receipt of the legal personal representatives of the insured shall be a discharge to the office for the sum secured by the policy, or for the value thereof, in whole or in part.

Note: This section has been extended to include adopted children (see the Adoption Act 1958, s. 14 (3)), and illegitimate children (see Family Law Reform Act 1969, s. 19 (1)).

Law Reform (Husband and Wife) Act (Northern Ireland) 1964

(C. 23)

Insurance for benefit of spouse or children

–05 **4.**—(1) This section applies to a policy of life assurance or endowment expressed to be for the benefit of, or by its express terms purporting to confer a benefit upon, the wife, husband or child of the insured.

(2) Such policy shall create a trust in favour of the objects therein named.

(3) The moneys payable under the policy shall not, so long as any part of the trust remains unperformed, form part of the estate of the insured or be subject to his or her debts.

(4) If it is proved that the policy was effected and the premiums paid with intent to defraud the creditors of the insured, they shall be entitled to receive, on account of their debts, payment out of the moneys payable under the policy, so, however, that the total amount of such payments shall not exceed the amount of the premiums so paid.

(5) The insured may by the policy, or by any memorandum under his or her hand, appoint a trustee or trustees of the moneys payable under the policy, and may from time to time appoint a new trustee or new trustees thereof, and may make provision for the appointment of a new trustee or trustees thereof and for the investment of the moneys payable under the policy.

(6) In default of any such appointment of a trustee, the policy, immediately on its being effected, shall vest in the insured and his or her legal personal representatives in trust for the purposes aforesaid.

(7) The receipt of a trustee or trustees duly appointed or, in default either of any such appointment or of notice thereof to the insurer, the receipt of the legal personal representative of the insured shall be a good discharge to the insurer for any sum paid by him under the policy.

(8) This section applies whether the policy was effected before or after the commencement of this Act.

Income and Corporation Taxes Act 1970

(as amended) (c.10)

Premiums under post-1916 life policies etc.

–06 **19.**—(1) Subject to the provisions of this section and of section 21 below, and subject also to section 227 (11) of this Act (retirement annuity premiums), if the claimant has paid any such premium as is specified in subsection (2) below, he shall be entitled to a deduction from the amount of income tax with which he is chargeable equal to income tax at one-half of the basic rate on the amount of the premium:

Provided that if, in any year of assessment, the total premiums in respect of which relief falls to be granted under this section do not exceed £20, the relief under this section shall be a deduction equal to income tax [at the basic rate (a)] on £10 or on the full amount of the premiums, whichever is the less.

(2) The premiums referred to in subsection (1) above are any premiums paid by the claimant under a policy of insurance or contract for a deferred annuity where—

(*a*) the insurance or contract was made after 22nd June 1916—

    (i) with any insurance company legally established within Her Majesty's dominions, any other country mentioned in section 1 (3) of the British Nationality Act 1948 or the Republic of Ireland, or lawfully carrying on business in the United Kingdom, or

    (ii) with underwriters, being members of Lloyd's or of any other association of underwriters approved by the Secretary of State or the Department of Commerce for Northern Ireland, who comply with the requirements set forth in section 73 of the Insurance Companies Act 1974 or, as the case may be, Schedule 1 to the Insurance Companies Act (Northern Ireland) 1968, or

    (iii) with a registered friendly society, or

    (iv) in the case of a deferred annuity, with the National Debt Commissioners, and

(*b*) the insurance or, as the case may be, the deferred annuity is on the life of the claimant or on the life of his spouse and

(*c*) the insurance or contract was made by him.

(3) No relief under this section shall—

(*a*) be given except in respect of premiums payable under policies for securing a capital sum on death, whether in conjunction with any other benefit or not, or

(*b*) be given in respect of premiums payable during the period of deferment in respect of a policy of deferred assurance:

Provided that this subsection shall not affect premiums payable—

(i) under policies or contracts made in connection with any superannuation or bona fide pension scheme for the benefit of the employees of any employer, or of persons engaged in any particular trade, profession, vocation or business, or for the benefit of the wife or widow of any such employee or person or of his children or other dependants, or

(ii) under policies taken out by teachers in the schools known in the year 1918 as secondary schools, pending the establishment of a superannuation or pension scheme for those teachers.

(4) Relief shall not be granted under this section in respect of premiums payable under any policy of life insurance issued in respect of an insurance made after 19th March 1968 unless the policy is a qualifying policy within the meaning of Part I of Schedule 1 to this Act:

Provided that this subsection shall not apply—

(*a*) to any policy of life insurance having as its sole object the provision on an individual's death or disability of a sum substantially the same as any amount then outstanding under a mortgage of his residence, or of any premises occupied by him for the purposes of a business, being a mortgage the principal amount secured by which is repayable by instalments payable annually or at shorter regular intervals, or

(*b*) to any policy of life insurance issued in connection with a sponsored superannuation scheme as defined in section 226 (11) of this Act, if one-half at least of the cost of the scheme is borne by the person or persons under whom the relevant offices or employments are held, or

(*c*) to any policy of life assurance issued in connection with an approved scheme as defined in Chapter II of Part II of the Finance Act 1970.

In the application of the above proviso to Scotland, for any reference to a mortgage there shall be substituted a reference to a heritable security within the meaning of the Conveyancing (Scotland) Act 1924 (but including a security constituted by ex facie disposition or assignation).

(5) A policy of life insurance issued in respect of an insurance made on or before 19th March 1968 shall be treated for the purposes of subsection (4) above as issued in respect of one made after that date if varied after that date so as to increase the benefits secured, or to extend the term of the insurance:

Provided that a variation effected before the end of the year 1968 shall be disregarded for the purposes of this subsection if its only effect was to bring into conformity with paragraph 2 of Schedule 1 to this Act (qualifying conditions for endowment policies) a policy previously conforming therewith except as respects the amount guaranteed on death, and no increase was made in the premiums payable under the policy.

(6) The provisions of Part II of Schedule 1 to this Act shall have effect with respect to the certification of policies which are qualifying policies within the meaning of Part I of that Schedule.

(7) Where in any year of assessment for which her husband's income includes or, if there were any, would include any of hers a premium is paid by a wife out of her separate income in respect of an insurance on her own life or the life of her husband, or a contract for any deferred annuity on her own life or the life of her husband, the same relief shall be given as if the premium were a premium paid by her husband for an insurance on his own life, or for a contract for a deferred annuity on his own life, and this section shall apply accordingly.

(8) *Repealed by I.C.T.A. 1970, s. 36 (8) & Sched. 8, Part VI.*

Premiums under pre-1916 life policies etc., and certain other payments

–07   **20.**—(1) Subject to the provisions of this section and of section 21 below, and subject also to sections 219 (3) and 227 (11) of this Act (retirement annuity premiums, and contributions under Superannuation Acts, National Insurance Acts etc.), if the claimant—

    (*a*) has paid any such premium as is specified in subsection (2) below, or

    (*b*) is under any Act of Parliament, or under the terms or conditions of his employment, liable to the payment of any sum, or to the deduction from his salary or stipend of any sum, for the purpose of securing a deferred annuity to his widow or provision for his children after his death,

he shall be entitled to a deduction from the amount of income tax with which he is chargeable equal to income tax at the appropriate rate on the amount of the premium paid by him or on the amount of the sum paid by him or deducted from his salary or stipend.

–08   (2) The premiums referred to in subsection (1) (*a*) above are any premiums paid by a person under a policy of insurance or contract for a deferred annuity where—

    (*a*) the insurance or contract was made on or before 22nd June 1916—

        (i) with any insurance company legally established within

169

the Crown's dominions, or lawfully carrying on business in the United Kingdom, or

(ii) with a registered friendly society, or

(iii) in the case of a deferred annuity, with the National Debt Commissioners, and

(*b*) the insurance or, as the case may be, the deferred annuity is on the life of that person or on the life of his wife, and

(*c*) the insurance or contract was made by him.

(3) For the purposes of this section, " the appropriate rate " means—

(*a*) where the total income of the claimant does not exceed £1,000, half the basic rate of income tax,

(*b*) where the total income of the claimant exceeds £1,000 but does not exceed £2,000, three-fourths of the basic rate of income tax,

(*c*) where the total income of the claimant exceeds £2,000, the basic rate of income tax:

Provided that, in relation to the premiums referred to in subsection (1) (*a*) above, this subsection shall, as respects any year for which the basic rate exceeds 35 per cent., have effect as if the basic rate were 35 per cent.

(4) No relief under subsection (1) above shall be given in respect of the amount, if any, by which the premiums or other sums in respect of which relief is claimed exceed the claimant's total income as reduced by any deductions made under this Chapter.

(5) Where the income tax ultimately payable by any person after deducting the relief under this section is greater than the amount of income tax at the basic rate which would be payable if the total income of that person exceeded £1,000, or £2,000, as the case may be, the relief under this section shall be increased by a sum representing the amount by which income tax at one-fourth of the basic rate on the amount of the premiums or payment in respect of which the relief is given exceeds the amount of the income tax at the basic rate on the amount by which the total income falls short of £1,000 or £2,000, as the case may be:

Provided that, in relation to the premiums referred to in subsection (1) (*a*) above, this subsection shall, as respects a year for which the basic rate of income tax exceeds 35 per cent., have effect as if the two last references therein to the basic rate were references to a rate of 35 per cent.

(6) Where a premium is paid by a wife out of her separate income in respect of an insurance on her own life or the life of her husband, or a contract for any deferred annuity on her own life or the life of her husband, the same relief shall be given as if the premium were a premium paid by her husband for an insurance on his own life, or for a contract for a deferred annuity on his own life, and this section shall apply accordingly.

Limits on relief under ss. 19 and 20

12–09   **21.**—(1) The aggregate of the premiums or other sums in respect of which relief is given to any person under sections 19 and 20 above shall not exceed one-sixth of that person's total income.

(1A) In relation to a year of assessment in which a woman is married and living with her husband but for which his income does not or, if there were any, would not include any of hers, subsection (1) above shall apply to each of them as if the maximum there specified were increased by an amount equal to the difference between—

(a) one-sixth of the other's total income; and

(b) the premiums or other sums in respect of which relief is given to the other.

(2) *Repealed by F.A.* 1975, *s.* 10 & *Sched.* 2 (6).

(3) The aggregate of the relief given under the said sections in respect of premiums or sums payable for securing any benefits other than capital sums on death shall not exceed the amount of the income tax calculated at the appropriate rate on £100.

(4) In subsection (3) above, " the appropriate rate "—

(a) in relation to premiums to which the said section 19 applies, means one-half of the basic rate, and

(b) in relation to other premiums or payments, has the same meaning as in the said section 20,

and the said subsection (3) shall not apply to premiums falling within the proviso to subsection (1) of the said section 19.

(5) War insurance premiums shall not be taken into account in calculating the limits of one-sixth of total income . . . or of £100 mentioned in this section.

In this subsection " war insurance premiums " means any additional premium or other sum paid in order to extend an existing life insurance policy to risks arising from war or war service abroad, and any part of any premium or other sum paid in respect of a life insurance policy covering those risks, or either of them, which appears to the inspector to be attributable to those risks, or either of them.

CHAPTER III

Retirement Annuities

226.—(1) Where, in any year of assessment, an individual—

(a) is (or would but for an insufficiency of profits or gains be) chargeable to income tax in respect of relevant earnings from any trade, profession, vocation, office or employment carried on or held by him, and

(b) pays a premium or other consideration under an annuity contract for the time being approved by the Board as having for its main object the provision for the individual of a life annuity in old age or under a contract for the time being approved under section 226A of this Act (hereafter in this Chapter referred to as " a qualifying premium "),

then relief from income tax may be given in respect of the qualifying premium under section 227 below, and any annuity payable to the same or another individual shall be treated as earned income of the annuitant to the extent to which it is payable in return for any amount on which relief is so given.

(2) Subject to subsection (3) below, the Board shall not approve a contract unless it appears to them to satisfy the conditions that it is made by the individual with a person lawfully carrying on in the United Kingdom the business of granting annuities on human life, and that it does not—

(a) provide for the payment by that person during the life of the individual of any sum except sums payable by way of annuity to the individual, or

(*b*) provide for the annuity payable to the individual to commence before he attains the age of sixty or after he attains the age of seventy-five, or

(*c*) provide for the payment by that person of any other sums except sums payable by way of annuity to the individual's widow or widower and any sums which, in the event of no annuity becoming payable either to the individual or to a widow or widower, are payable to the individual's personal representatives by way of return of premiums, by way of reasonable interest on premiums or by way of bonuses out of profits, or

(*d*) provide for the annuity, if any, payable to a widow or widower of the individual to be of a greater annual amount than that paid or payable to the individual, or

(*e*) provide for the payment of any annuity otherwise than for the life of the annuitant,

and that it does include provision securing that no annuity payable under it shall be capable in whole or in part of surrender, commutation or assignment:

Provided that the contract may give the individual the right to receive, by way of commutation of part of that annuity payable to him, a lump sum not exceeding three times the annual amount of the remaining part of the annuity, taking, where the annual amount is or may be different in different years, the initial annual amount, and shall make any such right depend on the exercise by the individual of an election at or before the time when the annuity first becomes payable to him.

12–11   (3) The Board may, if they think fit, and subject to any conditions they think proper to impose, approve a contract otherwise satisfying the preceding conditions, notwithstanding that the contract provides for one or more of the following matters—

(*a*) for the payment after the individual's death of an annuity to a dependant not the widow or widower of the individual,

(*b*) for the payment to the individual of an annuity commencing before he attains the age of sixty, if the annuity is payable on his becoming incapable through infirmity of body or mind of carrying on his own occupation or any occupation of a similar nature for which he is trained or fitted,

(*c*) if the individual's occupation is one in which persons customarily retire before attaining the age of sixty, for the annuity to commence before he attains that age (but not before he attains the age of fifty),

(*d*) for the annuity payable to any person to continue for a term certain (not exceeding ten years), notwithstanding his death within that term, or for the annuity payable to any person to terminate, or be suspended, on marriage (or re-marriage) or in other circumstances,

(*e*) in the case of an annuity which is to continue for a term certain, for the annuity to be assignable by will, and in the event of any person dying entitled to it, for it to be assignable by his personal representatives in the distribution of the estate so as to give effect to a testamentary disposition, or to the rights of those entitled on intestacy, or to an appropriation of it to a legacy or to a share or interest in the estate.

(4) So much of subsection (1) above as provides that an annuity shall be treated, in whole or in part, as earned income of the annuitant shall apply only in relation to the annuitant to whom the annuity is made payable by the terms of the contract.

12–12
(5) The preceding provisions of this section shall apply in relation to a contribution under a trust scheme approved by the Board as they apply in relation to a premium under an annuity contract so approved, with the modification that, for the condition as to the person with whom the contract is made, there shall be substituted a condition that the scheme—

    (*a*) is established under the law of any part of, and administered in, the United Kingdom, and

    (*b*) is established for the benefit of individuals engaged in or connected with a particular occupation (or one or other of a group of occupations), and for the purpose of providing retirement annuities for them, with or without subsidiary benefits for their families or dependants, and

    (*c*) is so established under irrevocable trusts by a body of persons comprising or representing a substantial proportion of the individuals so engaged in the United Kingdom, or of those so engaged in England, Wales, Scotland or Northern Ireland,

and with the necessary adaptations of other references to the contract or the person with whom it is made.

(6) Exemption from income tax shall be allowed in respect of income derived from investments or deposits of any fund maintained for the purpose mentioned in subsection (5) (*b*) above under a scheme for the time being approved under that subsection; (a) and a gain accruing to a person from his acquisition and disposal of assets held by him as part of any such fund . . . shall not be a chargeable gain for the purposes of capital gains tax.

(7) The Board may at any time, by notice in writing given to the persons by and to whom premiums are payable under any contract for the time being approved under this section, or to the trustees or other persons having the management of any scheme so approved, withdraw that approval on such grounds and from such date as may be specified in the notice.

2–13
(8) For the purposes of this Chapter, a married woman's relevant earnings shall not be treated as her husband's relevant earnings notwithstanding that her income chargeable to tax is treated as his income.

(9) Subject to subsection (8) above, " relevant earnings," in relation to any individual, means for the purposes of this Chapter any income of his chargeable to tax for the year of assessment in question, being either—

    (*a*) income arising in respect of remuneration from an office or employment held by him other than a pensionable office or employment, or

    (*b*) income from any property which is attached to or forms part of the emoluments of any such office or employment held by him, or

    (*c*) income which is chargeable under Schedule A, Schedule B or Schedule D and is immediately derived by him from the carrying on or exercise by him of his trade, profession or vocation either as an individual or, in the case of a partnership, as a partner personally acting therein, or

(*d*) income treated as earned income by virtue of section 383 of this Act (patent rights),

but does not include any remuneration as director of a company whose income consists wholly or mainly of investment income (construed in accordance with paragraph 11 of Schedule 16 to the Finance Act 1972), being a company of which he is a controlling director (as defined in section 224 (1) above.

(10) For the purposes of this Chapter, an office or employment is a pensionable office or employment if, and only if, service in it is service to which a sponsored superannuation scheme relates (not being a scheme under which the benefits provided in respect of that service are limited to a lump sum payable on the termination of the service through death or disability before the age of seventy-five or some lower age); but references to a pensionable office or employment apply whether or not the duties are performed wholly or partly in the United Kingdom or the holder is chargeable to tax in respect of it.

Service in an office or employment shall not for the purposes of this definition be treated as service to which a sponsored superannuation scheme relates by reason only of the fact that the holder of the office or employment might (though he does not) participate in the scheme by exercising or refraining from exercising an option open to him by virtue of that service.

12–14   (11) In subsection (10) above " a sponsored superannuation scheme " means a scheme or arrangement relating to service in particular offices or employments and having for its object or one of its objects to make provision in respect of persons serving therein against future retirement or partial retirement, against future termination of service through death or disability, or against similar matters, being a scheme or arrangement under which any part of the cost of the provision so made is or has been borne otherwise than by those persons by reason of their service (whether it is the cost or part of the cost of the benefits provided, or of paying premiums or other sums in order to provide those benefits, or of administering or instituting the scheme or arrangement); but for this purpose a person shall be treated as bearing by reason of his service the cost of any payment made or agreed to be made in respect of his service, if that payment or the agreement to make it is treated under the Income Tax Acts as increasing his income, or would be so treated if he were chargeable to tax under Case I of Schedule E in respect of his emoluments from that service.

(12) Nothing in sections 4 and 6 of the Policies of Assurance Act 1867 (which put on assurance companies certain obligations in relation to notices of assignment of policies of life assurance) shall be taken to apply to any contract approved under this section.

(13) For the purposes of any provision applying this subsection " approved annuities " means annuities under contracts approved by the Board under this section, being annuities payable wholly in return for premiums or other consideration paid by a person who (when the premiums or other consideration are or is payable) is, or would but for an insufficiency of profits or gains be, chargeable to tax in respect of relevant earnings from a trade, profession, vocation, office or employment carried on or held by him.

Contracts for dependants or life insurance

226A.—(1) The Board may approve under this section—

(*a*) a contract the main object of which is the provision of an annuity for the wife or husband of the individual, or for any one or more dependants of the individual,

(*b*) a contract the sole object of which is the provision of a lump sum on the death of the individual before he attains the age of 75, being a lump sum payable to his personal representatives.

(2) The Board shall not approve the contract unless it appears to them that it is made by the individual with a person lawfully carrying on in the United Kingdom the business of granting annuities on human life.

(3) The Board shall not approve a contract under subsection (1) (*a*) above unless it appears to them to satisfy all the following conditions, that is—

(*a*) that any annuity payable to the wife or husband or dependant of the individual commences on the death of the individual,

(*b*) that any annuity payable to the individual commences at a time after the individual attains the age of 60, and, unless the individual's annuity is one to commence on the death of a person to whom an annuity would be payable under the contract if that person survived the individual, can not commence after the time when the individual attains the age of 75,

(*c*) that the contract does not provide for the payment by the person contracting with the individual of any sum, other than any annuity payable to the individual's wife or husband or dependant, or to the individual except, in the event of no annuity becoming payable under the contract, any sums payable to the individual's personal representatives by way of return of premiums, by way of reasonable interest on premiums or by way of bonuses out of profits,

(*d*) that the contract does not provide for the payment of any annuity otherwise than for the life of the annuitant,

(*e*) that the contract does include provision securing that no annuity payable under it shall be capable in whole or in part of surrender, commutation or assignment.

(4) The Board may, if they think fit, and subject to any conditions that they think proper to impose, approve a contract under subsection (1) (*a*) above notwithstanding that, in one or more respects, they are not satisfied that the contract complies with the provisions of paragraphs (*a*) to (*e*) of subsection (3) above.

(5) Subsections (2) and (3) of section 226 above shall not apply to the approval of a contract under this section.

(6) The main purpose of a trust scheme, or part of a trust scheme, within section 226 (5) above may be to provide annuities for the wives, husbands and dependants of the individuals, or lump sums payable to the individuals' personal representatives on death and in that case—

(*a*) approval of the trust scheme shall be subject to the preceding provisions of this section with any necessary modifications, and not subject to subsections (2) and (3) of section 226 above,

(*b*) the provisions of this Chapter shall apply to the scheme or part of the scheme when duly approved as it applies to a contract approved under this section,

(c) section 226 (6) above (tax relief for investments or deposits of the fund) shall apply to any duly approved trust scheme, or part of a trust scheme.

(7) Except as otherwise provided in this chapter, any reference in the Tax Acts to a contract or scheme approved under section 226 above shall include a reference to a contract or scheme approved under this section.

Nature and amount of relief for qualifying premiums

12–16   227.[1]—(1) Relief shall be given under this section in respect of a qualifying premium paid by an individual only on a claim made for the purpose, and where relief is to be so given, the amount of that premium shall, subject to the provisions of this section, be deducted from or set off against his relevant earnings for the year of assessment in which the premium is paid.

(1A) Subject to the provisions of this section and of section 228 below, the amount which may be deducted or set off in any year of assessment (whether in respect of one or more qualifying premiums, and whether or not including premiums in respect of a contract approved under section 226A of this Act)—

(a) shall not be more than the sum of [£3,000], and

(b) shall not be more than 15 per cent. of the individual's net relevant earnings for that year.

(1B) Subject to the provisions of this section, the amount which may be deducted or set off in any year of assessment in respect of qualifying premiums paid under a contract approved under section 226A of this Act (whether in respect of one or more such premiums)—

(a) shall not be more than the sum of [£1,000], and

(b) shall not be more than 5 per cent. of the individual's net relevant earnings for that year.

(1C) Where the condition in section 226 (1) (a) above is satisfied as respects part only of the year, then for the said sums of [£3,000] and £1,000 mentioned above there shall be substituted sums which respectively bear to [£3,000] and [£1,000] the same proportion as that part bears to the whole year.

(2) If in any year of assessment a reduction or a greater reduction would be made under this section in the relevant earnings of an individual but for either or both of the following reasons, that is—

(a) an insufficiency of net relevant earnings, or

(b) the operation of paragraph (b) of subsection (1B) above (as respects a qualifying premium paid under a contract approved under section 226A of this Act),

the amount of the reduction which would be made but for those reasons less the amount of any reduction which is made in that year, shall be carried forward to the next following year, and shall be treated for the purposes of relief under this section as the amount of a qualifying premium paid in that following year.

(2A) If and so far as an amount once carried forward under subsection (2) above (and treated as the amount of a qualifying premium paid in the said following year) is not deducted from or set off against

---

[1] The figures in square brackets in this section were amended by F.A. 1977, s. 27.

the individual's net relevant earnings for that year of assessment, it shall be carried forward again to the next following year (and treated as the amount of a qualifying premium paid in that year), and so on for succeeding years (if necessary).

(2B) The provisions of this subsection have effect for determining whether and how far an amount carried forward under subsection (2) above is to be treated as paid under an individual's contract on the one hand or a contract approved under section 226A of this Act on the other.

If and so far as any such amount could not have been so carried forward but for a qualifying premium paid under an individual's contract, that amount, or any part of it, when so carried forward on the first or any subsequent occasion, shall be treated for the purposes of this Chapter as the amount of a qualifying premium paid under an individual's contract.

In this subsection "individual's contract" means an approved annuity contract other than one approved under section 226A of this Act.

(3) Where a relevant assessment to tax becomes final and conclusive at a time after 5th October in the year of assessment to which it relates, a qualifying premium paid—

(*a*) after that year of assessment, and
(*b*) not more than six months after that time,

may, if the individual so elects not more than six months after that time, be treated for the purposes of this section as paid in the year of assessment (and not in the year in which it is paid):

Provided that where either—

(i) the amount of that premium, together with any qualifying premiums paid by him in the year to which the assessment relates (or treated as so paid by virtue of any previous election under this subsection), exceeds the maximum amount of the reduction which may be made under this section in his relevant earnings for that year, or
(ii) the amount of that premium itself exceeds the increase in that maximum amount which is due to taking into account the income on which the assessment is made,

then the election shall have no effect as respects the excess.

In this subsection "a relevant assessment to tax" means an assessment on the individual's relevant earnings or on the profits or gains of a partnership from which the individual derives relevant earnings.

(4) For the purposes of relief under this section, an individual's relevant earnings are those earnings before giving effect to any capital allowances, other than deductions allowable in computing profits or gains, but after taking into account the amounts on which charges fall to be made under the Capital Allowances Act 1968 (including the enactments which under this Act are to be treated as contained in Part I of that Act); and references to income in the following provisions of this section (other than references to total income) shall be construed similarly.

(5) Subject to the following provisions of this section, "net relevant earnings" means, in relation to an individual, the amount of his relevant earnings for the year of assessment in question, less the amount of any deductions falling to be made from the relevant

earnings in computing for the purposes of income tax . . . his total income for that year, being either—

  (*a*) deductions in respect of payments made by him, or
  (*b*) deductions in respect of losses or of capital allowances, being losses or allowances arising from activities profits or gains of which would be included in computing relevant earnings of the individual or of the individual's wife or husband for the year 1956–57 or a later year of assessment.

(6) Where, in any year of assessment for which an individual claims and is allowed relief under this section, there falls to be made in computing the total income of the individual or that of the individual's wife or husband a deduction in respect or any such loss or allowance of the individual as is mentioned in subsection (5) (*b*) above, and the deduction or part of it falls to be so made from income other than relevant earnings, the amount of the deduction made from that other income shall be treated as reducing the individual's net relevant earnings for subsequent years of assessment (being deducted as far as may be from those of the immediately following year, whether or not he claims or is entitled to claim relief under this section for that year, and so far as it cannot be so deducted, then from those of the next year, and so on).

12–18 (7) Where an individual's income for any year of assessment consists partly of relevant earnings and partly of other income, then as far as may be any deductions which fall to be made in computing his total income, and which may be treated in whole or in part either as made from relevant earnings or as made from other income, shall be treated for the purposes of this section as being made from those relevant earnings in so far as they are deductions in respect of any such loss or allowance as is mentioned in subsection (5) (*b*) above, and otherwise as being made from that other income.

(8) An individual's net relevant earnings for any year of assessment are to be computed without regard to any relief which falls to be given for that year under this section either to the individual or to the individual's wife or husband.

(9) An individual's relevant earnings, in the case of partnership profits, shall be taken to be his share of the partnership income, estimated in accordance with the Income Tax Acts, but the amount to be included in respect of those earnings in arriving at his net relevant earnings shall be his share of that income after making therefrom all such deductions (if any) in respect of payments made by the partnership, or in respect of capital allowances falling to be made to the partnership for chargeable periods after the year 1955–56, as would be made in computing the tax payable in respect of that income.

(10) Where relief under this section for any year of assessment is claimed and allowed (whether or not relief then falls to be given for that year), and afterwards there is made any assessment, alteration of an assessment, or other adjustment of the claimant's liability to tax, there shall be made also such adjustments, if any, as are consequential thereon in the relief allowed or given under this section for that or any subsequent year of assessment.

(11) Where relief under this section is claimed and allowed for any year of assessment in respect of any payment, relief shall not be given in respect of it under any other provision of the Income Tax Acts for the same or a later year of assessment nor (in the case of a

payment under an annuity contract) in respect of any other premium or consideration for an annuity under the same contract; and references in the Income Tax Acts to relief in respect of life assurance premiums shall not be taken to include relief under this section.

(12) The allowances mentioned in subsections (5) (*b*) and (9) above shall not be treated as including amounts carried forward from a year of assessment earlier than the year 1956–57.

(13) If any person, for the purpose of obtaining for himself or any other person any relief from or repayment of tax under this section, knowingly makes any false statement or false representation, he shall be liable to a penalty not exceeding £500.

Application of the proviso to s. 227 (1) to holders of pensionable offices, etc. and persons born in or before 1915

12–19   **228.**[2]—(1) Subject to the provisions of this section, in the case of an individual who is the holder of a pensionable office or employment section 227 (1A) and (1C) of this Act shall have effect with the substitution for references to [£3,000] of references to [£3,000] less 15 per cent. of his pensionable emoluments for the year of assessment.

(2) Where an individual is the holder of a pensionable office or employment during part only of the year of assessment, then—

   (*a*) subsection (1) above shall not apply if the condition in section 226 (1) (*a*) above is not satisfied at any time during that part of the year, but

   (*b*) if that condition is satisfied at such a time and is also satisfied at a time during the remainder of the year, subsection (1) above shall apply, but for 15 per cent. of his pensionable emoluments there shall be substituted therein such less proportion thereof as may be just.

(3) For the purposes of this subsection and subsections (1) and (2) above, an individual's pensionable emoluments for any year of assessment shall be taken to be the amount, estimated in accordance with the provisions applicable to Case I of Schedule E, of any income of his for the year (but not including in the case of a married man income of his wife), being either—

   (*a*) income arising in respect of remuneration from any pensionable office or employment, or

   (*b*) income from any property which is attached to or forms part of the emoluments of any pensionable office or employment.

12–20   (4) Subject to subsection (5) below, in the case of an individual born at a time specified in the first column of the Table set out below, section 227 (1A) and (1C) of this Act, and subsections (1) and (2) above, shall have effect with the substitution for references to [£3,000] and to 15 per cent. of references respectively to such sum and such percentage as are specified for his case in the second and third columns of the Table.

TABLE

Year of birth					Sum	Percentage
1914 or 1915	..	..	..	..	£3,600	18
1912 or 1913	..	..	..	..	£4,200	21
1910 or 1911	..	..	..	..	£4,800	24
1908 or 1909	..	..	..	..	£5,400	27
1907 or any earlier year		..	..	..	£6,000	30

[2] The figures in square brackets in this section were amended by F.A. 1977, s. 27.

(5) Subsection (4) above shall not apply in relation to any year of assessment in which the individual, in respect of his past services in any office or employment formerly held by him (not being one in which he served part-time only), either—

(*a*) receives any income in respect of a pension payable under or in pursuance of a sponsored superannuation scheme or otherwise purchased or provided for him by another person, or

(*b*) has a right under a sponsored superannuation scheme to a pension which is not presently payable, whether because it is suspended or because it is to become payable only at a future time or on the happening of some contingency (but not including a right dependent also on service in an office or employment for the time being held by him).

In this subsection "pension" includes any superannuation or other allowance or deferred pay.

Annuity premiums of Ministers and other officers

12–21   **229.**—(1) For the purposes of this Chapter so much of any salary which—

(*a*) is payable to the holder of a qualifying office who is also a Member of the House of Commons, and

(*b*) is payable for a period in respect of which the holder elects not to be a participant under section 2 of the Parliamentary and other Pensions Act 1972, or for any part of such period,

as is equal to the difference between a Member's ordinary salary (in accordance with any resolution of the House of Commons relating to the remuneration of Members for the time being in force) and the salary which (in accordance with that resolution) is payable to him as a Member holding that qualifying office shall be treated as remuneration from the office of Member and not from the qualifying office, and shall accordingly be treated for the purposes of section 228 (1) to (3) of this Act as pensionable emoluments from the office of Member.

In this subsection "qualifying office" has the meaning assigned to it by section 2 (1) of the Parliamentary and other Pensions Act 1972 and "Member's ordinary salary" has the meaning assigned to it by section 3 (6) of that Act.

(2) For the purposes of this Chapter, so much of the salary of the holder of any office to which this subsection applies who is also a Member of the House of Commons of Northern Ireland as is equal to the salary to which, pursuant to any Resolution of that House relating to the remuneration of Members, he would be entitled if he did not hold that office shall be treated as remuneration from the office of Member, and not from the office to which this subsection applies, and shall accordingly be treated for the purposes of section 228 (1) to (3) of this Act as pensionable emoluments from the office of Member.

The offices to which this subsection applies are those of Chairman of Ways and Means of the House of Commons of Northern Ireland and Attorney General for Northern Ireland.

CHAPTER IV

Purchased Life Annuities

Purchased life annuities, other than retirement annuities

2–22
230.—(1) A purchased life annuity (not being of a description excepted by subsection (7) below) shall, for the purposes of the provisions of the Tax Acts relating to tax on annuities and other annual payments, be treated as containing a capital element and, to the extent of the capital element, as not being an annual payment or in the nature of an annual payment; but the capital element in such an annuity shall be taken into account in computing profits or gains or losses for other purposes of the Tax Acts in any circumstances in which a lump sum payment would be taken into account.

(2) In the case of any purchased life annuity to which this section applies—

    (*a*) the capital element shall be determined by reference to the amount or value of the payments made or other consideration given for the grant of the annuity, and

    (*b*) the proportion which the capital element in any annuity payment bears to the total amount of that payment shall be constant for all payments on account of the annuity, and

    (*c*) where neither the term of the annuity nor the amount of any annuity payment depends on any contingency other than the duration of a human life or lives, that proportion shall be the same proportion which the total amount or value of the consideration for the grant of the annuity bears to the actuarial value of the annuity payments as determined in accordance with the next following subsection, and

    (*d*) where paragraph (*c*) above does not apply, the said proportion shall be such as may be just, having regard to that paragraph and to the contingencies affecting the annuity.

(2A) Where, in the case of any purchased life annuity to which this section applies, the amount of any annuity payment (but not the term of the annuity) depends on any contingency other than the duration of a human life or lives—

    (*a*) the capital element shall be determined by reference—

        (i) to the amount or value of the payments made or other consideration given for the grant of the annuity (in this subsection referred to as the "purchase price" of the annuity), and

        (ii) to the expected term of the annuity, as at the date when the first annuity payment began to accrue, expressed in years (and any odd fraction of a year), and determined by reference to the prescribed tables of mortality,

    and in head (ii) above "term" means the period from the date when the first annuity payment begins to accrue to the date when the last payment becomes payable,

    (*b*) the capital element in any annuity payment made in respect of a period of twelve months shall be a fraction $\dfrac{1}{E}$ of the purchase price, where E is the said expected term,

    (*c*) the capital element in any annuity payment made in respect of

181

a period of less than, or more than, twelve months shall be the amount at (*b*) above reduced, or as the case may be increased, in the same proportion as the length of that period bears to a period of twelve months,

(*d*) subsection (2) above shall not apply, but paragraphs (*a*) and (*b*) of subsection (3) below shall apply as they apply to that subsection,

and in applying subsection (2) (*d*) above where both the amount and the term of the annuity depend on any contingency other than the duration of a human life or lives, regard shall be had to this subsection (and not to subsection (2) (*c*) above) as well as to the contingencies affecting the annuity.

(3) For the purposes of subsection (2) above—

(*a*) any entire consideration given for the grant of an annuity and for some other matter shall be apportioned as appears just (but so that a right to a return of premiums or other consideration for an annuity shall not be treated for this purpose as a distinct matter from the annuity),

(*b*) where it appears that the amount or value of the consideration purporting to be given for the grant of an annuity has affected, or has been affected by, the consideration given for some other matter, the aggregate amount or value of those considerations shall be treated as one entire consideration given for both and shall be apportioned under paragraph (*a*) above accordingly, and

(*c*) the actuarial value of any annuity payments shall be taken to be their value as at the date when the first of those payments begins to accrue, that value being determined by reference to the prescribed tables of mortality and without discounting any payment for the time to elapse between that date and the date it is to be made.

(4) Where a person making a payment on account of any life annuity has been notified in the prescribed manner of any decision as to its being or not being a purchased life annuity to which this section applies or as to the amount of the capital element (if any), and has not been notified of any alteration of that decision, the notice shall be conclusive as to those matters for the purpose of determining the amount of income tax which he is entitled or required to deduct from the payment, or for which he is chargeable in respect of it.

12–23   (5) Where a person making a payment on account of a purchased life annuity to which this section applies has not been notified in the prescribed manner of the amount of the capital element, the amount of income tax which he is entitled or required to deduct from the payment, or for which he is chargeable in respect of it, shall be the same as if the annuity were not a purchased life annuity to which this section applies.

(6) For the purposes of this section, " life annuity " means an annuity payable for a term ending with (or at a time ascertainable only by reference to) the end of a human life, whether or not there is provision for the annuity to end during the life on the expiration of a fixed term or on the happening of any event or otherwise, or to continue after the end of the life in particular circumstances, and " purchased life annuity " means a life annuity granted for con-

sideration in money or money's worth in the ordinary course of a business of granting annuities on human life.

(7) This section shall not apply—

    (*a*) to any annuity which would, apart from this section, be treated for the purposes of the provisions of the Tax Acts relating to tax on annuities and other annual payments as consisting to any extent in the payment or repayment of a capital sum, or

    (*b*) to any annuity where the whole or part of the consideration for the grant of the annuity consisted of sums satisfying the conditions for relief from income tax under section 19 or 20 of this Act (relief for life insurance premiums and certain other payments) or under section 227 above (retirement annuities), or

    (*c*) to any annuity purchased in pursuance of any direction in a will, or to provide for an annuity payable by virtue of a will or settlement out of income of property disposed of by the will or settlement (whether with or without resort to capital), or

    (*d*) to any annuity purchased under or for the purposes of any sponsored superannuation scheme (as defined in section 226 (11) above) or any scheme approved under that section or in pursuance of any obligation imposed, or offer or invitation made, under or in connection with any such scheme or to any other annuity purchased by any person in recognition of another's services (or past services) in any office or employment.

Supplementary

2–24   **231.**—(1) Any question whether an annuity is a purchased life annuity to which section 230 above applies, or what is the capital element in such an annuity, shall be determined by the inspector; but a person aggrieved by the inspector's decision on any such question may appeal within the prescribed time to the Special Commissioners.

(2) Save as otherwise provided in this Chapter, the procedure to be adopted in giving effect thereto shall be such as may be prescribed.

(3) The Board may by statutory instrument make regulations for prescribing anything which is to be prescribed under this Chapter, and the regulations may apply for the purposes of this Chapter or of the regulations any provision of the Income Tax Acts, with or without modifications.

2–25   (4) Regulations under subsection (3) above may in particular make provision as to the time limit for making any claim for relief from or repayment of tax under this Chapter and as to all or any of the following matters, that is to say—

    (*a*) as to the information to be furnished in connection with the determination of any question whether an annuity is a purchased life annuity to which section 230 above applies, or what is the capital element in an annuity, and as to the persons who may be required to furnish any such information,

    (*b*) as to the manner of giving effect to the decision on any such question, and (notwithstanding anything in section 52 of this Act) as to the making of assessments for the purpose on the person entitled to the annuity,

(c) as to the extent to which the decision on any such question is to be binding, and the circumstances in which it may be reviewed.

(5) If any person, for the purpose of obtaining for himself or for any other person any relief from or repayment of tax under this Chapter, knowingly makes any false statement or false representation, he shall be liable to a penalty not exceeding £500.

CHAPTER III

Life Policies, Life Annuities and Capital Redemption Policies

Introductory

12–26 393.—(1) This Chapter shall have effect for the purpose of imposing, in the manner and to the extent therein provided, charges to tax, including tax under Schedule 16 to the Finance Act 1972 (apportionment of income of close companies) in respect of gains to be treated in accordance with this Chapter as arising in connection with policies of life insurance, contracts for life annuities, and capital redemption policies.

(2) Nothing in this Chapter shall apply—

(a) to any policy of life insurance having as its sole object the provision on an individual's death or disability of a sum substantially the same as any amount then outstanding under a mortgage of his residence, or of any premises occupied by him for the purposes of a business, being a mortgage the principal amount secured by which is repayable by instalments payable annually or at shorter regular intervals, or

(b) to any policy of life insurance issued in connection with a sponsored superannuation scheme as defined in section 226 (11) of this Act if one-half at least of the cost of the scheme is borne by the person or persons under whom the relevant offices or employments are held or

(c) to any policy of life assurance issued in connection with an approved scheme as defined in Chapter II of Part II of the Finance Act 1970.

In the application of this subsection to Scotland, for the reference to a mortgage there shall be substituted a reference to a heritable security within the meaning of the Conveyancing (Scotland) Act 1924 (but including a security constituted by ex facie absolute disposition or assignation).

(2A) Nothing in this Chapter shall apply to a policy of insurance which constitutes, or is evidence of, a contract for the time being approved under section 226A of this Act.

(3) In this Chapter—

" life annuity " means any annuity to which section 230 of this Act (purchased life annuities) applies,

" capital redemption policy " means any insurance effected in the course of a capital redemption business as defined in section 324 (3) of this Act,

" assignment ", in relation to Scotland, means an assignation.

(4) This Chapter shall have effect only as respects policies of life

insurance issued in respect of insurances made after 19th March 1968, contracts for life annuities entered into after that date, and capital redemption policies effected after that date.

(5) A policy of life insurance issued in respect of an insurance made on or before 19th March 1968 shall be treated for the purposes of subsection (4) above and the following provisions of this Chapter as issued in respect of one made after that date if it is varied after that date so as to increase the benefits secured or to extend the term of the insurance:

Provided that a variation effected before the end of the year 1968 shall be disregarded for the purposes of this subsection if its only effect was to bring into conformity with paragraph 2 of Schedule 1 to this Act (qualifying conditions for endowment policies) a policy previously conforming therewith except as respects the amount guaranteed on death, and no increase was made in the premiums payable under the policy.

Life policies: chargeable event

12-27   **394.**—(1) Subject to the provisions of this section, in this Chapter " chargeable event " means, in relation to a policy of life insurance—

(a) unless it is a policy which falls within subsection (2) below, any of the following—

(i) any death giving rise to benefits under the policy,

(ii) the maturity of the policy,

(iii) the surrender in whole . . . of the rights conferred by the policy, and

(iv) the assignment for money or money's worth of those rights . . .; and

(v) an excess of the reckonable aggregate value mentioned in sub-paragraph (6) of paragraph 9 of Schedule 2 to the Finance Act 1975 over the allowable aggregate amount mentioned in sub-paragraph (7) of that paragraph, being an excess occurring at the end of any year (as defined in sub-paragraph (9) of that paragraph), except, if it ends with another chargeable event, the final year; and

(b) if it is a policy falling within subsection (2) below, any of the above events, but—

(i) in the case of death or maturity, only if the policy is converted into a paid-up policy before the expiry of ten years from the making of the insurance, or, if sooner, of three-quarters of the term for which the policy is to run if not ended by death or disability,

(ii) in the case of a surrender or assignment or such an excess as is mentioned in paragraph (a) (v) above only if it is effected or occurs within that time, or the policy has been converted into a paid-up policy within that time.

(2) A policy falls within this subsection if (whether or not the premiums thereunder are eligible for relief under section 19 of this Act) it is a qualifying policy within the meaning of Part I of Schedule 1 to this Act.

(3) The maturity of a policy is not a chargeable event in relation thereto if a new policy is issued in consequence of the exercise of an option conferred by the maturing policy unless the person making the insurance in respect of which the new policy is issued was an infant

when the former policy was issued, and the former policy was one securing a capital sum payable either on a specified date falling not later than one month after his attaining twenty-five or on the anniversary of the policy immediately following his attainment of that age.

(4) No event is a chargeable event in relation to a policy if the rights conferred by the policy have at any time before the event been assigned for money or money's worth and are not at the time of the event held by the original beneficial owner.

(5) No account shall be taken for the purposes of this section of any assignment effected by way of security for a debt, or on the discharge of a debt secured by the rights or share concerned, or of any assignment between spouses living together; . . .

(6) Where subsection (1) (*b*) above applies to a policy which has been varied so as to increase the premiums payable thereunder, it shall so apply as if the references in subsection (1) (*b*) (i) to the making of the insurance and the term of the policy were references respectively to the taking effect of the variation and the term of the policy as from the variation.

Life policies: computation of gain

12–28   395.—(1) On the happening of a chargeable event in relation to any policy of life insurance, there shall be treated as a gain arising in connection with the policy—

- (*a*) if the event is a death, the excess (if any) of the surrender value of the policy immediately before the death, plus the amount or value of any relevant capital payments over the sum of the following—

    (i) the total amount previously paid under the policy by way of premiums; and

    (ii) the total amount treated as a gain by virtue of paragraph (*d*) below on the previous happening of chargeable events;

- (*b*) if the event is the maturity of the policy, or the surrender in whole . . . of the rights thereby conferred, the excess (if any) of the amount or value of the sum payable or other benefits arising by reason of the event, plus the amount or value of any relevant capital payments over the sum of the following—

    (i) the total amount previously paid under the policy by way of premiums; and

    (ii) the total amount treated as a gain by virtue of paragraph (*d*) below on the previous happening of chargeable events;

- (*c*) if the event is an assignment, the excess (if any) of the amount or value of the consideration, plus the amount or value of any relevant capital payments or of any previously assigned share in the rights conferred by the policy, over the sum of the following—

    (i) the total amount previously paid under the policy by way of premiums; and

    (ii) the total amount treated as a gain by virtue of paragraph (*d*) below on the previous happening of chargeable events;

- (*d*) if the event is the occurrence of such an excess as is mentioned in section 394 (1) (v) above, the amount of the excess.

(2) Where, in a case falling within subsection (1) (*b*) above, a right to periodical payments arises by reason of the event, there shall be treated as payable by reason thereof an amount equal to the capital value of those payments at the time the right arises.

(3) Where, in a case falling within subsection (1) (*c*) above, the assignment is between persons who are connected with each other within the meaning of section 533 of this Act, the assignment shall be deemed to have been made for a consideration equal to the market value of the rights or share assigned.

(3A) Where there is an assignment, otherwise than for money or money's worth, of all the rights conferred by the policy the calculations required to be made by paragraph 9 of Schedule 2 to the Finance Act 1975 shall be made, in the first instance, without regard to any surrender or assignment of part of or a share in those rights which takes place after the assignment, and any gain treated as arising under subsection (1) (*d*) above on the calculation so made shall be treated as arising to the assignor.

(4) In this section, " relevant capital payments " means, in relation to any policy, any sum or other benefit of a capital nature, other than one attributable to a person's disability, paid or conferred under the policy before the happening of the chargeable event, . . . and references in this subsection and (in relation to premiums) in subsection (1) above to " the policy " include references to any related policy, that is to say, to any policy in relation to which the policy is a new policy within the meaning of paragraph 9 of Schedule 1 to this Act, any policy in relation to which that policy is such a policy, and so on.

Life annuity contracts: chargeable event

2–29   **396.**—(1) Subject to subsections (2) and (3) below, in this Chapter " chargeable event " means, in relation to any contract for a life annuity, the surrender in whole . . . of the rights conferred by the contract, or the assignment for money or money's worth of those rights . . . or an excess of the reckonable aggregate value mentioned in sub-paragraph (6) of paragraph 9 of Schedule 2 to the Finance Act 1975 over the allowable aggregate amount mentioned in sub-paragraph (7) of that paragraph, being an excess occurring at the end of any year (as defined in sub-paragraph (9) of that paragraph), except, if it ends with another chargeable event, the final year.

Where the terms of a contract provide for the payment of a capital sum as an alternative, in whole or in part, to payments by way of an annuity, the taking of the capital sum shall be treated for the purposes of this section and section 397 below as a surrender in whole or in part of the rights conferred by the contract and where the terms of the contract provide for the payment of a capital sum on death and the contract was made on or after 10th December 1974, the death shall be treated for the purposes of this section and section 397 below as a surrender in whole of the rights conferred by the contract.

(2) An event referred to in subsection (1) above is not a chargeable event in relation to any contract if the rights conferred by the contract have at any time before the event been assigned for money or money's worth and are not at the time of the event held by the original beneficial owner.

(3) Subsection (5) of section 394 above shall, with any necessary

modification, apply for the purposes of this section as it applies for the purposes of the said section 394.

Life annuity contracts: computation of gain

12–30   **397.**—(1) On the happening of a chargeable event in relation to any contract for a life annuity, there shall be treated as a gain arising in connection with the contract—

> (*a*) if the event is the surrender in whole . . . of the rights conferred by the contract, the excess (if any) of the amount payable by reason of the event plus the amount or value of any relevant capital payments over the sum of the following—
>
> > (i) the total amount previously paid under the contract, whether by way of premiums or as lump sum consideration, reduced, if before the happening of the event one or more payments have been made on account of the annuity, by the capital element in the said payment or payments, as determined in accordance with section 230 of this Act, and
> >
> > (ii) the total amount treated as a gain by virtue of paragraph (*c*) below on the previous happening of chargeable events;
>
> (*b*) if the event is an assignment, the excess (if any) of the amount or value of the consideration, plus the amount or value of any relevant capital payments or of any previously assigned share in the rights conferred by the contract, over the sum of the following—
>
> > (i) the amount specified in subsection (1) (*a*) (i) above; and
> >
> > (ii) any amount treated as a gain by virtue of paragraph (*c*) below on the previous happenings of chargeable events;
>
> (*c*) if the event is the occurrence of such an excess as is mentioned in section 396 (1) above, the amount of the excess.

(2) Subsection (3) of section 395 above shall apply for the purposes of subsection (1) above as it applies for the purposes of subsection (1) (*c*) of that section and subsection (3A) of that section shall apply for the purposes of this section with the substitution of references to the contract for references to the policy.

(3) In this section " relevant capital payments " means, in relation to any contract, any sum or other benefit of a capital nature paid or conferred under the contract before the happening of the chargeable event.

Capital redemption policies

12–31   **398.**—(1) Subject to subsection (2) below, in this Chapter " chargeable event " means, in relation to a capital redemption policy, any of the following—

> (i) the maturity of the policy, except where the sums payable on maturity are annual payments chargeable to tax under Schedule D
>
> (ii) the surrender in whole . . . of the rights conferred by the policy, and
>
> (iii) the assignment for money or money's worth of those rights . . . and
>
> (iv) an excess of the reckonable aggregate value mentioned in sub-paragraph (6) of paragraph 9 of Schedule 2 to the Finance

Act 1975 over the allowable aggregate amount mentioned in sub-paragraph (7) of that paragraph, being an excess occurring at the end of any year (as defined in sub-paragraph (9) of that paragraph), except, if it ends with another chargeable event, the final year.

(2) Subsection (5) of section 394 above shall apply for the purposes of this section as it applies for purposes of the said section 394.

(3) The provisions of section 395 above, except subsection (3) thereof, shall, so far as appropriate and subject to subsection (4) below, apply to capital redemption policies as they apply to policies of life insurance.

(4) Where a chargeable event happens in relation to a capital redemption policy which has previously been assigned for money or money's worth, the said section 395 shall have effect in relation thereto as if, for the references to the total amount previously paid under the policy by way of premiums, there were substituted references to the amount or value of the consideration given for the last such assignment, plus the total amount of the premiums paid under the policy since that assignment.

Method of charging gain to tax

12–32

399.—(1) Where, under the preceding provisions of this Chapter, a gain is to be treated as arising in connection with any policy or contract—

    (*a*) if, immediately before the happening of the chargeable event in question, the rights conferred by the policy or contract were vested in an individual as beneficial owner, or were held on trusts created by an individual (including trusts arising under section 11 of the Married Women's Property Act 1882, section 2 of the Married Women's Policies of Assurance (Scotland) Act 1880, or section 4 of the Law Reform (Husband and Wife) Act (Northern Ireland) 1964) or as security for a debt owed by an individual, the amount of the gain shall be deemed . . . to form part of that individual's total income for the year in which the event happened;

    (*b*) if, immediately before the happening of that event, the said rights were in the beneficial ownership of a close company, or were held on trusts created, or as security for a debt owed, by a close company, then, for the purposes of Schedule 16 to the Finance Act 1972—

        (i) the amount of the gain shall be deemed to form part of the company's income for the accounting period in which the event happened, and

        (ii) the company's distributable income (but not its estate or trading income) for that period shall be treated as increased by the amount of the gain;

    (*c*) if, immediately before the happening of that event, the said rights were vested in personal representatives within the meaning of Part XV of this Act, the amount of the gain shall, . . . be deemed for the purposes of the said Part XV to be part of the aggregate income of the estate of the deceased:

Provided that nothing in this subsection shall apply to any amount which is chargeable to tax apart from this subsection.

(2) Where, immediately before the happening of a chargeable event,

189

the rights conferred by any policy or contract were vested beneficially in two or more persons, or were held on trusts created, or as security for a debt owed, by two or more persons, paragraphs (*a*) and (*b*) of subsection (1) above shall have effect in relation to each of those persons as if he had been the sole owner, settlor or debtor, but with references to the amount of the gain construed as references to the part of it proportionate to his share in the rights at the time of the event or, as the case may require, when the trusts were created.

(3) References in subsections (1) and (2) above to the rights conferred by a policy or contract are, in the case of an assignment of a share only in any rights, references to that share.

(4) Subject to section 400 of this Act, where, by virtue of subsection (1) above, a sum is included in an individual's total income—

> (*a*) no assessment shall be made on him in respect of income tax at the basic rate on that sum but he shall be treated as having paid income tax at the basic rate on that sum or, if his total income is reduced by any deductions, on so much of that sum as is part of his total income as so reduced;
>
> (*b*) no repayment shall be made of the income tax treated by virtue of paragraph (*a*) above as having been paid; and
>
> (*c*) the sum so included shall be treated for the purposes of sections 52 and 53 of this Act as not brought into charge to income tax.

Relief where gain charged directly to surtax

12–33   **400.**—(1) The following provisions of this section shall have effect for the purpose of giving relief, on a claim in that behalf being made by him to the Board, in respect of any increase in an individual's liability to tax which is attributable to one or more amounts being included in his total income for a year of assessment by virtue of section 399 (1) (*a*) above.

(2) Where one amount only is so included, there shall be computed—

> (*a*) the tax which would be chargeable in respect of the amount if relief under this section were not available and it constituted the highest part of the claimant's total income for the year, and
>
> (*b*) the tax (if any) which would be chargeable in respect of the amount if calculated, in accordance with subsection (3) below, by reference to its appropriate fraction,

and the relief shall consist of a reduction or repayment of tax equal to the difference between the two amounts of tax so computed, or, if tax would not be chargeable on a calculation by reference to the appropriate fraction, of a reduction or repayment of the tax equal to the tax computed under paragraph (*a*) above.

(3) In subsection (2) above " appropriate fraction " means, in relation to any amount, such a sum as bears thereto the same proportion as that borne by one to the number of complete years for which the policy or contract has run before the happening of the chargeable event; and the computation required by paragraph (*b*) of that subsection shall be made by applying to the amount in question such rate or rates of income tax, other than the basic rate, as would apply if it were reduced to that fraction and, as so reduced, still constituted the highest part of the claimant's total income for the year.

For the purposes of this subsection, the number of years for which a policy of life insurance has run before the happening of a chargeable event shall be calculated, where appropriate, from the issue of the earliest related policy, meaning, any policy in relation to which the policy is a new policy within the meaning of paragraph 9 of Schedule 1 to this Act, any policy in relation to which that policy is such a policy, and so on.

(4) Where by virtue of the said section 399 (1) (*a*) two or more amounts are included in any individual's total income for any year of assessment, subsections (2) and (3) above shall apply as if they together constituted a single amount, but with the appropriate fraction of the whole determined by adding together the appropriate fractions of the individual amounts.

(5) A provision of this section requiring tax to be calculated as if an amount constituted the highest part of a claimant's total income shall apply notwithstanding any provision of the Income Tax Acts directing any other amount to be treated as the highest part thereof, but, for the purposes of this section, a claimant's total income shall be deemed not to include any amount in respect of which he is chargeable to tax under sections 80, 81 or 82 of this Act (premiums, etc. treated as rent) or section 187 of this Act (payments on retirement or removal from office or employment).

Right of individual to recover tax from trustees

?–34   **401.**—(1) Where an amount is included in an individual's income by virtue of section 399 (1) (*a*) above, and the rights or share in question were held immediately before the happening of the chargeable event on trust, the individual shall be entitled to recover from the trustees, to the extent of any sums, or to the value of any benefits, received by them by reason of the event, an amount equal to that (if any) by which the tax with which he is chargeable for the year of assessment in question, reduced by the amount of any relief available under section 400 above in respect of the amount so included, exceeds the tax with which he would have been chargeable for the year if the said amount had not been so included.

(2) Where, for the purposes of relief under the said section 400, two or more amounts are to be treated as one, the reduction required by subsection (1) above on account of the relief available in respect of any of them shall consist of a proportionate part of the relief available in respect of their aggregate.

(3) An individual may require the Board to certify any amount recoverable by him by virtue of this section, and the certificate shall be conclusive evidence of the amount.

Information: duty of insurers

?–35   **402.**—(1) Subject to subsection (2) below, where a chargeable event within the meaning of this Chapter has happened in relation to any policy or contract, the body by or with whom the policy or contract was issued, entered into or effected shall, within three months of the event or, if it is a death or an assignment, within three months of their receiving written notification thereof, deliver to the inspector a certificate specifying—

(*a*) the name and address of the policy holder,

(*b*) the nature of the event, and the date on which it happened,

(*c*) as may be required for computing the gain to be treated as arising by virtue of this Chapter—

(i) the surrender value of the policy, or the sum payable, or other benefits to be conferred, by the body in question by reason of the event,

(ii) the amount or value of any relevant capital payments,

(iii) the amounts previously paid under the policy or contract by way of premiums, or otherwise by way of consideration for an annuity, and

(iv) the capital element in any payment previously made on account of an annuity, and

(*d*) the number of years relevant for computing the appropriate fraction of the gain for the purposes of section 400 (3) above.

(2) Subsection (1) above shall not apply where—

(*a*) the body in question are satisfied that no gain is to be treated as arising by reason of the event, or

(*b*) the amount of the surrender value or sum, or the value of the other benefits, referred to in paragraph (*c*) (i) of that subsection, together with the amount or value of any payments within paragraph (*c*) (ii) thereof, does not exceed £500,

but the inspector may by notice in writing require a like certificate in any such case, and it shall be the duty of the body to deliver the certificate within thirty days of the receipt of the notice.

CHAPTER IV

Insurance: Borrowing to pay premiums and Borrowing against Life Policies

Interest on loans used for payment of premiums, etc.; disallowance as deduction for surtax

12–36   **403.**—(1) Subject to the exceptions contained in section 404 below, in computing for the purposes of excess liability the total income for any year of assessment of an individual who has entered into a contract of assurance, no deduction shall be allowed in respect of any interest on any borrowed money which has been applied directly or indirectly to or towards the payment of any premium under that contract, or of any sum paid in lieu of any such premium.

In this subsection " excess liability " means the excess of liability to income tax over what it would be if all income tax were charged at the basic rate to the exclusion of any other rate.

(2) Where the benefit of a contract of assurance entered into by any person has become vested in another person, being an individual, subsection (1) above shall apply in relation to that individual—

(*a*) as if the contract had been a contract entered into by him, and

(*b*) in a case where the benefit of the contract became vested in him by virtue of an assignment and any payment was made by him in consideration of the assignment, as if that payment were the payment of a premium under the contract, and

(*c*) in a case where, either as being the person in whom the said benefit is vested, or by reason of any agreement under or in pursuance of which the said benefit became vested in him, he pays any interest on any borrowed money, as if that money had been applied to the payment of a premium under the contract.

(3) The provisions of section 22 of the Taxes Management Act 1970 with regard to the delivery of particulars as to deductions claimed to be allowed shall be extended so as to enable the Board to require such particulars with respect to deductions and otherwise as they may consider necessary for the purpose of carrying this section and section 404 below into effect.

(4) In this section and the said section 404—

- (a) " contract of assurance " means a contract of assurance or a contract similar in character to a contract of assurance, being in either case a contract under which a capital sum is expressed to be payable in the future in return for one or more antecedent payments, and " premium " means any such antecedent payment,
- (b) " interest " includes any sum payable in respect of any borrowed money,
- (c) any reference to borrowed money applied to or towards any payment shall be deemed to include a reference to borrowed money applied directly or indirectly to or towards the replacement of any money so applied, and
- (d) any reference to a capital sum payable on death under a contract of assurance shall be construed as a reference to the actual capital sum assured on death, exclusive of any addition which has arisen or may arise from any bonus, share of profits, return of premiums or otherwise, and, in the case of a contract under which different capital sums are payable on death in different events, as a reference to the least of those sums.

Exceptions from disallowance for surtax

–37 404.—(1) Subject to the provisions of this section, section 403 above shall not, where the interest is payable at a rate not exceeding 10 per cent. per annum, apply to—

- (a) interest on money borrowed mainly on the security of property other than a contract of assurance, if the premium in question either—
    - (i) is payable under a contract of assurance entered into in order to provide against the failure of a contingent interest in any property, and to serve as additional security for the loan and for no other purpose, or
    - (ii) is the first of a series of premiums payable under a contract of assurance entered into solely in order to provide for the repayment of the money borrowed and does not exceed 10 per cent. of the sum assured under that contract, or
- (b) interest on borrowed money applied to or towards the payment of premiums under a contract of assurance which assures throughout the term of the contract a capital sum payable on death, if—
    - (i) neither the amount of the first premium under the contract, nor the amount subsequently payable by way of premiums thereunder in respect of any period of twelve months, exceeds one-eighth of the capital sum payable on death, and
    - (ii) it is shown to the satisfaction of the Board that it is exceptional for the individual in question to apply borrowed

money to or towards the payment of premiums to which this paragraph applies, and that no such money has been so applied by him in any of the three years of assessment immediately preceding that in which he so applies the money on which the interest in question is payable, or

(c) interest on borrowed money applied to or towards the payment of premiums which—

    (i) are not premiums such as those specified in paragraph (a), (d) or (e) of this subsection, and

    (ii) are either premiums payable under a policy of life insurance which is a qualifying policy within the meaning of Part I of Schedule 1 to this Act or premiums each of which is one of a series of equal premiums payable at equal intervals of not more than one year,

except so far as such interest exceeds in the year of assessment £100 in all, or

(d) interest on borrowed money applied to or towards the payment of any premium under a contract of assurance entered into before 15th April 1930 which assures a fixed capital sum payable either—

    (i) on death only, or

    (ii) on the expiry of a period of not less than ten years from the date of the commencement of the contract or on earlier death, or

(e) interest on money borrowed before 6th April 1929, unless—

    (i) the money was borrowed from an insurance company, and

    (ii) the repayment thereof was secured on a contract of assurance, and

    (iii) the premium in question was a premium under that contract.

(2) In relation to—

(a) interest on borrowed money applied to or towards the payment of premiums under any policy of life insurance falling within paragraph (a) or (b) of section 393 (2) of this Act (mortgage repayments and sponsored superannuation schemes), and

(b) interest on money borrowed on or before 19th March 1968,

subsection (1) above shall have effect with the omission of paragraph (b) (ii) and paragraph (c), but subsection (3) below shall apply.

(3) Section 403 above shall not apply to interest—

(a) which is payable at a rate not exceeding 10 per cent. per annum, and

(b) which is within subsection (2) (a) or (b) above, and

(c) which is interest on borrowed money applied to or towards the payment of premiums which—

    (i) are not premiums such as those specified in paragraph (a), (b), (d) or (e) of subsection (1) above, and

    (ii) are premiums each of which is one of a series of equal premiums payable at equal intervals of not more than one year,

except so far as such interest exceeds in the year of assessment £100 in all.

Borrowings against life policies to be treated as income in certain cases

–38   **405.**—(1) Where—

(*a*) under any contract or arrangements made on or after 7th April 1949, provision is made for the making to any person, at intervals until the happening of an event or contingency dependent on human life, of payments by way of loan; and

(*b*) under the contract or arrangements, the loans are secured upon a policy of life assurance which assures moneys payable on the happening of such an event or contingency and need not be repaid until the policy moneys become payable; and

(*c*) the amount of the moneys payable on the happening of the event or contingency is made by the policy to increase by reference to the length of a period ending on the happening thereof,

the payments by way of loan shall be treated for tax purposes as annual payments falling within Case III of Schedule D, or, if they are made to a person residing in the United Kingdom and the contract or arrangements were made outside the United Kingdom, as income from a possession out of the United Kingdom and, for income tax, as falling within section 122 (1) of this Act.

(2) The amount of the moneys payable under a policy of life assurance shall not be deemed for the purposes of this section to be made to increase by reference to the length of a period ending on the happening of an event or contingency dependent on human life by reason only that those moneys are to increase from time to time if profits are made by the persons liable under the policy.

(3) This section shall not apply to any payments by way of loan if the Board are satisfied as respects those payments that it is not one of the objects of the contract or arrangements under which the payments are made that the recipient thereof should enjoy the advantages which would, apart from any question of liability to tax, be enjoyed by a person in receipt of payments of the same amounts paid at the same times by way of annuity.

SCHEDULE 1

Sections 19, 394 (2) and 404 (1)

Life Policies: Qualification for Relief on Premiums

Part I

Qualifying Conditions

General rules applicable to whole life and term assurances

–39   **1.**—(1) Subject to the following provisions of this Part of this Schedule, if a policy secures a capital sum which is payable only on death, or one payable either on death or on earlier disability, it is a qualifying policy if—

(*a*) it satisfies the conditions appropriate to it under sub-paragraphs (2) to (4A) below, and (*b*) except to the extent permitted by sub-paragraph (5) below it does not secure any other benefits.

(2) If the capital sum referred to in sub-paragraph (1) above is payable whenever the event in question happens, or if it happens at any time during the life of a specified person—

    (*a*) the premiums under the policy must be payable at yearly or shorter intervals, and either—

        (i) until the happening of the event, or, as the case may require, until the happening of the event or the earlier death of the specified person, or

        (ii) until the time referred to in sub-paragraph (i) above or the earlier expiry of a specified period ending not earlier than ten years after the making of the insurance, and

    (*b*) the total premiums payable in any period of twelve months must not exceed—

        (i) twice the amount of the total premiums payable in any other such period, or

        (ii) one-eighth of the total premiums which would be payable if the policy were to continue in force for a period of ten years from the making of the insurance, or, in a case falling within paragraph (*a*) (ii) above, until the end of the period therein referred to.

(3) If the capital sum referred to in sub-paragraph (1) above is payable only if the event in question happens before the expiry of a specified term ending more than ten years after the making of the insurance, or only if it happens both before the expiry of such a term and during the life of a specified person—

    (*a*) the premiums under the policy must be payable at yearly or shorter intervals, and either—

        (i) until the happening of the event or the earlier expiry of the said term, or, as the case may require, until the happening of the event or, if earlier, the expiry of the term or the death of the specified person, or

        (ii) as in sub-paragraph (i) above, but with the substitution for references to the term of references to a specified shorter period, being one ending not earlier than ten years after the making of the insurance or, if sooner, the expiry of three-quarters of the said term, and

    (*b*) the total premiums payable in any period of twelve months must not exceed—

        (i) twice the amount of the total premiums payable in any other such period, or

        (ii) one-eighth of the total premiums which would be payable if the policy were to continue in force for the term referred to in paragraph (*a*) (i) above, or, as the case may require, for the shorter period referred to in paragraph (*a*) (ii) above.

(4) If the capital sum referred to in sub-paragraph (1) above is payable only if the event in question happens before the expiry of a specified term ending not more than ten years after the making of the insurance, or only if it happens both before the expiry of such a term and during the life of a specified person, the policy must provide that any payment made by reason of its surrender during the period is not to exceed the total premiums previously paid thereunder.

(4A) Except where—

(*a*) the capital sum referred to in sub-paragraph (1) above is payable only in the circumstances mentioned in sub-paragraph (3) or (4) above, and

(*b*) the policy does not provide for any payment on the surrender in whole or in part of the rights conferred by it, and

(*c*) the specified term mentioned in sub-paragraph (3) or, as the case may be, (4) above ends at or before the time when the person whose life is insured attains the age of seventy-five years,

the capital sum, so far as payable on death, must not be less than 75 per cent. of the total premiums that would be payable if the death occurred at the age of seventy-five years, the age being, if the sum is payable on the death of the first to die of two persons, that of the older of them, if on the death of the survivor of them, that of the younger of them, and, in any other case, that of the person on whose death it is payable; and if the policy does not secure a capital sum in the event of death occurring before the age of sixteen or some lower age, it must not provide for the payment in that event of an amount exceeding the total premiums previously paid under it.

(5) Notwithstanding sub-paragraph (1) (*b*) above, if a policy secures a capital sum payable only on death, it may also secure benefits (including benefits of a capital nature) to be provided in the event of a person's disability; and no policy is to be regarded for the purposes of that provision as securing other benefits by reason only of the fact that it confers a right to participate in profits, that it provides for a payment on the surrender in whole or in part of the rights conferred by the policy, that it gives an option to receive payments by way of annuity, or that it makes provision for the waiver of premiums by reason of a person's disability, or for the effecting of a further insurance or insurances without the production of evidence of insurability.

(6) In applying sub-paragraph (2) or (3) above to any policy—

(*a*) no account shall be taken of any provision for the waiver of premiums by reason of a person's disability, and

(*b*) if the term of the policy runs from a date earlier, but not more than three months earlier, than the making of the insurance, the insurance shall be treated as having been made on that date, and any premium paid in respect of the period before the making of the insurance, or in respect of that period and a subsequent period, as having been payable on that date.

(7) References in this paragraph to a capital sum payable on any event include references to any capital sum, or series of capital sums, payable by reason of that event but where what is so payable is either an amount consisting of one sum or an amount made up of two or more sums, the 75 per cent. mentioned in sub-paragraph (4A) above shall be compared with the smaller or smallest amount so payable and a policy secures a capital sum payable either on death or on disability notwithstanding that the amount payable may vary with the event.

General rules applicable to endowment assurances

2.—(1) Subject to the following provisions of this Part of this Schedule, a policy which secures a capital sum payable either on survival for a specified term or on earlier death, or earlier death or disability, including a policy securing the sum on death only if occurring after the

197

attainment of a specified age not exceeding sixteen, is a qualifying policy
if it satisfies the following conditions—

(*a*) the term must be one ending not earlier than ten years after the
making of the insurance,

(*b*) premiums must be payable under the policy at yearly or shorter
intervals, and—

(i) until the happening of the event in question, or

(ii) until the happening of the event, or the earlier expiry of
a specified period shorter than the term but also ending not
earlier than ten years after the making of the insurance, or

(iii) if the policy is to lapse on the death of a specified person,
until one of those times or the policy's earlier lapse,

(*c*) the total premiums payable under the policy in any period of
twelve months must not exceed—

(i) twice the amount of the total premiums payable in any
other such period, or

(ii) one-eighth of the total premiums which would be payable
if the policy were to run for the specified term,

(*d*) the policy—

(i) must guarantee that the capital sum payable on death,
or on death occurring after the attainment of a specified age
not exceeding sixteen, will, whenever that event may happen,
be equal to 75 per cent. at least of the total premiums which
would be payable if the policy were to run for that term,
disregarding any amounts included in those premiums by
reason of their being payable otherwise than annually except
that if, at the beginning of that term, the age of the person
concerned exceeds fifty-five years, the capital sum so
guaranteed may, for each year of the excess, be less by 2 per
cent. of that total than 75 per cent. thereof, the person concerned being, if the capital sum is payable on the death of the
first to die of two persons, the older of them, if on the death
of the survivor of them, the younger of them and, in any
other case, the person on whose death it is payable, and

(ii) if it is a policy which does not secure a capital sum in
the event of death before the attainment of a specified age
not exceeding sixteen, must not provide for the payment in
that event of an amount exceeding the total premiums
previously paid thereunder, and

(*e*) the policy must not secure the provision (except by surrender in
whole or in part of the right conferred by the policy) at any
time before the happening of the event in question of any benefit
of a capital nature other than a payment falling within paragraph
(*d*) (ii) above, or benefits attributable to a right to participate in
profits or arising by reason of a person's disability.

(2) For the purposes of sub-paragraph (1) (*d*) (i) above, 10 per cent.
of the premiums payable under any policy issued in the course of an
industrial insurance business as defined in section 1 (2) of the Industrial
Assurance Act 1923 shall be treated as attributable to the fact that they
are not paid annually.

(3) Sub-paragraphs (6) and (7) of paragraph 1 above shall, with any
necessary modifications, have effect for the purposes of this paragraph
as they have effect for the purposes of that paragraph.

Special types of policy
(i) *Friendly Society policies*

2–41 **3.** A policy issued by any friendly society, or branch of a friendly society, in the course of its tax exempt life or endowment business, as defined in section 337 (3) of this Act, is a qualifying policy notwithstanding that it does not comply with the conditions specified in paragraph 1 or 2 above.

(ii) *Industrial Assurance policies*

2–42 **4.**—(1) A policy issued in the course of an industrial assurance business, as defined in section 1 (2) of the Industrial Assurance Act 1923, and not constituting a qualifying policy by virtue of paragraph 1 or 2 above, is nevertheless a qualifying policy if—

(*a*) the sums guaranteed by the policy, together with those guaranteed at the time the assurance is made by all other policies issued in the course of such a business to the same person and not constituting qualifying policies apart from this paragraph, do not exceed £1,000,

(*b*) it satisfies the conditions with respect to premiums specified in paragraph 1 (2) above,

(*c*) except by reason of death or surrender, no capital sum other than one falling within paragraph (*d*) below can become payable under the policy earlier than ten years after the making of the assurance, and

(*d*) where the policy provides for the making of a series of payments during its term—

(i) the first such payment is due not earlier than five years after the making of the assurance, and the others, except the final payment, at intervals of not less than five years, and

(ii) the amount of any payment, other than the final payment, does not exceed four-fifths of the premiums paid in the interval before its payment, and

(iii) if the first such payment is due earlier than ten years after the making of the assurance, or any other such payment except the last is due earlier than ten years after the preceding one, the sums guaranteed by the policy, together with the other sums referred to in paragraph (*a*) above so far as guaranteed by policies the payments under which also fall within this sub-paragraph, do not exceed £500.

(2) For the purposes of this paragraph, the sums guaranteed by a policy do not include any bonuses, or, in the case of a policy providing for a series of payments during its term, any of those payments except the first, or any sum payable on death during the term by reference to one or more of those payments except so far as that sum is referable to the first such payment.

(iii) *Family income policies and mortgage protection policies*

2–43 **5.**—(1) The following provisions apply to any policy which is not a qualifying policy apart from those provisions, and the benefits secured by which consist of or include the payment on or after a person's death of—

(*a*) one capital sum which does not vary according to the date of death, plus a series of capital sums payable if the death occurs during a specified period, or (*b*) a capital sum, the amount of which is less if the death occurs in a later part of a specified period than if it occurs in an earlier part of that period.

(2) A policy falling within sub-paragraph (1) (*a*) above is a qualifying policy if—

(*a*) it would be one if it did not secure the series of capital sums there referred to, and the premiums payable under the policy were such as would be chargeable if that were in fact the case, and

(*b*) it would also be one if it secured only that series of sums, and the premiums thereunder were the balance of those actually so payable.

(3) A policy falling within sub-paragraph (1) (*b*) above is a qualifying policy if—

(*a*) it would be one if the amount of the capital sum there referred to were equal throughout the period to its smallest amount, and the premiums payable under the policy were such as would be chargeable if that were in fact the case, and

(*b*) it would also be one if it secured only that capital sum so far as it from time to time exceeds its smallest amount, and the premiums payable thereunder were the balance of those actually so payable.

Other special provisions

(i) *Exceptional mortality risk*

12–44　　**6.** For the purpose of determining whether any policy is a qualifying policy, there shall be disregarded—

(*a*) so much of any premium thereunder as is charged on the grounds that an exceptional risk of death is involved, and

(*b*) any provision under which, on those grounds, any sum may become chargeable as a debt against the capital sum guaranteed by the policy on death.

(ii) *Connected policies*

12–45　　**7.** Where the terms of any policy provide that it is to continue in force only so long as another policy does so, neither policy is a qualifying policy unless, if they had constituted together a single policy issued in respect of an insurance made at the time of the insurance in respect of which the first-mentioned policy was issued, that single policy would have been a qualifying policy.

(iii) *Premiums paid out of sums due under previous policies*

12–46　　**8.**—(1) Where, in the case of a policy under which a single premium only is payable, liability for the payment of that premium is discharged in accordance with sub-paragraph (2) below, the policy is a qualifying policy notwithstanding anything in paragraph 1 (2) or 1 (3) above, or in paragraph (*b*) or (*c*) of paragraph 2 (1); and where, in the case of any other policy, liability for the payment of the first premium thereunder, or of any part of that premium, is so discharged, the premium or part shall be disregarded for the purposes of paragraph 1 (2) (*b*) and 1 (3) (*b*) above, and of paragraph (*c*) of paragraph 2 (1).

(2) Liability for the payment of a premium is discharged in accordance with this sub-paragraph if it is discharged by the retention by the company with whom the insurance is made of the whole or a part of any sum which has become payable on the maturity of, or on the

surrender more than ten years after its issue of the rights conferred by, a policy—

(*a*) previously issued by the company to the person making the insurance, or, if it is made by trustees, to them or any predecessors in office, or

(*b*) issued by the company when the person making the insurance was an infant, and securing a capital sum payable either on a specified date falling not more than one month after his attaining twenty-five, or on the anniversary of the policy immediately following his attainment of that age,

being, unless it is a policy falling within paragraph (*b*) above and the premium in question is a first premium only, a policy which was itself a qualifying policy, or which would have been a qualifying policy had it been issued in respect of an insurance made after 19th March 1968.

(iv) *Substitutions and variations*

9.—(1) Where one policy (hereafter referred to as " the new policy ") is issued in substitution for, or on the maturity of and in consequence of an option conferred by, another policy (hereafter referred to as " the old policy "), the question whether the new policy is a qualifying policy shall, to the extent provided by the rules in sub-paragraph (2) below, be determined by reference to both policies.

(2) The said rules (for the purposes of which, the question whether the old policy was a qualifying policy shall be determined in accordance with this Part of this Schedule, whatever the date of the insurance in respect of which it was issued), are as follows—

(*a*) if the new policy would apart from this paragraph be a qualifying policy, but the old policy was not, the new policy is not a qualifying policy unless the person making the insurance in respect of which it is issued was an infant when the old policy was issued, and the old policy was one securing a capital sum payable either on a specified date falling not later than one month after his attaining twenty-five or on the anniversary of the policy immediately following his attainment of that age;

(*b*) if the new policy would apart from this paragraph be a qualifying policy, and the old policy was also a qualifying policy, the new policy is a qualifying policy unless—

(i) it takes effect before the expiry of ten years from the making of the insurance in respect of which the old policy was issued, and

(ii) the highest total of premiums payable thereunder for any period of twelve months expiring before that time is less than one half of the highest total paid for any period of twelve months under the old policy, or under any related policy issued less than ten years before the issue of the new policy ("related policy" meaning any policy in relation to which the old policy was a new policy within the meaning of this paragraph, any policy in relation to which that policy was such a policy, and so on);

(*c*) if the new policy would not apart from this paragraph be a qualifying policy, and would fail to be so by reason only of paragraph 1 (2) or 1 (3) above or of paragraph (*a*), (*b*) or (*c*) of paragraph 2 (1), it is nevertheless a qualifying policy if the old policy was a qualifying policy and—

201

(i) the old policy was issued in respect of an insurance made more than ten years before the taking effect of the new policy, and the premiums payable for any period of twelve months under the new policy do not exceed the smallest total paid for any such period under the old policy, or

(ii) the old policy was issued outside the United Kingdom, and the circumstances are as specified in sub-paragraph (3) below.

(3) The said circumstances are—

(*a*) that the person in respect of whom the new insurance is made became resident in the United Kingdom, during the twelve months ending with the date of its issue,

(*b*) that the issuing company certify that the new policy is in substitution for the old, and that the old was issued either by a branch or agency of theirs outside the United Kingdom or by a company outside the United Kingdom with whom they have arrangements for the issue of policies in substitution for ones held by persons coming to the United Kingdom, and

(*c*) that the new policy confers on the holder benefits which are substantially equivalent to those which he would have enjoyed if the old policy had continued in force.

10.—(1) Subject to the provisions of this paragraph, where the terms of a policy are varied, the question whether the policy after the variation is a qualifying policy shall be determined in accordance with the rules in paragraph 9 above, with references in those rules to the new policy and the old policy construed for that purpose as references respectively to the policy after the variation and the policy before the variation, and with any other necessary modifications.

(2) In applying any of those rules by virtue of this paragraph, the question whether a policy after a variation would be a qualifying policy apart from the rule shall be determined as if any reference in paragraphs 1 to 7 of this Schedule to the making of an insurance, or to a policy's term, were a reference to the taking effect of the variation or, as the case may be, to the term of the policy as from the variation.

(3) This paragraph does not apply by reason of—

(*a*) any variation which, whether or not of a purely formal character, does not affect the terms of a policy in any significant respect, or

(*b*) any variation effected before the end of the year 1968 for the sole purpose of converting into a qualifying policy any policy issued (but not one treated by virtue of section 19 (5) of this Act as issued) in respect of an insurance made after 19th March 1968.

Part II

Certification of Qualifying Policies

12–48   **11.**—(1) Subject to sub-paragraph (3) below, a body issuing any policy of life insurance which is certified by the Board as being a qualifying policy within the meaning of Part I of this Schedule or which conforms with such a form as is mentioned in paragraph 1 (1) (*b*) of Schedule 2 to the Finance Act 1975 and is in the opinion of the body issuing it a qualifying policy shall, within three months of the date of issue, give to the policy holder a duly authenticated certificate to that effect, specifying in the certificate the name of the policy holder, the name of the person whose life is assured, the reference number or other means of identification allocated to the policy, the reference number of the relevant Inland Revenue certificate (if any), the capital sum or sums assured, and the amounts and dates for payment of the premiums.

(2) Subject to the said sub-paragraph (3), where a policy of life insurance is varied, and, after the variation, it either is certified by the Board as a qualifying policy or conforms with such a form as is referred it was issued a qualifying policy, that body shall, within three months of the making of the variation, give to the policy holder a like certificate with respect to the policy as varied.

(3) Where, in the case of any policy, or any policy after a variation, the total premiums payable in any period of twelve months do not exceed £52, a certificate need be given under sub-paragraph (1) or (2) above only if requested in writing by the policy holder, and, if so requested, shall be given within three months of receipt of the request; and sub-paragraph (2) above shall not apply by reason of—

    (*a*) any variation which, whether or not of a purely formal character, does not affect the terms of a policy in any significant respect, or

    (*b*) any variation of a policy issued in respect of an insurance made on or before 19th March 1968, other than a variation by virtue of which the policy falls, under section 19 (5) of this Act, to be treated as issued in respect of an insurance made after that date.

Finance Act 1975

(As amended by Finance Act 1976)

(c. 7)

An Act to grant certain duties, to alter other duties, and to amend the law relating to the National Debt and the Public Revenue, and to make further provision in connection with Finance.

PART II

INCOME TAX AND CORPORATION TAX

Early surrender or conversion of life policies

7.—(1) Where a policy of life insurance to which this section applies has been issued and, within four years from the making of the insurance in respect of which it was issued, any of the following events happens, that is to say—

    (*a*) the surrender of the whole or part of the rights conferred by the policy;

    (*b*) the falling due (otherwise than on death) of a sum payable in pursuance of a right conferred by the policy to participate in profits; and

    (*c*) the conversion of the policy into a paid-up or partly paid-up policy;

the body by whom the policy was issued shall pay to the Board, out of the sums payable by reason of the surrender or, as the case may be, out of the sum falling due or out of the fund available to pay the sums which will be due on death or on the maturity of the policy, a sum determined in accordance with the following provisions of this section, unless the body is wound up and the event is a surrender or conversion effected in connection with the winding-up.

(2) The sum payable under subsection (1) above shall, subject to the following provisions of this section, be equal to the lower of the following, that is to say—

(a) the appropriate percentage of the premiums payable under the policy up to the happening of the event; and

(b) the surrender value of the policy at the time of the happening of the event less the complementary percentage of the premiums mentioned in paragraph (a) above.

(3) If the event is one of those mentioned below, the sum payable to the Board shall not exceed the following limit, that is to say,—

(a) if it is the surrender of part of the rights conferred by the policy, the value of the rights surrendered at the time of the surrender;

(b) if it is the conversion of the policy into a partly paid-up policy, the surrender value, at the time of the conversion, of so much of the policy as is paid up; and

(c) if it is the falling due of a sum, that sum.

(4) If the event was preceded by the happening of such an event as is mentioned in subsection (1) above, subsection (2) above shall apply—

(a) as if the lower of the amounts mentioned therein were reduced by the sum paid under this section in respect of the earlier event; and

(b) if the earlier event was such an event as is mentioned in paragraph (a) or (c) of subsection (3) above, as if the surrender value of the policy were increased by the amount which, under that paragraph, limited or might have limited the sum payable under this section in respect of the earlier event.

(5) For the purposes of this section, the appropriate percentage, in relation to any event, is the percentage equal to the following fraction of the basic rate of income tax in force for the year of assessment in which the event happens, that is to say,—

(a) if the event happens in the first two of the four years mentioned in subsection (1) above, three-sixths;

(b) if it happens in the third of those years, two-sixths; and

(c) if it happens in the last of those years, one-sixth;

and the complementary percentage, in relation to any event, is 100 per cent. less the appropriate percentage.

(6) Where the annual amount of the premiums payable under a policy of life insurance is at any time increased (whether under the policy or by any contract made after its issue) so as to exceed by more than 25 per cent. the first annual amount so payable, the additional rights attributable to the excess shall be treated for the purposes of this section as conferred by a new policy issued in respect of an insurance made at that time, and the excess shall be treated as premiums payable under the new policy.

(7) Subject to subsection (8) below, this section applies to any policy of life insurance issued in respect of an insurance made after 26th March 1974; but where it applies by virtue of subsection (6) above to a policy treated as having been issued in respect of an insurance made after that date by reason of an increase in the annual amount of the

premiums payable under an earlier policy, it shall apply with the modification that the excess referred to in that subsection shall be taken to be the excess over the annual amount of the premiums at 26th March 1974.

(8) This section does not apply to a policy unless it is a qualifying policy within the meaning of Schedule 1 to the Taxes Act, and does not in any case apply to such a policy as is mentioned in paragraph (*b*) or (*c*) of the proviso to section 19 (4) of that Act.

Surrender, etc. of policies after four years

2–50   **8.**—(1) Where a policy of life insurance to which this section applies has been issued and, in the fifth or any later year from the making of the insurance in respect of which it was issued, either of the following events happens, that is to say—

    (*a*) the surrender of the whole or part of the rights conferred by the policy; and

    (*b*) the falling due (otherwise than on death or maturity) of a sum payable in pursuance of a right conferred by the policy to participate in profits;

then, if either of those events has happened before, the body by whom the policy was issued shall pay to the Board, out of the sums payable by reason of the surrender, or, as the case may be, out of the sum falling due, a sum determined in accordance with the following provisions of this section.

(2) The sum payable under subsection (1) above shall, subject to the following provisions of this section, be equal to the applicable percentage of the lower of the following—

    (*a*) the total of the premiums which are payable in that year under the policy; and

    (*b*) the sums payable by reason of the surrender or, as the case may be, the sum falling due;

and the percentage to be applied for this purpose shall be a percentage equal to one half of the basic rate of income tax in force in the year of assessment in which the event happens.

(3) Where, after a sum has become payable under subsection (1) above, and within the same year from the making of the insurance, another such event happens as is mentioned therein, the sums payable under that subsection in respect of both or all of the events shall not exceed the applicable percentage of the total mentioned in subsection (2) (*a*) above.

(4) Where, on the happening of an event in the fifth or any later year from the making of the insurance, any sum is payable under subsection (1) of section 7 of this Act as applied by subsection (6) of that section, as well as under subsection (1) above, subsection (2) above shall apply as if the sums or sum mentioned in paragraph (*b*) thereof were reduced by the sum payable under section 7 of this Act.

(5) This section applies to any policy of life insurance issued in respect of an insurance made after 26th March 1974, but only if it is a qualifying policy within the meaning of Schedule 1 to the Taxes Act; but does not apply to a policy issued in the course of an industrial insurance business, as defined in section 1 (2) of the Industrial Assurance Act 1923 or of the Industrial Assurance Act (Northern Ireland) 1924.

Provisions supplementary to sections 7 and 8

12–51   **9.**—(1) Where on the happening of an event in relation to a policy of life insurance a sum is payable under section 7 or 8 of this Act, relief under section 19 of the Taxes Act in respect of the relevant premiums paid under the policy shall be reduced by the sum so payable or, as the case may be, by so much of that sum as does not exceed the amount of that relief (or does not exceed so much of that amount as remains after any previous reduction under this section).

(2) For the purposes of this section the relevant premiums are—

    (*a*) in relation to a sum payable under section 7 of this Act, the premiums payable under the policy up to the happening of the event by reason of which the sum is payable; and

    (*b*) in relation to a sum payable under section 8 of this Act, the premiums payable in the year (from the making of the insurance) in which the event happens by reason of which the sum is payable.

(3) Where the relevant premiums are payable in more than one year of assessment the reduction in relief under this section shall, so far as possible, reduce relief for an earlier year of assessment before reducing relief for a later one.

(4) Any sum paid under section 7 or 8 of this Act by reason of any event shall be treated—

    (*a*) as between the parties, as received by the person by whom the premiums under the policy were paid; and

    (*b*) for the purposes of income tax, as income tax paid by that person in satisfaction of the increase in liability resulting from the reduction of relief under this section;

and where that sum exceeds that increase in liability he shall be entitled, on a claim made by him not later than six years after the end of the year of assessment in which the event happens, to repayment of the excess.

(5) Schedule 1 to this Act shall have effect with respect to the payment of sums payable under section 7 or 8 of this Act and related matters.

Life policies, life annuities and capital redemption policies

12–52   **10.** Sections 19 and 21 and Chapter III of Part XIV of the Taxes Act and Schedule 1 to that Act shall have effect subject to the provisions of Schedule 2 to this Act; and in those provisions references to any section not otherwise identified are to sections of that Act and " Schedule 1 " means Schedule 1 to that Act.

Capital transfer tax

19.—(1) A tax, to be known as capital transfer tax, shall be charged on the value transferred by a chargeable transfer.

(2) Schedule 4 to this Act shall have effect with respect to the administration and collection of the tax.

Transfers and chargeable transfers

12–53   **20.**—(1) The following provisions of this section shall have effect, subject to the other provisions of this Part of this Act, for determining for the purposes of capital transfer tax what is a chargeable transfer and what value is transferred by a chargeable transfer.

(2) Subject to subsections (3) and (4) below, a transfer of value is any disposition made by a person ("the transferor") as a result of which the value of his estate immediately after the disposition is less than it would be but for the disposition; and the amount by which it is less is the value transferred by the transfer.

(3) For the purposes of subsection (2) above no account shall be taken of the value of excluded property which ceases to form part of a person's estate as a result of a disposition.

(4) A disposition is not a transfer of value if it is shown that it was not intended, and was not made in a transaction intended, to confer any gratuitous benefit on any person and either—

(*a*) that it was made in a transaction at arm's length between persons not connected with each other, or

(*b*) that it was such as might be expected to be made in a transaction at arm's length between persons not connected with each other;

but this subsection does not apply to a disposition by which a reversionary interest is acquired in the circumstances mentioned in section 23 (3) of this Act and does not apply to a sale of shares or debentures not quoted on a recognised stock exchange unless it is shown that the sale was at a price freely negotiated at the time of the sale or at a price such as might be expected to have been freely negotiated at the time of the sale.

In this subsection " transaction " includes a series of transactions and any associated operations.

(5) A chargeable transfer is any transfer of value made by an individual after 26th March 1974 other than an exempt transfer.

(6) A transfer of value made by an individual after that date and exempt only to a limited extent—

(*a*) is, if all the value transferred by it is within the limit, an exempt transfer; and

(*b*) is, if that value is partly within and partly outside the limit, a chargeable transfer of so much of that value as is outside the limit as well as an exempt transfer of so much of that value as is within the limit.

(7) For the purposes of this section, where the value of a person's estate is diminished and that of another person's estate is increased by the first-mentioned person's omission to exercise a right he shall be treated as having made a disposition at the time, or the latest time, when he could have exercised the right, unless it is shown that the omission was not deliberate.

Settled property

21. Schedule 5 to this Act shall have effect with respect to settled property.

Transfer on death

22.—(1) On the death of any person after the passing of this Act tax shall be charged as if, immediately before his death, he had made a transfer of value and the value transferred by it had been equal to the value of his estate immediately before his death, but subject to the following provisions of this section.

(2) Where the deceased was entitled to an interest in possession in settled property which on his death but during the life of the settlor reverted to the settlor, then, unless the settlor had acquired a rever-

sionary interest in the property for a consideration in money or money's worth, the value of the settled property shall be left out of account in determining for the purposes of this Part of this Act the value of the deceased's estate immediately before his death.

(3) Where the deceased was entitled to an interest in possession in settled property and on his death the settlor's spouse became beneficially entitled to that property, then if—

    (*a*) the settlor's spouse was at the time of the death domiciled in the United Kingdom . . . ; and

    (*b*) neither the settlor nor the settlor's spouse had acquired a reversionary interest in the property for a consideration in money or money's worth;

the value of the settled property shall be left out of account in determining for the purposes of this Part of this Act the value of the deceased's estate immediately before his death.

The references in this subsection to the settlor's spouse include, in a case where the settlor died less than two years before the deceased or the deceased died before 1st April 1977, references to the settlor's widow or widower.

(4) Where one party to a marriage has died before 13th November 1974 and the other party dies after the passing of this Act, then, in determining for the purposes of this Part of this Act the value of the other party's estate immediately before his death, there shall be left out of account the value of any property which, if estate duty were chargeable on that death, would be excluded from the charge by section 5 (2) of the Finance Act 1894 (relief on death of surviving spouse).

(5) Where a person who dies after the passing of this Act—

    (*a*) had, before 27th March 1974 but not more than seven years before his death, made a gift inter vivos of any property; or

    (*b*) had, before 27th March 1974 but not at any time thereafter, a beneficial interest in possession in any property comprised in a settlement;

and by reason thereof any property would, had estate duty been chargeable on his death, have been included by virtue of section 2 (1) (*c*) or 2 (1) (*b*) (i) of the Finance Act 1894 in the property passing on his death, then, in determining for the purposes of capital transfer tax the value of his estate immediately before his death, there shall be included the value which for the purposes of estate duty chargeable on his death would have been the principal value of the property so included (or, in a case where, under paragraph 3 of Part II of Schedule 17 to the Finance Act 1969 the duty chargeable on the property would have been charged on a reduced value, that reduced value).

(6) Where estate duty on the whole or part of the value of any property which would have been included as mentioned in subsection (5) above would, by virtue of section 23 of the Finance Act 1925 or section 28 of the Finance Act 1954 have been chargeable at 55 per cent. of the estate rate, the tax chargeable on that value or part by virtue of subsection (5) above shall be charged at 55 per cent. of the rate represented by the fraction of which—

    (*a*) the numerator is the amount of tax which (apart from this subsection) would be chargeable on the value of the deceased's estate immediately before his death; and

    (*b*) the denominator is that value.

(7) Where any part of the property which would have been included as mentioned in subsection (5) above would, by virtue of section 40 (2) (c) of the Finance Act 1969, have formed an estate by itself, the tax chargeable under this section shall be the aggregate of—

(a) the tax that would have been so chargeable if that part had not been so included; and

(b) the tax (if any) that would have been so chargeable if that part only had formed the estate of the deceased and the deceased had made no previous chargeable transfers;

but in a case where (by reason of an excess over £25,000) the part referred to in paragraph (b) above would have been a fraction only of any property, the tax that would have been chargeable as mentioned in that paragraph shall be taken to be the like fraction of the tax that would have been so chargeable if the remainder of that property had also been included in the estate of the deceased.

(8) Where the estate duty would have been estate duty under the law of Northern Ireland—

(a) subsection (5) above shall have effect with the substitution of a reference to four years for the reference in paragraph (a) to seven years, and of a reference to Schedule 1 to the Finance Act (Northern Ireland) 1969 for the reference to Schedule 17 to the Finance Act 1969; and

(b) subsection (6) shall have effect with the substitution of references to section 3 of the Finance (No. 2) Act (Northern Ireland) 1947 and section 3 of the Finance Act (Northern Ireland) 1954 for the references to section 23 of the Finance Act 1925 and section 28 of the Finance Act 1954; and

(c) subsection (7) shall have effect with the substitution of a reference to section 7 (2) (c) of the Finance Act (Northern Ireland) 1969 for the reference to section 40 (2) (c) of the Finance Act 1969.

(9) For the purposes of this section, where it cannot be known which of two or more persons who have died survived the other or others they shall be assumed to have died at the same instant.

Exempt transfers and miscellaneous exemptions and reliefs

2–56   **29.** Schedule 6 to this Act shall have effect with respect to exempt transfers and Schedule 7 to this Act with respect to the exemptions and reliefs mentioned therein.

Annuity purchased in conjunction with life policy

2–57   **42.**—(1) Where—

(a) a policy of life insurance is issued in respect of an insurance made on or after 27th March 1974 or is on or after that date varied or substituted for an earlier policy; and

(b) at the time the insurance is made or at any earlier or later date an annuity on the life of the insured is purchased; and

(c) the benefit of the policy is vested in a person other than the person who purchased the annuity;

then, unless it is shown that the purchase of the annuity and the making of the insurance (or, as the case may be, the substitution or variation) were not associated operations, the person who purchased the annuity shall be treated as having made a transfer of value by a disposition made at the time the benefit of the policy became so vested (to the exclusion of any transfer of value which, apart from this section, he might have made as a result of the vesting or of the purchase and the vesting being associated operations).

(2) The value transferred by that transfer of value shall be equal to whichever of the following is less, namely,—

(a) the aggregate of—

(i) the value of the consideration given for the annuity; and

(ii) any premium paid or other consideration given under the policy on or before the transfer; and

(b) the value of the greatest benefit capable of being conferred at any time by the policy, calculated as if that time were the date of the transfer.

(3) The preceding provisions of this section shall apply, with the necessary modifications, where a contract for an annuity payable on a person's death is on or after 27th March 1974 made or varied or substituted for or replaced by such a contract or a policy of life insurance as they apply where a policy of life insurance is issued, varied or substituted as mentioned in subsection (1) above.

Associated operations

12–58   **44.**—(1) In this Part of this Act " associated operations " means, subject to subsection (2) below, any two or more operations of any kind, being—

(a) operations which affect the same property, or one of which affects some property and othe other or others of which affect property which represents, whether directly or indirectly, that property, or income arising from that property, or any property representing accumulations of any such income; or

(b) any two operations of which one is effected with reference to the other, or with a view to enabling the other to be effected or facilitating its being effected, and any further operation having a like relation to any of those two, and so on;

whether those operations are effected by the same person or different persons, and whether or not they are simultaneous; and " operation " includes an omission.

(2) The granting of a lease for full consideration in money or money's worth shall not be taken to be associated with any operation effected more than three years after the grant, and no operation effected on or after 27th March 1974 shall be taken to be associated with an operation effected before that date.

(3) Where a transfer of value is made by associated operations carried out at different times it shall be treated as made at the time of the last of them; but where any one or more of the earlier operations also constitute a transfer of value made by the same transferor, the value transferred by the earlier operations shall be treated as reducing the value transferred by all the operations taken together, except to the extent that the transfer constituted by the earlier operations but not that made by all the operations taken together is exempt under paragraph 1 of Schedule 6 to this Act.

SCHEDULE 1

Section 9

COLLECTION OF SUMS PAYABLE UNDER SECTION 7 OR 8

1. Any body by whom a policy to which section 7 or 8 of this Act applies has been issued shall, within thirty days of the end of the period ending with 31st March 1976 and of every subsequent period of twelve months make a return to the collector of the sums which, in that period, have become payable by it under either of those sections.

2.—(1) Any sum which is to be included in a return made under paragraph 1 above shall be due at the time by which the return is to be made and shall be paid without being demanded.

(2) Where any sum which was or ought to have been included in such a return is not paid by the end of the period for which the return was to be made it may be recovered by an assessment as if it were income tax for the year of assessment in which that period ends; and where it appears to the inspector that a sum which ought to have been so included had not been included or that a return is not correct he may make such an assessment to the best of his judgment.

(3) All the provisions of the Income Tax Acts relating to the assessment and collection of tax, interest on unpaid tax, appeals and penalties shall, with the necessary modifications, apply in relation to sums due under this paragraph; and for the purposes of those provisions so far as they relate to interest on unpaid tax, a sum assessed in pursuance of this paragraph shall be treated as having been payable when it would have been payable had it been included in a return under paragraph 1 above.

(4) Where, on an appeal against an assessment made in pursuance of this paragraph, it is determined that a greater sum has been assessed than was payable, the excess, if paid, shall be repaid.

3.—Where a body has paid a sum which is payable under section 7 or 8 of this Act it shall give within thirty days to the person by whom the sum is, under section 9 (4) of this Act, treated as received a statement specifying that sum and showing how it has been arrived at.

4.—(1) The Board or an inspector may, by notice in writing served on the body by whom a policy to which section 7 or 8 of this Act applies has been issued, require the body, within such time, not being less than thirty days, as may be specified in the notice—

(*a*) to furnish such particulars; or

(*b*) to make available for inspection by an officer authorised by the Board such books and other documents in the possession or under the control of the body;

as the Board or officer may reasonably require for the purposes of those sections or this Schedule.

(2) In section 98 of the Taxes Management Act 1970 (penalty for failure to furnish information) there shall be added in the first column of the Table the words " paragraph 4 of Schedule 1 to the Finance Act 1975."

Section 10.

SCHEDULE 2

LIFE POLICIES, LIFE ANNUITIES AND CAPITAL REDEMPTION POLICIES

PART I

QUALIFYING POLICIES—CERTIFICATION

12–60   **1.**—(1) A policy of life insurance issued in respect of an insurance made on or after such day as the Treasury may by order made by statutory instrument appoint (in this Schedule referred to as " the appointed day ") or varied on or after the appointed day shall not be a qualfying policy within the meaning of Schedule 1 unless—

    (*a*) it is certified as such by the Board; or

    (*b*) it conforms with a form which, at the time the policy is issued or varied, is either—

        (i) a standard form certified by the Board as a standard form of qualifying policy; or

        (ii) a form varying from a standard form so certified in no other respect than by making such additions thereto as are, at the time the policy is issued, certified by the Board as compatible with a qualifying policy when made to that standard form and satisfy any conditions subject to which they are so certified;

and any certificate issued in pursuance of paragraph (*a*) above shall be conclusive evidence that the policy is a qualifying policy within the meaning of that Schedule.

   (2) In issuing a certificate in pursuance of sub-paragraph (1) above the Board may disregard any provision of the policy, standard form or addition which appears to them insignificant.

   (3) Where the Board refuse to certify a policy as being a qualifying policy within the meaning of Schedule 1, the person to whom it is issued may appeal to the General Commissioners or, if he so elects, to the Special Commissioners.

   (4) The preceding provisions of this paragraph do not apply in relation to such a policy as is mentioned in paragraph 3 of Schedule 1 (friendly societies policies).

   2.—(1)–(3) *See* I.C.T.A. 1970, Sched. 1, para. 11.

PART II

AMENDMENT OF QUALIFYING CONDITIONS

12–61   **3.**—(1) The following provisions of this paragraph shall have effect for determining for the purposes of Schedule 1 and this Schedule whether a policy has been varied or whether a policy which confers on the person to whom it is issued an option to have another policy substituted for it or to have any of its terms changed is a qualifying policy.

   (2) If the policy is one issued in respect of an insurance made before the appointed day—

    (*a*) any such option shall, until it is exercised, be disregarded in determining whether the policy is a qualifying policy; and

    (*b*) any change in the terms of the policy which is made in pursuance of such an option shall be deemed to be a variation of the policy.

(3) If the policy is one issued in respect of an insurance made on or after the appointed day, the policy shall not be a qualifying policy unless it satisfies the conditions applicable to it under Schedule 1 before any such option is exercised and—

(*a*) each policy that might be substituted for it in pursuance of such an option would satisfy those conditions under the rules of paragraph 9 of that Schedule; and

(*b*) the policy would continue to satisfy those conditions under the rules of that paragraph as applied by paragraph 10 of that Schedule if each or any of the changes capable of being made in pursuance of such an option had been made and were treated as a variation;

and it shall not be treated as being varied by reason only of any change made in pursuance of such an option.

12–62   **4.**—(1) In relation to any policy issued in respect of an insurance made on or after the appointed day paragraphs 1 and 2 of Schedule 1 shall have effect subject to the following provisions of this paragraph.

(2) *See* I.C.T.A. 1970, Sched. 1, para. 1 (1) (*a*).

(3) *See* I.C.T.A. 1970, Sched. 1, para. 1 (4A).

(4) In determining, for the purposes of sub-paragraph (3) above, whether a capital sum is less than 75 per cent. of the total premiums, any amount included in the premiums by reason of their being payable otherwise than annually shall be disregarded, and if the policy is issued in the course of an industrial assurance business as defined in section 1 (2) of the Industrial Assurance Act 1923 or of the Industrial Assurance Act (Northern Ireland) 1924, 10 per cent. of the premiums payable under the policy shall be treated as so included.

(5) *See* I.C.T.A. 1970, Sched. 1, para. 1 (5).

(6) *See* I.C.T.A. 1970, Sched. 1, para. 1 (7).

(7) *See* I.C.T.A. 1970, Sched. 1, para. 2 (1) (*d*) (i).

(8) *See* I.C.T.A. 1970, Sched. 1, para. 2 (1) (*e*).

5. Where the new policy referred to in paragraph 9 of Schedule 1 is one issued on or after the appointed day then, in determining under sub-paragraph (2) of that paragraph whether that policy would or would not (apart from that paragraph) be a qualifying policy there shall be left out of account so much of the first premium payable thereunder as is accounted for by the value of the old policy.

PART III

RELIEF UNDER SECTION 19 OR 20

12–63   **6.**—(1) *See* I.C.T.A. 1970, s. 21.

(2) This paragraph has effect for the year 1976–77 and subsequent years of assessment.

7.—(1) Where a policy issued in the course of an industrial assurance business, as defined in section 1 (2) of the Industrial Assurance Act 1923 or of the Industrial Assurance Act (Northern Ireland) 1924, is not a qualifying policy by virtue of paragraph 1 or 2 of Schedule 1 but is a policy with respect to which the conditions in paragraphs (*b*) and (*c*) of sub-paragraph (1) of paragraph 4 of Schedule 1 are satisfied, it shall be a qualifying policy whether or not the conditions of paragraphs (*a*) and (*d*) (iii) of that sub-paragraph are satisfied with respect to it; but where they are not satisfied relief under section 19 in respect of premiums paid under the policy shall be given only on such amount (if any) as would have been the amount of the premiums had those conditions been satisfied.

(2) This paragraph has effect in relation to any policy issued in respect of an insurance made after the appointed day.

Part IV

Charges in Connection with Policies of Life Insurance, Contracts for Life Annuities and Capital Redemption Policies

12–64   **8.** This Part of this Schedule shall have effect in relation to any event happening in any year (as defined in paragraph 9 (9) below) which falls wholly after the passing of this Act, but without prejudice to the operation in relation to earlier events of paragraphs 10 (1), 12 (2), 16 and 17 below.

9.—(1) *See* I.C.T.A. 1970, s. 394 (1) (*a*).

(2) *See* I.C.T.A. 1970, s. 394 (1) (*b*) (ii).

(3) *See* I.C.T.A. 1970, s. 396 (1).

(4) *See* I.C.T.A. 1970, s. 398 (1).

(5) For the purposes of sections 394, 396 and 398 as amended by the preceding sub-paragraphs there shall be calculated at the end of each year, but subject to sub-paragraph (8) below,—

> (*a*) the value, as at the time of surrender or assignment, of any part of or share in the rights conferred by the policy or contract which has been assigned or surrendered up to the end of the year; and

> (*b*) the appropriate portion of any payment made up to the end of the year by way of premium or as a lump sum consideration;

and the appropriate portion of any payment shall be one-twentieth for the year in which it is made, increased by a further one-twentieth for each of the subsequent nineteen years, but subject to sub-paragraph (8) below.

(6) The reckonable aggregate value referred to in those sections shall be—

> (*a*) the sum of the values calculated under sub-paragraph (5) above; less

> (*b*) the sum of the values so calculated for the previous year and brought into account on the previous happening of a chargeable event.

(7) The allowable aggregate amount referred to in those sections shall be—

> (*a*) the aggregate of the appropriate portions calculated under sub-paragraph (5) above; less

> (*b*) the aggregate of the appropriate portions so calculated for a previous year and brought into account on the previous happening of a chargeable event.

(8) In making the calculations required by sub-paragraph (5) above there shall be excluded—

> (*a*) from the value mentioned in paragraph (*a*) thereof, the value of

any part of or share in the rights conferred by the policy or contract which has been assigned or surrendered before the commencement of the first year which falls wholly after the passing of this Act; and

(b) from the appropriate portion mentioned in paragraph (b) thereof, the one-twentieth mentioned therein for any year before that first year.

(9) In this paragraph " year " means the twelve months beginning with the making of the insurance or contract and any subsequent period of twelve months; except that—

(a) death, the maturity of the policy or the surrender of the whole of the rights conferred by the policy or contract shall be treated as ending the final year; and

(b) if the final year would by virtue of paragraph (a) above begin and end in the same year of assessment, the final year and the year preceding it shall together be one year.

10.—(1) *See* I.C.T.A. 1970, s. 394 (4).

(2) *See* I.C.T.A. 1970, s. 394 (5) *and* s. 395 (4).

(3) Sub-paragraph (1) above applies in relation to any event happening on or after 10th December 1974.

11.—(1) *See* I.C.T.A. 1970, s. 395 (1).

(2) *See* I.C.T.A. 1970, s. 395 (3A).

12.—(1) *See* I.C.T.A. 1970, s. 396 (1).

(2) *See* I.C.T.A. 1970, s. 396 (2).

(3) Sub-paragraph (2) above applies in relation to any event happening on or after 10th December 1974.

13.—(1) *See* I.C.T.A. 1970, s. 397 (1).

(2) *See* I.C.T.A., s. 397 (2).

(3) *See* I.C.T.A. 1970, s. 397 (3).

14. *See* I.C.T.A. 1970, s. 398 (1).

15. For the purposes of sections 394 to 402 and of this Schedule the falling due of a sum payable in pursuance of a right conferred by a policy or contract to participate in profits shall be treated as the surrender of rights conferred by the policy or contract.

16.—(1) Where—

(a) under section 399, a gain arising in connection with a policy or contract would be treated as forming part of an individual's total income; and

(b) the policy was issued in respect of an insurance made after 26th March 1974 or the contract was made after that date and;

(c) any sum is at any time after the making of the insurance or contract lent to or at the direction of that individual by or by arrangement with the body issuing the policy or, as the case may be, the body with which the contract was made;

then, subject to sub-paragraph (3) below, the same results shall follow under sections 7 to 9 of this Act, this Schedule and sections 394 to 402, as if at the time the sum was lent there had been a surrender of part of the rights conferred by the policy or contract and the sum had been paid as consideration for the surrender (and if the policy is one falling within subsection (2) of section 394, those results shall follow under section 8 of this Act, whether or not a gain would be treated as arising on the surrender).

(2) If the whole or any part of the sum is repaid the repayment shall be treated, for the purpose of computing any gain arising on the happening, at the end of the final year, of a chargeable event, as a payment of a premium or lump sum consideration.

(3) The preceding provisions of this paragraph do not apply in relation to a policy if—

(*a*) it is a qualifying policy within the meaning of Schedule 1; and

(*b*) either interest at a commercial rate is payable on the sum lent or the sum is lent to a full-time employee of the body issuing the policy for the purpose of assisting him in the purchase or improvement of a dwelling used or to be used as his only or main residence.

(4) In this paragraph " final year " has the same meaning as in paragraph 9 above.

17. Where, under section 397, a gain is to be treated as arising in connection with a contract for a life annuity made after 26th March 1974—

(*a*) section 399 shall have effect, in relation to the gain, as if subsection (4) were omitted; and

(*b*) the gain shall be chargeable to tax under Case VI of Schedule D; but

(*c*) any relief under section 400 shall be computed as if this paragraph had not been enacted.

18. Where a chargeable event on the happening of which an amount is included in an individual's total income by virtue of section 399 (1) (*a*) follows the happening of another chargeable event in relation to the same policy or contract, and each of the events in such an excess as is mentioned in section 394 (1) (*a*) (v), 396 (1) or 398 (1) (iv), subsection (3) of section 400 (top slicing relief) shall have effect in relation to that amount as if the number of complete years referred to in it were the number of complete years elapsing between that other event (or, if more than one, the last of them) and the first-mentioned event.

19.—(1) Subject to sub-paragraph (1A) below where such an excess as is mentioned in paragraph (*a*) or (*b*) of section 395 (1) or paragraph (*a*) of section 397 (1) would be treated as a gain arising in connection with a policy or contract and would form part of an individual's total income for the year of assessment in which the final year ends, a corresponding deficiency occurring at the end of the final year shall be allowable as a deduction from his total income for that year of assessment, so far as it does not exceed the total amount treated as a gain by virtue of section 395 (1) (*d*) or 397 (1) (*c*) on the previous happenings of chargeable events.

(1A) Except where the deficiency mentioned in sub-paragraph (1) above occurs in connection with a contract for a life annuity made after 26th March 1974, the deduction allowable under that sub-paragraph shall be made only for the purpose of ascertaining the individual's excess liability, that is to say, the excess (if any) of his liability to income tax over what it would be if all income tax were chargeable at the basic rate to the exclusion of any other rate.

(2) In this paragraph " final year " has the same meaning as in paragraph 9 above.

12–66 **20.**—(1) Section 402 shall have effect subject to the following provisions of this paragraph.

(2) Where the chargeable event is an assignment of all the rights conferred by the policy or contract the certificate shall also specify any such excess as is mentioned in section 394 (1) (*a*) (v), 396 (1) or 398 (1) (iv) which has occurred since the relevant date, the date on which it occurred and the value of the part of or share in the rights which have been surrendered or assigned since the relevant date.

(3) Where the chargeable event is the occurrence of such an excess as is mentioned in section 394 (1) (*a*) (v), 396 (1) or 398 (1) (iv), section 402 shall apply with the omission of subsection (2) (*b*) and the certificate shall also specify the value of the part of or share in the rights surrendered or assigned in any year since the relevant date and the amounts paid by way of premiums in any year since the relevant date.

(4) In this paragraph " year " has the meaning assigned to it by paragraph 9 (9) above and " the relevant date," in relation to any certificate, means the date of the chargeable event in respect of which the last certificate under section 402 was delivered or, if none was delivered, the commencement of the policy or contract.

SCHEDULE 5

Section 21.

SETTLED PROPERTY

Definition of " settlement " and related expressions

12–67 **1.**—(1) The following provisions of this paragraph apply for determining what is to be taken for the purposes of capital transfer tax to be a settlement, and what property is, accordingly, referred to as property comprised in a settlement or as settled property; and who is the settlor and a trustee in relation to a settlement.

(2) " Settlement " means any disposition or dispositions of property, whether effected by instrument, by parol or by operation of law, or partly in one way and partly in another, whereby the property is for the time being—

    (*a*) held in trust for persons in succession or for any person subject to a contingency; or

    (*b*) held by trustees on trust to accumulate the whole or part of any income of the property or with power to make payments out of that income at the discretion of the trustees or some other person, with or without power to accumulate surplus income; or

    (*c*) charged or burdened (otherwise than for full consideration in money or money's worth paid for his own use or benefit to the person making the disposition), with the payment of any annuity or other periodical payment payable for a life or any other limited or terminable period;

or would be so held or charged or burdened if the disposition or dispositions were regulated by the law of any part of the United Kingdom; or whereby, under the law of any other country, the administration of the property is for the time being governed by provisions equivalent

217

in effect to those which would apply if the property were so held, charged or burdened.

(3) A lease of property which is for life or lives, or for a period ascertainable only by reference to a death, or which is terminable on, or at a date ascertainable only by reference to, a death, shall be treated as a settlement and the property as settled property, unless the lease was granted for full consideration in money or money's worth, and where a lease not granted as a lease at a rack rent is at any time to become a lease at an increased rent it shall be treated as terminable at that time.

(4) In relation to Scotland " settlement " also includes—
  (a) an entail;
  (b) any deed by virtue of which an annuity is charged on, or on the rents of, any property (the property being treated as the property comprised in the settlement).

(5) In sub-paragraph (4) above, " deed " includes any disposition, arrangement, contract, resolution, instrument or writing.

(6) " Settlor," in relation to a settlement, includes any person by whom the settlement was made directly or indirectly, and in particular (but without prejudice to the generality of the preceding words) includes any person who has provided funds directly or indirectly for the purpose of or in connection with the settlement or has made with any other person a reciprocal arrangement for that other person to make the settlement.

(7) " Trustee," in relation to a settlement in relation to which there would be no trustees apart from this sub-paragraph, means any person in whom the settled property or its management is for the time being vested.

(8) Where more than one person is a settlor in relation to a settlement and the circumstances so require, this Schedule and section 25 (3) (d) of this Act shall apply in relation to it as if the settled property were comprised in separate settlements.

(9) In the application of this Part of this Act to Scotland, any reference to an interest in possession in settled property is a reference to an interest of any kind under a settlement by virtue of which the person in right of that interest is entitled to the enjoyment of the property or would be so entitled if the property were capable of enjoyment and the person in right of such an interest at any time shall be deemed to be entitled to a corresponding interest in the whole or any part of the property comprised in the settlement.

(10) In the application of this Part of this Act to Northern Ireland this paragraph shall have effect as if references to property held in trust for persons included references to property standing limited to persons and as if the lease referred to in sub-paragraph (3) did not include a lease in perpetuity within the meaning of section 1 of the Renewable Leasehold Conversion Act 1849 or a lease to which section 37 of that Act applies.

Excluded property

12–68   2.—(1) Where property comprised in a settlement is situated outside the United Kingdom—
  (a) the property (but not a reversionary interest in the property) is excluded property unless the settlor was domiciled in the United Kingdom at the time the settlement was made; and

(*b*) section 24 (2) of this Act applies to a reversionary interest in the property but does not otherwise apply in relation to the property.

(2) In determining whether property comprised in a settlement which became so comprised before 10th December 1974 is excluded property section 45 of this Act shall be disregarded.

Interests in possession

12-69 **3.**—(1) A person beneficially entitled to an interest in possession in settled property shall be treated as beneficially entitled to the property in which the interest subsists.

(2) Where the person entitled to the interest is entitled to part only of the income (if any) of the property, the interest shall be taken to subsist in such part only of the property as bears to the whole thereof the same proportion as the part of the income to which he is entitled bears to the whole of the income.

(3) Where the part of the income of any property to which a person is entitled is a specified amount (or the whole less a specified amount) in any period, his interest in the property shall be taken, subject to sub-paragraph (4) below, to subsist in such part (or in the whole less such part) to the property as produces that amount in that period.

(4) The Treasury may from time to time by order made by statutory instrument prescribe a higher and a lower rate for the purposes of this paragraph; and where tax is chargeable in accordance with sub-paragraph (3) above by reference to the value of the part of a property which produces a specified amount or by reference to the value of the remainder (but not where chargeable transfers are made simultaneously and tax is chargeable by reference to the value of the remainder) the value of the part producing that specified amount—

(*a*) shall, if tax is chargeable by reference to the value of that part, be taken to be not less than it would be if the property produced income at the higher rate so prescribed; and

(*b*) shall, if tax is chargeable by reference to the value of the remainder, be taken to be not more than it would be if the property produced income at the lower rate so prescribed;

but the value to be taken by virtue of paragraph (*a*) above as the value of part of a property shall not exceed the value of the whole of the property.

(5) Where the person entitled to the interest is not entitled to any income of the property but is entitled, jointly or in common with one or more other persons, to the use and enjoyment of the property, his interest shall be taken to subsist in such part of the property as corresponds to the proportion which the annual value of his interest bears to the aggregate of the annual values of his interest and that or those of the other or others.

(6) Where, under paragraph 1 (3) of this Schedule, a lease of property is to be treated as a settlement, the lessee's interest in the property shall be taken to subsist in the whole of the property less such part of it as corresponds to the proportion which the value of the lessor's interest (as determined under Schedule 10 to this Act) bears to the value of the property.

(7) A statutory instrument made under this paragraph shall be subject to annulment in pursuance of a resolution of the House of Commons.

Termination of interest in possession treated as transfer of value

12–70   **4.**—(1) Where a person beneficially entitled to an interest in possession in any property comprised in a settlement disposes of his interest the disposal—

(*a*) is not a transfer of value; but

(*b*) shall be treated for the purposes of this Schedule as the coming to an end of his interest;

and tax shall be charged accordingly under the following provisions of this paragraph.

(2) Where at any time during the life of a person beneficially entitled to an interest in possession in any property comprised in a settlement his interest comes to an end, tax shall be charged, subject to the following provisions of this paragraph, as if at that time he had made a transfer of value and the value transferred had been equal to the value of the property in which his interest subsisted.

(3) If the person whose interest in the property comes to an end becomes on the same occasion beneficially entitled to the property or to another interest in possession in the property tax shall not be chargeable under this paragraph, except in the case mentioned in sub-paragraph (10) (*b*) below.

(4) If the interest comes to an end by being disposed of by the person beneficially entitled thereto and the disposal is for a consideration in money or money's worth, tax shall be chargeable under this paragraph as if the value of the property in which the interest subsisted were reduced by the amount of the consideration; but in determining that amount the value of a reversionary interest in the property or of any interest in other property comprised in the same settlement shall be left out of account.

(5) If the interest comes to an end during the settlor's life and on the same occasion the property in which the interest subsisted reverts to the settlor, tax shall not be chargeable under this paragraph unless the settlor had acquired a reversionary interest in the property for a consideration in money or money's worth.

(6) If the interest comes to an end and on the same occasion the settlor's spouse becomes beneficially entitled to the settled property, then if—

(*a*) the settlor's spouse is then domiciled in the United Kingdom . . .; and

(*b*) neither the settlor nor the settlor's spouse had acquired a reversionary interest in the property for a consideration in money or money's worth;

tax shall not be chargeable under this paragraph.

The references in this sub-paragraph of the settlor's spouse include, in a case where the settlor has died less than two years before the interest comes to an end or the interest comes to an end before 1st April 1977, references to the settlor's widow or widower.

(7) Where the person beneficially entitled to the interest is the surviving spouse of a person who has died before 13th November 1974, tax shall not be chargeable under this paragraph if the value of the property in which the interest subsists would, by virtue of section 22 (4) of this Act, have been left out of account in determining the value of his estate had he died immediately before the coming to an end of the interest.

(8) The tax chargeable under this paragraph in a case where—

(*a*) the settlement was made before 27th March 1974; and

(*b*) the interest comes to an end before 10th December 1974;

shall not in any case exceed the tax that would be so chargeable if the values transferred by previous chargeable transfers made by the person beneficially entitled to the interest had been equal to the values (if any) on which tax is chargeable under this paragraph on the earlier termination of an interest in the settled property.

(9) Where a transaction is made between the trustees of the settlement and a person who is, or is connected with,—

(*a*) the person beneficially entitled to an interest in the property; or

(*b*) a person beneficially entitled to any other interest in that property or to any interest in any other property comprised in the settlement; or

(*c*) a person for whose benefit any of the settled property may be applied,

and, as a result of the transaction, the value of the first-mentioned property is less than it would be but for the transaction, a corresponding part of the interest shall be deemed for the purposes of this paragraph to come to an end, unless the transaction is such that, were the trustees beneficially entitled to the settled property, it would be a transfer of value.

(10) References in this paragraph to any property and to an interest in any property include references to part of any property or interest; and—

(*a*) the tax chargeable under this paragraph on the coming to an end of part of an interest shall be charged as if the value of the property (or part) in which the interest subsisted were a corresponding part of the whole thereof; and

(*b*) if the value of the property (or part) to which or to an interest in which a person becomes entitled as mentioned in sub-paragraph (3) above is less than the value on which tax would be chargeable apart from that sub-paragraph, tax shall be chargeable on a value equal to the difference.

(11) Tax shall not be chargeable under this paragraph if the settled property is excluded property.

Relief for successive charges on interest in possession

2–71   5.—(1) Where the value transferred by a chargeable transfer falls to be determined by reference to the value of any settled property in which there subsists an interest in possession to which the transferor is entitled, and—

(*a*) the value transferred by an earlier chargeable transfer also fell to be determined by reference to the value of that property; and

(*b*) that earlier transfer either was or included the making of the settlement or was made after the making of the settlement;

then, if the period between those transfers is not more than four years, tax shall be charged as if the value of that property were reduced—

  (i) by 80 per cent. if that period is one year or less;

 (ii) by 60 per cent. if that period is more than one year but not more than two years;

(iii) by 40 per cent. if that period is more than two years but not more than three years; and

(iv) by 20 per cent. if that period is more than three years.

(2) Where the transferor became entitled to the interest—
    (*a*) on a death on which estate duty was payable in respect of the settled property; or
    (*b*) in consequence of—
        (i) a gift inter vivos; or
        (ii) a disposition or determination of a beneficial interest in possession in any property comprised in a setttlement, where, by reason of the gift or interest, estate duty or capital transfer tax under section 22 (5) of this Act was payable on a subsequent death in respect of the settled property,
sub-paragraph (1) above shall apply as if the period referred to therein were the period between the death and the chargeable transfer.

Charge on capital distributions of settled property

12–72   **6.**—(1) Where a distribution payment is made out of property comprised in a settlement and at the time the payment is made no interest in possession subsists in the property or in the part of it out of which the payment is made, the payment is in this Schedule referred to as a capital distribution.

(2) Where a person becomes entitled to an interest in possession in the whole or any part of the property comprised in a settlement at a time when no such interest subsists in the property or that part, a capital distribution shall be treated as being made out of the property or that part of the property; and the amount of the distribution shall be taken to be equal to the value at that time of the property or, if the interest is in part only of that property, of that part.

(3) Where, at a time when no interest in possession subsists in property comprised in a settlement or in a part of that property, a transaction is made between the trustees of the settlement and a person who is, or is connected with,—
    (*a*) a person beneficially entitled to an interest in any of the settled property; or
    (*b*) a person for whose benefit any of the settled property may be applied;
and, as a result of the transaction, the value of the property or part is less than it would be but for the transaction, a capital distribution shall be treated as being made out of the property or part of an amount equal to that by which that value is less, unless the transaction is such that, were the trustees beneficially entitled to the settled property, it would not be a transfer of value.

(4) Tax shall be charged on any capital distribution as on the value transferred by a chargeable transfer where—
    (*a*) The value transferred less the tax payable on it is equal to the amount of the capital distribution; and
    (*b*) the rate applicable is that specified in paragraphs 7 to 9 below;
and in those paragraphs " the assumed transferor " means the person who would be the transferor in relation to the chargeable transfer assumed by this sub-paragraph and the appropriate Table for the purposes of those paragraphs (including the calculation of any tax that would have been chargeable as mentioned in paragraph 7 (2) (*a*) below) is the Second Table set out in section 37 (3) of this Act.

(5) The reference in sub-paragraph (4) (*a*) above to the tax payable on a capital distribution does not include any tax which is payable by a

person to whom a distribution payment is made; for in the case of a capital distribution treated as made under sub-paragraph (2) above or paragraph 15 (3) below, any tax which is payable out of the property whose value is taken as the amount of the capital distribution; and in relation to a capital distribution treated as made under sub-paragraph (3) above or paragraph 12 or 24 (2) below, sub-paragraph (4) (*a*) above shall have effect as if the words " less the tax payable on it " were omitted.

(6) Notwithstanding sub-paragraph (1) above, a distribution payment which is made to the settlor or the settlor's spouse shall not be a capital distribution if the settlor or, as the case may be, the settlor's spouse is domiciled in the United Kingdom at the time the payment is made . . .

The references in this sub-paragraph to the settlor's spouse include, in the case of a distribution payment made less than two years after the settlor's death or made before 1st April 1977, references to the settlor's widow or widower.

(6A) Where the person referred to in sub-paragraph (2) above is the settlor, the settlor's spouse or, if the settlor had died less than two years before the time there referred to, the settlor's widow or widower, and is domiciled in the United Kingdom at that time, that sub-paragraph shall have effect as if the reference in it to a capital distribution were a reference to a distribution payment to the settlor or, as the case may be, the settlor's spouse, widow or widower.

(7) *Repealed by F.A. 1976.*

(8) Where a person entitled to an interest in possession in part of the property comprised in a settlement became so entitled as a member of a class, sub-paragraph (2) above shall not apply on his becoming entitled, as such a member, to an interest in possession in another part of that property, if he becomes so entitled on the death under full age of another member of that class.

Rates of charge on capital distributions following chargeable transfers

7.—(1) This paragraph applies where, at or after the relevant time and before the capital distribution, there has been a transfer of value which satisfies the conditions stated in paragraph 11 (2) below.

(2) So far as the amount on which tax is chargeable, when added to the amount of all previous distribution payments made out of property comprised in the settlement, does not exceed the initial value, the rate chargeable shall be equal to the fraction of which—

  (*a*) the numerator is the amount of the tax which would have been charged on the value transferred by the relevant transfer, or such part of that amount as is attributable to the initial value, if the value so transferred had been equal to the aggregate of the initial values of the settlement and any related settlement; and

  (*b*) the denominator is the initial value.

(3) So far as the amount on which tax is chargeable, when so added, exceeds the initial value, the rate or rates chargeable shall be the rate or rates that would be applicable if the assumed transferor had made previous chargeable transfers and the aggregate of the values transferred by them were equal to the aggregate of—

  (*a*) the values transferred by any chargeable transfers which the person who made the relevant transfer had made before the relevant transfer;

(b) the aggregate of the initial values of the settlement and any related settlement; and

(c) the amounts of any previous distribution payments out of property comprised in the settlement, so far as the tax (if any) chargeable thereon is chargeable in accordance with this sub-paragraph.

Rate of charge on other capital distributions

12–73
    8.—(1) This paragraph applies where paragraph 7 above does not apply.

(2) The rate or rates chargeable shall be the rate or rates that would be applicable if the assumed transferor—

(a) had made previous chargeable transfers in any case where there had been previous distribution payments made on or after 27th March 1974 out of the settled property; but

(b) had made no previous chargeable transfers in any other case;

and, where paragraph (a) above applies, the aggregate of the values transferred by the previous chargeable transfers were equal to the aggregate amounts of the previous distribution payments mentioned therein.

Further property added by settlor

12–74
    9.—(1) The following provisions of this paragraph apply where, by a transfer of value made by the settlor at any time after the making of the settlement and after 26th March 1974 (in this paragraph referred to as " the subsequent transfer ") further property is added to the property comprised in the settlement immediately before the subsequent transfer (in this paragraph referred to as " the previous property ").

(2) The subsequent transfer shall be treated for the purposes of paragraphs 6 to 8 above as the making of a separate settlement and the further property comprised in that separate settlement, and the following provisions of this paragraph shall apply for determining the property out of which any capital distributions made after the subsequent transfer are to be treated as made.

(3) If paragraph 7 above would have applied to a capital distribution made immediately before the subsequent transfer, any capital distribution made after the subsequent transfer shall be treated as made—

(a) out of the previous property, if or to the extent that the amount of the distribution, when added to the amount of all previous distribution payments made out of the settled property, does not exceed the previous value defined in sub-paragraph (4) below; and

(b) out of the further property in any other case.

(4) For the purposes of sub-paragraph (3) above the previous value is the initial value, increased, if there was an earlier transfer which is a " subsequent transfer " as defined above, by the value, immediately after the earlier transfer, of any property added by it to the settled property.

(5) If paragraph 7 above would not have applied to a capital distribution made immediately before the subsequent transfer, any capital distribution made after the subsequent transfer shall be treated as made—

(a) out of the previous property, if or to the extent that the amount of the distribution, when added to the amount of any previous distribution payment made since the subsequent transfer, does not exceed the value of the settled property immediately before the subsequent transfer; and

(*b*) out of further property in any other case;

and accordingly, where paragraph (*b*) above applies, the rate or rates chargeable shall be determined in accordance with paragraph 7 above (and, where there is a further subsequent transfer, in accordance with sub-paragraphs (3) and (4) above).

Capital distributions after termination of interest of settlor or settlor's spouse

12-75

10. Where, after the termination of an interest in possession in a part (in this paragraph referred to as the chargeable part) of any property comprised in a settlement made after 26th March 1974, a capital distribution is made out of the chargeable part, and—

(*a*) the settlor or settlor's spouse was the person entitled to the interest before its termination, and either the settlor or the settlor's spouse was entitled to an interest in possession in the chargeable part immediately after the making of the settlement; and

(*b*) the making of the settlement either was not a transfer of value or was an exempt transfer or a transfer exempt to the extent of the value of the chargeable part;

paragraphs 6 to 9 above shall apply as if the chargeable part were comprised in a separate settlement made by the person entitled to the first-mentioned interest on its termination and the termination of the interest were the relevant transfer; and as if the subsequent termination of any interest of his in any other part of the settled property were an addition made by him to the property comprised in that separate settlement.

10A. Where a capital distribution is made on the same day and out of property comprised in the same settlement as a distribution payment that is not a capital distribution, the capital distribution shall for the purpose of paragraphs 7 to 9 above be treated as made before the distribution payment.

Interpretation of paragraphs 6 to 10

12-76

11.—(1) The following provisions apply for the interpretation of paragraphs 6 to 10 above.

(2) The relevant transfer, in relation to any settlement, is the first transfer of value made at or after the relevant time which satisfies the conditions—

(*a*) that the value of the property comprised in the settlement or of that part of it out of which the capital distributions are made was taken into account in determining the value transferred; and

(*b*) that the transfer was, or would but for paragraph 19 (2) below or paragraphs 2 to 7 of Schedule 6 to this Act or section 76 of the Finance Act 1976 have been, a chargeable transfer; and

(*c*) that, if the settlement was made before 27th March 1974, the transfer was made neither under paragraph 4 above nor on death;

and where it was not a chargeable transfer (or it was a chargeable transfer of some only of the value transferred by it) the reference in paragraph 7 (2) (*a*) above to the tax which would have been charged is a reference to the tax which would have been charged but for paragraph 19 (2) below or paragraphs 2 to 7 of Schedule 6 to this Act or section 76 of the Finance Act 1976.

(3) The relevant time, in relation to any settlement, is, if the settled property became comprised in the settlement on the death of any person, the time immediately before his death, and, in any other case, the time when the settlement was made.

(4) Where, by the same disposition, property ceases to be comprised in one settlement and becomes comprised in another settlement, the property shall be treated as remaining comprised in the first settlement.

(5) The amount of any distribution payment which is a capital distribution shall be taken (except for the purposes of paragraph 6 (4) (*a*)) to be the amount on which tax is chargeable in respect of it.

(6) A settlement is related to another if the same transfer of value is the relevant transfer in relation to both; and for this purpose transfers of value made by the same person on the same day shall be treated as one.

(7) "Distribution payment" means, subject to sub-paragraph (8) below, any payment which—

(*a*) is not income of any person for any of the purposes of income tax and would not for any of those purposes be income of a person not resident in the United Kingdom if he were so resident; and

(*b*) is not a payment in respect of costs or expenses; and "payment" includes the transfer of assets other than money.

(8) The amount of any capital distribution treated as made under paragraph 6 (2) or (3) above or paragraph 15 (3) or 24 (2) below shall also be deemed to be a distribution payment; but where, after an amount has been taken into account by virtue of this sub-paragraph or paragraph 6 (6A) above as a distribution payment made out of the whole or part of any property, one or more distribution payments are made (otherwise than under this sub-paragraph or paragraph 6 (6A) above) out of that property or part, the amount so taken into account shall be treated as reducing the amount of those payments.

(9) "Initial value", in relation to any settlement, means the value, immediately after the relevant transfer, of the property then comprised in the settlement.

(10) "Interest in possession" means an interest in possession to which an individual is beneficially entitled or, if the following conditions are satisfied, an interest in possession to which a company is beneficially entitled, the conditions being—

(*a*) that the business of the company consists wholly or mainly in the acquisition of interests in settled property; and

(*b*) that the company has acquired the interest for full consideration in money or money's worth from an individual who was beneficially entitled to the interest.

(11) References to settled property shall be construed as referring only to property which is not excluded property.

Periodic charge to tax

12–77 12.—(1) Where, at a relevant anniversary, no interest in possession subsists in the property comprised in a settlement or in a part of that property, a capital distribution of an amount equal to the value immediately before that anniversary of that property or part shall be treated as made out of that property or part, and tax shall be charged on a capital distribution so treated as made at 30 per cent. of the rate at which it would be chargeable under paragraphs 6 to 10 above on a capital distribution of the same amount made at the same date, but subject to any reduction under sub-paragraph (4) below.

(2) Where the trustees of the settlement are not resident in the United Kingdom a capital distribution of a corresponding amount shall also be treated as made if no interest in possession subsists in the property or in a part thereof at the end of any year in the period of ten years ending with a relevant anniversary, except the last and except any year ending before 1st January 1976; and tax shall be charged on a capital distribution so treated as made at 3 per cent. of the rate at which it would be chargeable under paragraphs 6 to 10 above on a capital distribution of the same amount made at the same date.

(3) Any tax charged by virtue of sub-paragraph (2) above shall be allowed as a credit against the tax chargeable on the next capital distribution made out of the property or, as the case may be, out of the part concerned, not being a capital distribution treated as made under that sub-paragraph.

(4) Where the whole or part of the value mentioned in sub-paragraph (1) above is attributable to property—

(*a*) which was added by the settlor after the end of the first of the ten years ending with the relevant anniversary; or

(*b*) in which an interest in possession subsisted throughout at least one of those ten years;

the rate at which, under sub-paragraph (1) above, tax is chargeable on that value or that part of it shall be reduced by one-tenth for each of those ten years throughout which either the settled property did not include that property, or an interest in possession subsisted in that property.

(5) For the purposes of this paragraph trustees of a settlement shall be regarded as not resident in the United Kingdom unless the general administration of the settlement is ordinarily carried on in the United Kingdom and the trustees or a majority of them (and, where there is more than one class of trustees, a majority of each class) are for the time being resident in the United Kingdom.

(6) For the purposes of this paragraph a relevant anniversary, in relation to a settlement, is the end of the ten years beginning with the date of the transfer of value which is the relevant transfer in relation to the settlement (or would be the relevant transfer in relation to it if dispositions made or events happening at that date could be chargeable transfers and paragraph (*c*) of paragraph 11 (2) above were omitted) and the end of every subsequent ten years; but no date falling before 1st April 1980 is a relevant anniversary.

(7) Paragraph 11 above shall apply for the interpretation of this paragraph as it applies for the interpretation of paragraphs 6 to 10, except that paragraph 11 (4) shall be disregarded in determining in relation to any settled property whether the trustees are resident in the United Kingdom.

(8) *Repealed by F.A. 1976.*

Tax credit for periodic charge

13.—(1) Subject to sub-paragraph (2) below, where tax is charged at a relevant anniversary on any capital distribution treated by virtue of paragraph 12 (1) above as made out of any property, the effective rate at which that tax is charged (taking into account any reduction under paragraph 12 (4) above) shall reduce the rate at which, apart from this paragraph, tax would be chargeable on any capital distribution made out of that property on or not later than twenty years after that relevant anniversary not being a capital distribution treated as made under paragraph 12 above.

(2) The amounts by which tax on any capital distribution is reduced under sub-paragraph (1) above by reason of any tax charged under paragraph 12 (1) above shall not together exceed the amount of the tax so charged.

(3) In this paragraph " relevant anniversary " has the same meaning as in paragraph 12 above.

Transitional relief for settlements made before 27th March 1974

14.—(1) In relation to a settlement made before 27th March 1974 paragraphs 6 to 12 above shall apply with the following modifications.

(2) Subject to sub-paragraphs (3) to (5) below, the rate at which tax is chargeable on any capital distribution made before 1st April 1980 out of property comprised in the settlement (but not on any capital distribution which, under paragraph 9 above, is treated as made out of property comprised in a separate settlement made after 26th March 1974) shall be the following percentage of the rate at which it would be chargeable apart from this paragraph, that is to say—

(*a*) 10 per cent. if the capital distribution is made before 1st April 1976;

(*b*) 12½ per cent. if it is made after 31st March 1976 but before 1st April 1977;

(*c*) 15 per cent. if it is made after 31st March 1977 but before 1st April 1978;

(*d*) 17½ per cent. if it is made after 31st March 1978 but before 1st April 1979; and

(*e*) 20 per cent. if it is made after 31st March 1979.

(3) Where any capital distribution made after 31st March 1976 but before 1st April 1977 could not have been made except as the result of some proceedings before a court, this paragraph shall have effect in relation to it as if it had been made before 1st April 1976.

(4) Sub-paragraph (2) above does not apply in relation to a capital distribution treated as made under paragraph 12 (2) above.

(5) Sub-paragraph (2) above does not apply—

(*a*) in relation to a capital distribution treated as made under paragraph 6 (2) above, unless the person becoming entitled as mentioned therein; or

(*b*) in relation to a capital distribution treated as made under paragraph 15 (3) below, unless each of the beneficiaries referred to therein living at the time of the capital distribution; or

(*c*) in relation to a distribution payment made for the benefit of any person, unless that person;

is an individual who is domiciled in the United Kingdom at the time the capital distribution is made . . .

(6) In this paragraph expressions defined for the purposes of paragraphs 6 to 10 above have the same meanings as in those paragraphs.

Accumulation and maintenance settlements

2–80   **15.**—(1) This paragraph applies to any settlement where—

(a) one or more persons (in this paragraph referred to as beneficiaries) will, on or before attaining a specified age not exceeding twenty-five, become entitled to, or to an interest in possession in, the settled property or part of it; and

(b) no interest in possession subsists in the settled property or part and the income from it is to be accumulated so far as not applied for the maintenance, education or benefit of a beneficiary; and

(c) either—

(i) not more than twenty-five years have elapsed since the day on which the settlement was made or, if it was later, since the time (or latest time) when the conditions stated in paragraphs (a) and (b) above became satisfied with respect to the property or part; or

(ii) all the persons who are or have been beneficiaries are or were either grandchildren of a common grandparent or children, widows or widowers of such grandchildren who were themselves beneficiaries but died before the time when, had they survived, they would have become entitled as mentioned in paragraph (a) above.

(2) Where this paragraph applies to a settlement—

(a) a payment made to a beneficiary out of the settled property or part concerned shall not be a capital distribution and a capital distribution shall not be treated as made under paragraph 6 (2) above on a beneficiary's becoming entitled to an interest in the property or part; and

(b) no capital distribution shall be treated as made out of the property or part by virtue of paragraph 12 above at any time during the period for which the income is to be accumulated as mentioned in sub-paragraph (1) (b) above.

(3) Where no interest in possession subsists in the property comprised in a settlement or some part of that property but the conditions stated in paragraphs (a) and (b) of sub-paragraph (1) above are not satisfied with respect to the property or part, then, if those conditions become satisfied with respect to the property or any part thereof a capital distribution shall be treated as being made out of the property or part and the amount of the distribution shall be taken to be equal to the value of the property with respect to which those conditions become satisfied.

(4) Where the conditions stated in paragraphs (a) and (b) of sub-paragraph (1) above were satisfied on 15th April 1976 with respect to any property comprised in a settlement made before that day, paragraph (c) (i) of that sub-paragraph shall have effect with the substitution of a reference to that day for the reference to the day on which the settlement was made, and the condition stated in paragraph (c) (ii) shall be treated as satisfied if—

229

(*a*) it is satisfied in respect of the period beginning with 15th April 1976; or

(*b*) it is satisfied in respect of the period beginning with 1st April 1977 and either there was no beneficiary living on 15th April 1976 or the beneficiaries on 1st April 1977 include a living beneficiary; or

(*c*) there is no power under the terms of the settlement whereby it could have become satisfied in respect of the period beginning with 1st April 1977, and the trusts of the settlement have not been varied at any time after 15th April 1976.

(5) In sub-paragraph (1) above " persons " includes unborn persons; but the conditions stated in paragraphs (*a*) and (*b*) of that sub-paragraph shall be treated as not satisfied unless there is or has been a living beneficiary.

(6) Paragraph 11 above shall apply for the interpretation of this paragraph as it applies for the interpretation of paragraphs 6 to 10; and for the purposes of this paragraph a person's children shall be taken to include his illegitimate children, his adopted children and his step-children.

Superannuation schemes

16.—(1) This paragraph applies to any scheme or fund mentioned in subsection (1) or subsection (2) of section 221 of the Taxes Act, to any fund to which section 218 of that Act applies, to any scheme approved under section 226 or 226A of that Act, to any exempt approved scheme or statutory scheme as defined in Chapter II of Part II of the Finance Act 1970 and to any other sponsored superannuation scheme as defined in section 226 (11) of the Taxes Act.

(2) An interest in or under a fund or scheme to which this paragraph applies which comes to an end on the death of the person entitled to it shall be left out of account in determining for the purposes of this Part of this Act the value of his estate immediately before his death, if the interest—

(*a*) is, or is a right to, a pension or annuity; and

(*b*) is not an interest resulting (whether by virtue of the instrument establishing the fund or scheme or otherwise) from the application of any benefit provided under the fund or scheme otherwise than by way of a pension or annuity.

(3) Paragraphs 3 and 4 above shall not apply in relation to an interest satisfying the conditions of paragraphs (*a*) and (*b*) of sub-paragraph (2) above; and where any tax chargeable on a transfer of value is attributable to the value of such an interest, the persons liable for it shall not include the trustees of the scheme or fund but shall, where the transfer is made on the death of the person entitled to the interest, include his personal representatives.

(4) In relation to an interest in or under a fund or scheme to which this paragraph applies, section 23 (2) of this Act shall apply as if the words " other than settled property " were omitted (in both places).

(5) Paragraphs 6 to 12 above shall not apply in relation to any property which is part of or held for the purposes of a fund or scheme to which this paragraph applies.

(6) The reference in sub-paragraph (5) above to property which is part of or held for the purposes of a fund or scheme does not

include a reference to a benefit which, having become payable under the fund or scheme, becomes comprised in a settlement; and where in such a case the settlement is made by a person other than the person entitled to the benefit, the settlement shall for the purposes of this Part of this Act be treated as made by the person so entitled.

Trusts for benefit of employees, etc.

12-81 17.—(1) Where settled property is held on trusts which, either indefinitely or until the end of a period (whether defined by a date or in some other way) do not permit any of the settled property to be applied otherwise than for the benefit of—

    (*a*) persons of a class defined by reference to employment in a particular trade, profession or undertaking or employment by, or office with, a body carrying on a trade, profession or undertaking; or

    (*b*) persons of a class defined by reference to marriage or relationship to, or dependence on, persons of a class defined as mentioned in paragraph (*a*) above; or

    (*c*) charities;

then, subject to sub-paragraph (2) below, this paragraph applies to that settled property or, as the case may be, applies to it during that period.

(2) Where any such class is defined by reference to employment by or office with a particular body this paragraph applies to the settled property only if the class comprises all or most of the persons employed by or holding office with that body.

(3) Where this paragraph applies to any settled property—

    (*a*) the property shall be treated as comprised in one settlement, whether or not it would fall to be so treated apart from this paragraph; and

    (*b*) an interest in possession in any part of the settled property shall be disregarded for the purposes of this Schedule if that part is less than 5 per cent. of the whole; and

    (*c*) subject to sub-paragraph (4) below, a payment out of the settled property shall not be a capital distribution and shall not be taken into account as a distribution payment; and

    (*d*) paragraph 7 above shall not apply to any capital distribution made out of the settled property; and

    (*e*) paragraph 12 above shall apply subject to sub-paragraph (5) below, and paragraph 13 above shall not apply.

(4) Sub-paragraph (3) (*c*) above does not apply in relation to any payment made for the benefit of a person who is, or is connected with,—

    (*a*) a person who has directly or indirectly provided any of the settled property otherwise than by additions not exceeding in value £1,000 in any one year; or

    (*b*) in a case where the employment in question is employment by a close company, a person who is a participator in relation to that company and would, on a winding-up of the company, be entitled to not less than 5 per cent. of its assets.

(4A) Where any property to which this paragraph applies ceases to be comprised in a settlement and, either immediately or not more than one month later, the whole of it becomes comprised in another settlement, then, if this paragraph again applies to it when it becomes comprised in the second settlement, it shall be treated for all the purposes of this Part of this Act as if it had remained comprised in the first settlement.

(5) Where this paragraph applies to any settled property, tax which would otherwise be chargeable at a relevant anniversary under paragraph 12 (1) above shall be deferred until either a capital distribution is made or this paragraph ceases to apply to the settled property; and when any deferred tax becomes chargeable it shall be charged—

(a) at the rate at which it would be chargeable if the relevant anniversary fell on the date on which the tax becomes chargeable; and

(b) on an amount determined in accordance with the following provisions of this paragraph.

(6) Where any deferred tax becomes chargeable when this paragraph ceases to apply to the settled property it shall be chargeable on an amount equal to the current value of the settled property, except that if more than one relevant anniversary has passed and, accordingly, more than one deferred tax becomes chargeable—

(a) the second deferred tax shall be charged on that value less the amount of the first deferred tax; and

(b) the third deferred tax (if any) shall be charged on the amount found under paragraph (a) above less the amount of the second deferred tax;

and so on.

(7) Where any of the deferred tax becomes chargeable when a capital distribution is made—

(a) it shall be chargeable on an amount determined under sub-paragraph (8) below; and

(b) the amount of the tax shall reduce the amount on which tax is chargeable on that capital distribution (and if it exceeds that amount the excess shall reduce the amount on which tax is chargeable on the next capital distribution, and so on).

(8) So far as any tax which would otherwise be chargeable on a relevant anniversary becomes chargeable when a capital distribution is made it shall be charged on an amount (in this sub-paragraph referred to as the first amount) equal to the proper proportion of the current value of the property out of which the capital distribution is made; and where the capital distribution is made after the next relevant anniversary and, accordingly, more than one deferred tax becomes chargeable—

(a) the second deferred tax shall be charged on the first amount less the amount of the first deferred tax; and

(b) the third deferred tax (if any) shall be charged on the amount found under paragraph (a) above less the amount of the second deferred tax;

and so on.

(9) For the purposes of this paragraph—

(a) the current value of any property is its value at the time any tax deferred under this paragraph becomes chargeable; and

(b) the proper proportion of the current value of any property out of which a capital distribution is made is the proportion which the amount on which tax would, apart from sub-paragraph (7) (b) above, be chargeable on the capital distribution bears to that current value;

and in this paragraph " close company " and " participator " have the same meanings as in section 39 of this Act, " relevant anniversary " has the same meaning as in paragraph 12 above and " year " has the same meaning as in paragraph 2 of Schedule 6 to this Act.

17A.—(1) In relation to property comprised in a settlement to which this paragraph applies, paragraph 17 above shall have effect as if newspaper publishing companies were included among the persons within paragraphs (*a*) to (*c*) of sub-paragraph (1) of that paragraph.

(2) This paragraph applies to a settlement if shares in a newspaper publishing company or a newspaper holding company are the only or principal property comprised in the settlement.

(3) In this paragraph—

"newspaper publishing company" means a company whose business consists wholly or mainly in the publication of newspapers in the United Kingdom; and

" newspaper holding company " means a company which—

(*a*) has as its only or principal asset shares in a newspaper publishing company, and

(*b*) has powers of voting on all or most questions affecting the publishing company as a whole which if exercised would yield a majority of the votes capable of being exercised thereon;

and for the purposes of this paragraph shares shall be treated as the principal property comprised in a settlement or the principal asset of a company if the remaining property comprised in the settlement or the remaining assets of the company are such as may be reasonably required to enable the trustees or the company to secure the operation of the newspaper publishing company concerned.

Protective trusts

18.—(1) This paragraph applies to settled property held on trusts to the like effect as those specified in section 33 (1) of the Trustee Act 1925; and in this paragraph " the principal beneficiary " and " the trust period " have the same meanings as in that section.

(2) Where this paragraph applies to any settled property—

(*a*) tax shall not be charged under paragraph 4 (2) above on the coming to an end of the principal beneficiary's interest in the property if the property is then held on discretionary trusts to the like effect as those specified in paragraph (ii) of the said section 33 (1); and

(*b*) a distribution payment made out of the settled property for the benefit of the principal beneficiary shall not be a capital distribution.

(3) Sub-paragraphs (5) to (9) of paragraph 17 above shall apply where this paragraph applies to any settled property as if the references to that paragraph were references to this paragraph and references to that paragraph ceasing to apply to the settled property included references to the coming to an end of the trust period.

Trusts for benefit of mentally disabled persons

19.—(1) This paragraph applies to settled property held on trusts under which, during the life of a mentally disabled person, no interest in possession in the settled property subsists and which secure that

233

any of the settled property which is applied during his life is applied only or mainly for his benefit.

(2) Where this paragraph applies to any settled property, then—

    (*a*) if the mentally disabled person is the settlor, neither the making of the settlement nor any addition made by him to the settled property shall be a chargeable transfer; and

    (*b*) a distribution payment made out of the settled property for the benefit of the mentally disabled person shall not be a capital distribution.

(3) Sub-paragraphs (5) to (9) of paragraph 17 above shall apply where this paragraph applies to any settled property as if the references to that paragraph were references to this paragraph and references to that paragraph ceasing to apply to the settled property included references to the death of the mentally disabled person.

(4) In this paragraph " mentally disabled person " means a person who by reason of mental disorder within the meaning of the Mental Health Act 1959 is incapable of administering his property or managing his affairs.

Trustees' annuities etc.

12–84   **19A.** Where under the terms of a settlement a person is entitled by way of remuneration for his services as trustee to an interest in possession in property comprised in the settlement, then, except to the extent that the interest represents more than a reasonable amount of remuneration,—

    (*a*) the interest shall be left out of account in determining for the purposes of this Part of this Act the value of his estate immediately before his death, and

    (*b*) tax shall not be charged under paragraph 4 (2) above when the interest comes to an end.

Charitable trusts

12–85   **20.** Paragraphs 6 to 12 above do not apply in relation to settled property held for charitable purposes only.

Compensation funds

21. Paragraphs 6 to 12 above do not apply in relation to any fund which is maintained or administered by a representative association of persons carrying on a trade or profession and the only or main objects of which are compensation for or relief of losses or hardship incurred or likely to be incurred through the default or alleged default of persons carrying on the trade or profession or of their agents or servants.

Administration period

12–86   **22.**—(1) Where a person would have been entitled to any interest in possession in the whole or part of the residue of the estate of a deceased person had the administration of that estate been completed the same consequences shall follow under this Schedule as if he had become entitled to an interest in possession in the unadministered estate and in the property (if any) representing ascertained residue, or in a corresponding part of it, on the date as from which the whole or part of the income of the residue would have been attributable to his interest had the residue been ascertained immediately after the death of the deceased person.

(2) In this paragraph—

    (*a*) " unadministered estate " means all the property for the time being held by personal representatives as such, excluding property devolving on them otherwise than as assets for the payment of debts and excluding property that is the subject of a specific disposition, and making due allowance for outstanding charges on residue and for any adjustments between capital and income remaining to be made in due course of administration;

    (*b*) " ascertained residue " means property which, having ceased to be held by the personal representatives as such, is held as part of the residue;

    (*c*) " charges on residue," and " specific disposition " have the same meanings as in Part XV of the Taxes Act and the reference to the completion of the administration of an estate shall be construed as if contained in that Part.

Survivorship clauses

12–87   **22A.**—(1) Where under the terms of a will or otherwise property is held for any person on condition that he survives another for a specified period of not more than six months, this Part of this Act shall apply as if the dispositions taking effect at the end of the period or, if he does not survive until then, on his death (including any such disposition which has effect by operation of law or is a separate disposition of the income from the property) had had effect from the beginning of the period.

(2) Sub-paragraph (1) above does not affect the application of this Part of this Act in relation to any distribution or application of property occurring before the dispositions there mentioned take effect.

(3) Where the death with which the period mentioned in sub-paragraph (1) begins occurred before 13th March 1975, that sub-paragraph shall not apply in relation to any property if or to the extent that, by virtue of section 121 (1) (*c*) of the Finance Act 1972 (relief for property given to a surviving spouse), the value attributable to it was disregarded for the purposes of estate duty chargeable on that death.

Sales and mortgages of reversionary interests

2–88   **23.**—(1) Where a reversionary interest in settled property was before 27th March 1974 sold or mortgaged for full consideration in money or money's worth, no greater amount of tax shall be payable by the purchaser or mortgagee when the interest falls into possession than the amounts of estate duty that would have been payable by him if none of the provisions of this Act had been passed; and any tax which, by virtue of this paragraph, is not payable by the mortgagee but which is payable by the mortgagor shall rank as a charge subsequent to that of the mortgagee.

(2) Where the interest was sold or mortgaged to a close company in relation to which the person entitled to the interest was a participator, sub-paragraph (1) above applies only to the extent that other persons had rights and interests in the company.

(3) Sub-paragraph (2) above shall be construed as if contained in section 39 of this Act.

12–89 24.—(1) In relation to a person who is a participator in his capacity as trustee of a settlement, subsection (1) of section 39 of this Act shall not apply; and

    (*a*) the references in that section to subsection (1) thereof shall have effect as references to sub-paragraph (2) below; and

    (*b*) in relation to tax chargeable by virtue of sub-paragraph (2) below, subsections (4) and (8D) of that section shall apply with the necessary modifications.

(2) Where any part of the value transferred by a close company is apportioned to a trustee of a settlement under section 39 of this Act, then—

    (*a*) if an interest in possession subsists in the settled property a part of that interest corresponding to such part of the property as is of a value equal to the part so apportioned less the amount specified in sub-paragraph (3) below shall be treated for the purposes of this Schedule as having come to an end on the making of the transfer; and

    (*b*) if no interest in possession subsists in the settled property, the part of the value so apportioned less the amount specified in sub-paragraph (3) below shall be treated as a capital distribution made at the time of the transfer;

and where an interest in possession subsists in part only of the settled property paragraphs (*a*) and (*b*) above shall apply with the necessary adjustments of the values and amounts referred to therein.

(3) The amount referred to in paragraphs (*a*) and (*b*) of sub-paragraph (2) above is the amount (if any) by which the value of the settled property is more than it would be apart from the company's transfer, leaving out of account the value of any rights or interests in the company.

(4) Nothing in subsection (4) of section 39 of this Act shall be taken to prevent a transfer of value assumed to have been made by a person falling under subsection (3) (*a*) of that section from being a relevant transfer as defined in paragraph 11 above.

(5) Where a close company is entitled to an interest in possession in settled property the persons who are participators in relation to the company shall be treated for the purposes of this Schedule as being the persons beneficially entitled to that interest according to their respective rights and interests in the company.

(6) In this paragraph expressions defined in section 39 of this Act have the same meanings as in that section.

SCHEDULE 6

Section 29

EXEMPT TRANSFERS

PART I

DESCRIPTION

Transfer between spouses

12–90 1.—(1) Subject to the provisions of Part II of this Schedule and the following provisions of this paragraph, a transfer of value is an exempt transfer to the extent that the value transferred is attributable to property which becomes comprised in the estate of the transferor's spouse or, so far as the value transferred is not so attributable, to the extent that that estate is increased.

(2) If, immediately before the transfer, the transferor but not the transferor's spouse is domiciled in the United Kingdom the value in respect of which the transfer is exempt (calculated as a value on which no tax is payable) shall not exceed £15,000 less any amount previously taken into account for the purposes of the exemption conferred by this paragraph.

(3) Where the transfer is made on death and the whole or part of the value of any property which devolved on or was given to the spouse (within the meaning of section 121 of and Schedule 26 to the Finance Act 1972) would have been included under section 22 (5) of this Act had it not fallen to be disregarded under section 121 of that Act, the value that would have been so included shall reduce the £15,000 mentioned in sub-paragraph (2) above.

(4) In its application to Northern Ireland, sub-paragraph (3) above shall have effect as if for the references to section 121 of and Schedule 26 to the Finance Act 1972 there were substituted references to Article 5 of and Schedule 2 to the Finance (Northern Ireland) Order 1972.

Values not exceeding £2,000

2.—(1) Transfers of value made by a transferor in any one year are exempt to the extent that values transferred by them (calculated as values on which no tax is payable) do not exceed £2,000.

(2) Where those values (if any) fall short of £2,000, the amount by which they so fall short shall, in relation to the next following year, be added to the £2,000 mentioned in sub-paragraph (1) above; and where they exceed £2,000 the excess—

  (*a*) shall, as between transfers made on different days, be attributed so far as possible, to a later rather than an earlier transfer; and

  (*b*) shall, as between transfers made on the same day, be attributed to them in proportion to the values transferred by them.

(3) In this paragraph "year" means the period beginning with 27th March 1974 and ending with 5th April 1974, and any subsequent period of twelve months ending with 5th April.

3.—(1) In relation to the period beginning with 27th March 1974 and ending with 5th April 1974 and the period of twelve months ending with 5th April 1975, paragraph 2 above shall have effect as if for the references to £1,000 there were substituted references to whichever of the following is the greater—

  (*a*) £1,000, and

  (*b*) the aggregate value of gifts made by the transferor in that period and qualifying for small gifts relief from estate duty.

(2) For the purposes of this paragraph a gift qualifying for small gifts relief from estate duty is a gift which would by virtue of section 59 (2) of the Finance (1909–10) Act 1910 or section 33 of the Finance Act 1949 or section 6 of the Finance Act (Northern Irland) 1949 have been excluded from the property passing on the donor's death for the purposes of estate duty if he had died immediately after making the gift.

Small gifts to same person

4.—(1) Transfers of value made by a transferor in any one year by outright gifts to any one person are exempt to the extent that the values transferred by them (calculated as values on which no tax is chargeable) do not exceed £100.

(2) In this paragraph " year " has the same meaning as in paragraph 2 above.

Normal expenditure out of income

5.—(1) A transfer of value is an exempt transfer if, or to the extent that, it is shown—

    (*a*) that it was made as part of the normal expenditure of the transferor; and

    (*b*) that (taking one year with another) it was made out of his income; and

    (*c*) that, after allowing for all transfers of value part of his normal expenditure, the transferor was left with sufficient income to maintain his usual standard of living.

(2) A payment of a premium on a policy of insurance on the transferor's life, or a gift of money or money's worth applied, directly or indirectly, in payment of such a premium, shall not for the purposes of this paragraph be regarded as part of his normal expenditure if, when the insurance was made, or at any earlier or later time, an annuity was purchased on his life, unless it is shown that the purchase of the annuity and the making or any variation of the insurance or of any prior insurance for which the first-mentioned insurance was directly or indirectly substituted, were not associated operations.

(3) Where a purchased life annuity (within the meaning of section 230 of the Taxes Act) was purchased after 12th November 1974 then, in relation to transfers of value made after 5th April 1975, so much of the annuity as is, for the purposes of the provisions of the Tax Acts relating to income tax on annuities and other annual payments, treated as the capital element contained in the annuity, shall not be regarded as part of the transferor's income for the purposes of this paragraph.

Gifts in consideration of marriage

6.—(1) Transfers of value made by gifts in consideration of marriage are exempt to the extent that the values transferred by such transfers made by any one transferor in respect of any one marriage (calculated as values on which no tax is payable) do not exceed—

    (*a*) in the case of gifts within sub-paragraph (2) below by a parent of a party to the marriage, £5,000;

    (*b*) in the case of other gifts within sub-paragraph (2) below, £2,500; and

    (*c*) in any other case £1,000;

any excess being attributed to the transfers in proportion to the values transferred.

(2) A gift is within this sub-paragraph if—

    (*a*) it is an outright gift to a child or remoter descendant of the transferor, or

    (*b*) the transferor is a parent or remoter ancestor of either party to the marriage, and either the gift is an outright gift to the other party to the marriage or the property comprised in the gift is settled by the gift, or (*c*) the transferor is a party to the marriage, and either the gift is an outright gift to the other party to the marriage or the property comprised in the gift is settled by the gift;

and in this paragraph " child " includes an illegitimate child, an adopted child and a step-child and " parent ", " descendant " and " ancestor " shall be construed accordingly.

(3) A disposition shall not be treated for the purposes of this paragraph as a gift made in consideration of marriage—

(*a*) in the case of an outright gift, if or in so far as it is a gift to a person other than a party to the marriage;

(*b*) in the case of any other disposition, if the persons who are or may become entitled to any benefit under the disposition include any person other than—

(i) the parties to the marriage, issue of the marriage, or a wife or husband of any such issue;

(ii) persons becoming entitled on the failure of trusts for any such issue under which trust property would (subject only to any power of appointment to a person falling within sub-paragraph (i) or (iii) of this paragraph) vest indefeasibly on the attainment of a specified age or either on the attainment of such an age or on some earlier event, or persons becoming entitled (subject as aforesaid) on the failure of any limitation in tail;

(iii) a subsequent wife or husband of a party to the marriage, or any issue, or the wife or husband of any issue, of a subsequent marriage of either party;

(iv) persons becoming entitled under such trusts, subsisting under the law of England or of Northern Ireland, as are specified in section 33 (1) of the Trustee Act 1925 or section 34 (1) of the Trustee Act (Northern Ireland) 1958 (protective trusts), the principal beneficiary being a person falling within sub-paragraph (i) or (iii) of this paragraph, or under such trusts, modified by the enlargement, as respects any period during which there is no such issue as aforesaid in existence, of the class of potential beneficiaries specified in paragraph (ii) of the said section 33 (1) or paragraph (*b*) of the said section 34 (1);

(v) persons becoming entitled under trusts subsisting under the law of Scotland and corresponding with such trusts as are mentioned in sub-paragraph (iv) above;

(vi) as respects a reasonable amount of remuneration, the trustees of the settlement.

(4) References in sub-paragraph (3) above to issue shall apply as if any person legitimated by a marriage, or adopted by the husband and wife jointly, were included among the issue of that marriage.

7. In relation to the marriages before the passing of this Act paragraph 6 above shall have effect with the substitution of a reference to £5,000 for the reference in sub-paragraph (1) to £2,500.

Interpretation of paragraphs 2 to 7

8. Section 51 (2) of this Act does not apply to the interpretation of paragraphs 2 to 7 above [but references in paragraph 2 above to transfers of value made by a transferor and to the values transferred by them (calculated as there mentioned) include references to apportionments made to a person under section 39 of this Act and the amounts for the tax on which (if charged) he would be liable].

9. *Repealed by F.A. 1976.*

Gifts to charities

12–94   **10.**—(1) Subject to the provisions of Part II of this Schedule, transfers of value are exempt to the extent that the values transferred by them—

(*a*) are attributable to property which is given to charities; and

(*b*) so far as made on or within one year of the death of the transferor, do not exceed £100,000.

(2) Subject to the provisions of Part II of this Schedule, where property comprised in a settlement is given to a charity, the payment or transfer of the property out of the settlement shall not be a distribution payment for the purposes of Schedule 5 to this Act.

(3) For the purposes of this paragraph property is given to charities if it becomes the property of charities or is held on trust for charitable purposes only.

(4) Where, in the case of a transfer of value made on death, the whole or part of the value of any property which was given (within the meaning of section 121 of and Schedule 26 to the Finance Act 1972) to charities would have been included under section 22 (5) of this Act had it not fallen to be disregarded under section 121 of that Act, the value that would have been so included shall reduce the £100,000 mentioned in sub-paragraph (1) above.

(5) In its application to Northern Ireland, sub-paragraph (4) above shall have effect as if for the references to section 121 of and Schedule 26 to the Finance Act 1972 there were substituted references to Article 5 of and Schedule 2 to the Finance (Northern Ireland) Order 1972.

Gifts to political parties

12–95   **11.**—(1) Subject to the provisions of Part II of this Schedule, transfers of value are exempt to the extent that the values transferred by them—

(*a*) are attributable to property which becomes the property of a political party qualifying for exemption under this paragraph; and

(*b*) so far as made on or within one year of the death of the transferor, do not exceed £100,000.

(1A) Subject to the provisions of Part II of this Schedule, where property comprised in a settlement becomes the property of a political party qualifying for exemption under this paragraph, the payment or transfer of the property out of the settlement shall not be a distribution payment for the purposes of Schedule 5 to this Act.

(2) A political party qualifies for exemption under this paragraph if, at the last general election preceding the transfer of value,—

(*a*) two members of that party were elected to the House of Commons; or

(*b*) one member of that party was elected to the House of Commons and not less than one hundred and fifty thousand votes were given to candidates who were members of that party.

Gifts for national purposes etc.

12–96   **12.**—(1) Subject to the provisions of Part II of this Schedule a transfer of value is an exempt transfer to the extent that the value transferred by it is attributable to property which becomes the propery of—

The National Gallery.

The British Museum.

The Royal Scottish Museum.

The National Museum of Wales.

The Ulster Museum.

Any other similar national institution which exists wholly or mainly for the purpose of preserving for the public benefit a collection of scientific, historic or artistic interest and which is approved for the purposes of this paragraph by the Treasury.

Any museum or art gallery in the United Kingdom which exists wholly or mainly for that purpose and is maintained by a local authority or university in the United Kingdom.

Any library the main function of which is to serve the needs of teaching and research at a university in the United Kingdom.

The National Trust for Places of Historic Interest or Natural Beauty.

The National Trust for Scotland for Places of Historic Interest or Natural Beauty.

The National Art Collections Fund.

The Friends of the National Libraries.

The Historic Churches Preservation Trust.

The Nature Conservancy Council.

Any local authority.

Any Government department (including the National Debt Commissioners).

Any university or university college in the United Kingdom.

(2) Subject to the provisions of Part II of this Schedule, where property comprised in a settlement becomes the property of a body mentioned in sub-paragraph (1) above, the payment or transfer of the property out of the settlement shall not be a distribution payment for the purposes of Schedule 5 to this Act.

Gifts for public benefit

12–97   **13.**—(1) Subject to the provisions of Part II of this Schedule, a transfer of value is an exempt transfer to the extent that—

(a) the value transferred by it is attributable to property within sub-paragraph (2) below which becomes property of a body not established or conducted for profit; and

(b) the Treasury so direct (whether before or after the time of the transfer).

(1A) Subject to the provisions of Part II of this Schedule, where—

(a) property comprised in a settlement becomes at any time the property of a body not established or conducted for profit, and

(b) the Treasury so direct (whether before or after that time),

the payment or transfer of the property out of the settlement shall not be a distribution payment for the purposes of Schedule 5 to this Act.

(2) Property is within this sub-paragraph if it is—

(a) land which in the opinion of the Treasury is of outstanding scenic or historic or scientific interest;

(b) a building for the preservation of which special steps should in the opinion of the Treasury be taken by reason of its outstanding historic or architectural or aesthetic interest and the cost of preserving it;

(c) land used as the grounds of a building within paragraph (b) above;

(d) an object which at the time of the transfer is ordinarily kept in, and which is given with, a building within paragraph (b) above;

(e) property given as a source of income for the upkeep of property within any of the paragraphs of this sub-paragraph;

(f) a picture, print, book, manuscript, work of art or scientific collection which in the opinion of the Treasury is of national scientific, historic or artistic interest.

(3) The Treasury shall not give a direction under this paragraph—

(a) in relation to land within sub-paragraph (2) (a) above, unless in their opinion the body whose property it becomes is an appropriate one to be responsible for the preservation of its character;

(b) in relation to property within sub-paragraph (2) (b) or (f) above, unless in their opinion the body whose property it becomes is an appropriate one to be responsible for its preservation;

(c) in relation to property within sub-paragraph (2) (e) above, if or to the extent that, in the opinion of the Treasury, the property will produce more income than is needed (with a reasonable margin) for the upkeep of the other property in question.

(4) Before giving a direction under this paragraph in relation to any property (other than property within sub-paragraph (2) (e) above) the Treasury may require such undertakings to be entered into, including undertakings restricting the use or disposal of the property, as they think appropriate for securing the preservation of the property or its character and reasonable access to it for the public.

(5) Any undertaking entered into by virtue of sub-paragraph (4) above may be varied from time to time by agreement between the Treasury and the person bound by the undertaking, and the Treasury may require further undertakings to be entered into as a condition for agreeing to any such variation or consenting to anything for which their consent is required by any undertaking.

(6) The obligations imposed by any undertaking entered into by virtue of this paragraph shall be enforceable for the public benefit by injunction (or, in Scotland, by interdict or by petition under section 91 of the Court of Session Act 1868), and any purported disposition of property in contravention of an undertaking shall be void, as if the obligation had been imposed by Act of Parliament.

(7) Property is given with other property for the purposes of this paragraph if the value transferred by a transfer of value is attributable to both and both become the property of the same body or if both become the property of the same body on the making of the same payment or transfer out of a settlement.

(8) In this paragraph "national interest" includes interest within any part of the United Kingdom.

Gifts made before 10*th December* 1974 *and not relevant to estate duty*

12–98 **14.** A transfer of value made by any person before 10th December 1974 is exempt to the extent that the value transferred thereby is attributable to the value of any property which, if the transferor had died immediately after the transfer, would not have been treated for the purposes of estate duty as passing on his death.

PART II

EXCEPTIONS

12–99 **15.**—(1) Paragraphs 1 and 10 to 13 above and section 84 of the Finance Act 1976 do not apply in relation to any property if the testamentary or other disposition by which it is given takes effect on the termination after the transfer of value of any interest or period; but paragraph 1 above is not excluded by virtue of this sub-paragraph by reason only that the property is given to a spouse only if he survives the other spouse for a specified period.

(2) Paragraphs 1 and 10 to 13 above and section 84 of the Finance Act 1976 do not apply in relation to any property if the testamentary or other disposition by which it is given depends on a condition which is not satisfied within twelve months after the transfer.

(3) Paragraphs 10 to 13 above and section 84 of the Finance Act 1976 do not apply in relation to any property if—

(*a*) the testamentary or other disposition by which it is given is defeasible; or

(*b*) the property is an interest in other property and that interest is less than the donor's or the property . . . is given for a limited period; or

(*ba*) the property is an interest in possession in settled property and the settlement does not come to an end in relation to that settled property on the making of the transfer; or

(*bb*) the property is land or a building and is given subject to an interest reserved or created by the donor which entitles him, his spouse or a person connected with him to possession of, or to occupy, the whole or any part of the land or building rent-free or at a rent less than might be expected to be obtained in a transaction at arm's length between persons not connected with each other; or

(*bc*) the property is not land or a building and is given subject to an interest reserved or created by the donor other than—

(i) an interest created by him for full consideration in money or money's worth; or

(ii) an interest which does not substantially affect the enjoyment of the property by the person or body to whom it is given; or

(*c*) the property or any part of it may become applicable for purposes other than charitable purposes or those of a body mentioned in paragraph 11, 12 or 13 above;

except that paragraph (*b*) above shall not prevent paragraph 12 above from applying in relation to property consisting of the benefit of an agreement restricting the use of land.

(4) For the purposes of sub-paragraph (3) above—

(*a*) any question whether any interest is less than the donor's or whether property is given subject to an interest shall be decided as at a time twelve months after the transfer of value; and

(b) any disposition which has not been defeated at that time and is not defeasible after that time shall be treated as not being defeasible, whether or not it was capable of being defeated before that time.

(4A) Where a person or body acquires a reversionary interest in any settled property for a consideration in money or money's worth, paragraphs 1 and 10 to 13 above do not apply in relation to the property when it becomes the property of that person or body on the termination of the interest on which the reversionary interest is expectant.

(5) For the purposes of this paragraph property is given to any person or body if it becomes the property of or is held on trust for that person or body, and " donor " shall be construed accordingly.

(6) In a case where property is given by a payment or transfer out of a settlement this paragraph shall have effect as if—

(a) any reference to a transfer of value were a reference to the payment or transfer, and

(b) paragraphs (b) to (bc) of sub-paragraph (3) above were omitted.

PART III

SUPPLEMENTARY PROVISIONS

Preliminary

12–100   **16.** Where any one or more of paragraphs 1 and 10 to 13 above and sections 76 and 84 of the Finance Act 1976 apply in relation to a transfer of value but the transfer is not wholly exempt—

(a) any question as to the extent to which it is exempt or, where it is exempt up to a limit, how an excess over the limit is to be attributed to the gifts concerned shall be determined in accordance with paragraphs 17 to 21 below; and

(b) paragraph 22 shall have effect as respects the burden of tax.

Abatement not attributable to tax

12–101   **17.** Where a gift would be abated owing to an insufficiency of assets and without regard to any tax chargeable, the gift shall be treated for the purposes of the following provisions of this Part of this Schedule as so abated.

Abatement for tax—specific gifts

12–102   **18.** Where the value attributable, in accordance with paragraph 19 below, to specific gifts exceeds the value transferred the gifts shall be treated as reduced to the extent necessary to reduce their value to that of the value transferred; and the reduction shall be made in the order in which, under the terms of the relevant disposition or any rule of law, it would fall to be made on a distribution of assets.

Attribution of value to specific gifts

12–103   **19.**—(1) Such part of the value transferred shall be attributable to specific gifts as corresponds to the value of the gifts; but if or to the extent that the gifts—

(*a*) are not gifts with respect to which the transfer is exempt or are outside the limit up to which the transfer is exempt, and

(*b*) do not bear their own tax,

the amount corresponding to the value of the gifts shall be taken to be the amount arrived at in accordance with sub-paragraphs (3) to (3B) below.

(2) Where any question arises as to which of two or more specific gifts are outside the limit up to which a transfer is exempt or as to the extent to which a specific gift is outside that limit—

(*a*) the excess shall be attributed to gifts not bearing their own tax before being attributed to gifts bearing their own tax; and

(*b*) subject to paragraph (*a*) above, the excess shall be attributed to gifts in proportion to their values.

(3) Where the only gifts with respect to which the transfer is or might be chargeable are specific gifts which do not bear their own tax, the amount referred to in sub-paragraph (1) above is the aggregate of—

(*a*) the sum of the value of those gifts, and

(*b*) the amount of tax which would be chargeable if the value transferred equalled that aggregate.

(3A) Where the specific gifts not bearing their own tax are not the only gifts with respect to which the transfer is or might be chargeable, the amount referred to in sub-paragraph (1) above is such amount as, after deduction of tax at the assumed rate specified in sub-paragraph (3B) below, would be equal to the sum of the value of those gifts.

(3B) For the purposes of sub-paragraph (3A) above—

(*a*) the assumed rate is the rate found by dividing the assumed amount of tax by that part of the value transferred with respect to which the transfer would be chargeable on the hypothesis that—

(i) the amount corresponding to the value of specific gifts not bearing their own tax is equal to the aggregate referred to in sub-paragraph (3) above, and

(ii) the parts of the value transferred attributable to specific gifts and to gifts of residue or shares in residue are determined accordingly; and

(*b*) the assumed amount of tax is the amount that would be charged on the value transferred on the hypothesis mentioned in paragraph (*a*) above.

(4) For the purposes of this paragraph, any liability of the transferor which is not to be taken into account under paragraph 1 (3) of Schedule 10 to this Act shall be treated as a specific gift.

Attribution of value to residuary gifts

2–104   **20.** Such part only of the value transferred shall be attributed to gifts of residue or shares in residue as is not attributed under paragraph 19 above to specific gifts.

Gifts made separately out of different funds

2–105   **21.** Where gifts taking effect on a transfer of value take effect separately out of different funds the preceding provisions of this Part of this Schedule shall be applied separately to the gifts taking effect out of each of those funds, with the necessary adjustments of the values and amounts referred to in those provisions.

Burden of tax

12–106   **22.** Notwithstanding the terms of any disposition—
(*a*) none of the tax on the value transferred shall fall on any specific gift if or to the extent that the transfer is exempt with respect to the gift; and
(*b*) none of the tax attributable to the value of property comprised in residue shall fall on any gift of a share of residue if or to the extent that the transfer is exempt with respect to the gift.

Legal rights in Scotland

12–107   **22A.**—(1) Where on the death of a person legal rights are claimed by a person entitled to claim such rights, those rights shall be treated as a specific gift which bears its own tax.

(2) In determining the value of legal rights mentioned in sub-paragraph (1) above, any capital transfer tax payable on the estate of the deceased shall be left out of account.

(3) In the case of any death occurring after 13th March 1975 and before the passing of the Finance Act 1976, the executors of the deceased may elect that this paragraph shall apply to the estate of the deceased.

(4) This paragraph extends to Scotland only.

Interpretation

12–108   **23.**—(1) In this Part of this Schedule—
" gift ", in relation to any transfer of value, means the benefit of any disposition or rule of law by which, on the making of the transfer, any property becomes (or would but for any abatement become) the property of any person or applicable for any purpose and
" given " shall be construed accordingly;
" specific gift " means any gift other than a gift of residue or of a share in residue.

(2) For the purposes of this Part of this Schedule a gift bears its own tax if the tax attributable to it falls on the person who becomes entitled to the property given or (as the case may be) is payable out of property applicable for the purposes for which the property given becomes applicable.

(3) Where—
(*a*) the whole or part of the value transferred by a transfer of value is attributable to property which is the subject of two or more gifts, and
(*b*) the aggregate of the values of the property given by each of those gifts is less than the value transferred or, as the case may be, that part of it,

then for the purposes of this Part of this Schedule (and notwithstanding the definition of a gift in sub-paragraph (1) above) the value of each gift shall be taken to be the relevant proportion of the value transferred or, as the case may be, that part of it; and the relevant proportion in relation to any gift is the proportion which the value of the property given by it bears to the said aggregate.

FINANCE ACT 1976

(c. 40)

Retirement annuities

12–109   **30.**—(1) See I.C.T.A., ss. 227 and 228.

(2) See I.C.T.A., ss. 226 and 226A.

(3) This section does not affect relief for any year of assessment before the year 1976–77.

Certification of life insurance policies

12–110   **33.**—(1) Until such day as the Treasury may by order made by statutory instrument appoint, paragraph 1 (1) of Schedule 2 to the Finance Act 1975 (which requires qualifying policies to be certified or to conform with a form certified by the Board) shall not apply to a policy issued in respect of an insurance made before 1st April 1976 which is varied on or after that date.

(2) In relation to the variation before the day appointed under sub-section (1) above of any such policy as is there mentioned paragraph 11 (2) of Schedule 1 to the Taxes Act (which was amended by the said Schedule 2 so as to transfer the function of certification from the body issuing the policy to the Board) shall have effect as originally enacted and not as so amended.

Relief on life policies etc.

12–111   **34.** For the year 1979–80 and subsequent years of assessment sections 19 to 21 of the Taxes Act and the other enactments mentioned in Schedule 4 to this Act shall have effect subject to the provisions of that Schedule.

Loan annuity contracts by the elderly

12–112   **35.** Paragraph 16 (1) and (2) of Schedule 2 to the Finance Act 1975 (charge in connection with contract for life annuity where money is lent to the annuitant etc.) shall not apply in relation to a contract if and to the extent that interest on the sum lent is eligible for relief under section 75 of the Finance Act 1972 by virtue of paragraph 24 of Schedule 1 to the Finance Act 1974 (loan to elderly person for purchase of life annuity).

Section 34.

SCHEDULE 4 [1]

LIFE POLICIES, ETC.

Preliminary

12–113   **1.** In this Schedule references to any sections not otherwise identified are to sections of the Taxes Act and " Schedule 1 " means Schedule 1 to that Act.

Short-term assurances

12–114   **2.** A policy which secures a capital sum payable only on death or payable either on death or on earlier disability shall not be a qualify-

---

[1] The amendments in this Schedule come into effect in 1979–80 and therefore are not yet incorporated in the Acts to be amended.

ing policy within the meaning of Schedule 1 if the capital sum is payable only if the event in question happens before the expiry of a specified term ending less than one year after the making of the insurance.

Relief by deduction from premiums

12–115   **3.**—(1) In section 19 (1) for the words " if the claimant " to the end there shall be substituted the words " an individual who pays any such premium as is specified in subsection (2) below shall (without making any claim) be entitled to relief under this section, and Schedule 4 to the Finance Act 1976 shall apply with respect to that relief."

(2) In section 19 (2)—

    (*a*) for the words from " by the claimant " to " (ii) with underwriters " there shall be substituted the words " by an individual under a policy of insurance or contract for a deferred annuity, where—

        (*a*) the payments are made to—

            (i) any insurance company legally established in the United Kingdom or any branch in the United Kingdom of an insurance company lawfully carrying on in the United Kingdom life assurance business (as defined in section 323 (2) of this Act); or

            (ii) underwriters ";

    (*b*) in sub-paragraphs (iii) and (iv) of paragraph (*a*) the word " with " shall be omitted;

    (*c*) in paragraph (*b*) for the word " claimant " there shall be substituted the word " individual "; and

    (*d*) at the end of paragraph (*c*) there shall be added the words " or his spouse ".

4.—(1) Relief under section 19 in respect of any premiums paid by an individual in a year of assessment shall be given by making good to the person to whom they are paid any deficiency arising from the deductions authorised under paragraph 5 below.

(2) Where the individual is not resident in the United Kingdom but is entitled to relief by virtue of subsection (2) of section 27, sub-paragraph (1) above shall not apply but (subject to the proviso to that subsection) the like relief shall be given to him under paragraph 15 below.

5. Subject to the following provisions of this Schedule,—

    (*a*) an individual resident in the United Kingdom who is entitled to relief under section 19 in respect of any premium may deduct from any payment in respect of the premium and retain an amount equal to $17\frac{1}{2}$ per cent. thereof; and

    (*b*) the person to whom the payment is made shall accept the amount paid after the deduction in discharge of the individual's liability to the same extent as if the deduction had not been made and may recover the deficiency from the Board.

Limit on deductions authorised under paragraph 5

6.—(1) Where the premiums payable in any year in respect of any policy or contract exceed £1,500 the percentage mentioned in paragraph 5 (*a*) above is a percentage of such part only of any payment as bears to the whole thereof the same proportion as £1,500 bears to the total amount of the premiums so payable; but without prejudice to the operation of paragraph 15 below in any case where by virtue of this paragraph the relief given under section 19 is reduced below the limit specified in section 21.

(2) In this paragraph " year " means the twelve months beginning with the making of the assurance or contract and any subsequent period of twelve months.

Husband and wife

12–116   **7.** Subsection (7) of section 19 shall be omitted.

8. The references in section 19 to an individual's spouse shall include any person who was that individual's spouse at the time the insurance or contract was made, unless the marriage was dissolved before 6th April 1979.

9. Where an election under section 23 of the Finance Act 1971 is in force, the relief to which either the husband or the wife is entitled under section 19 in respect of an insurance or contract on the life of the other or made by the other shall not be affected by paragraph 3 of Schedule 4 to that Act (which requires relief to be determined as if the husband and the wife were not married).

10. Where, throughout a year of assessment, a woman is a married woman living with her husband, then—

(*a*) if no election under section 38 is in force, section 21 and paragraph 15 below shall apply as if any relief to which the wife is entitled under section 19 were relief to which the husband is entitled; and

(*b*) if an election under section 38 is in force, section 21 and paragraph 15 below shall apply separately to the amounts paid by each of them, but as if for the limit specified in section 21 there were substituted, in relation to each of them, a limit of £750 or one-twelfth of their total income, whichever is the greater, plus any amount by which the payments in respect of which relief can be given to the other fall short of the limit so substituted.

Industrial assurance policies

12–117   **11.**—(1) This paragraph applies to—

(*a*) a policy issued in the course of an industrial assurance business as defined in section 1 (2) of the Industrial Assurance Act 1923 or the Industrial Assurance Act (Northern Ireland) 1924; and

(*b*) a policy issued by a registered friendly society in the course of tax exempt life or endowment business (as defined in section 337 (3)).

(2) If a policy to which this paragraph applies was issued before the passing of this Act section 19 shall have effect in relation to it as if subsections (2) (*b*), (3) and (4) were omitted; and if a policy to which this paragraph applies was issued after the passing of this Act, paragraph (*b*) of section 19 (2) shall have effect in relation to it as if it permitted the insurance to be on the life of the individual's parent or grandparent or, subject to sub-paragraph (3) below, on the life of the individual's child or grandchild.

(3) Relief may be given in respect of premiums under a policy of insurance on the life of an individual's child or grandchild which is issued after the passing of this Act as if paragraph (*b*) of section 19 (3) were omitted, but may be given only if the annual amount of

the premiums, together with that of any relevant premiums, does not exceed £52; and for this purpose a relevant premium, in relation to an insurance made at any time on the life of an individual's child or grandchild, is any premium under a policy of insurance on the same life, where the insurance is made at the same time or earlier, whether it is made by the individual or any other person.

(4) In this paragraph " child " has the same meaning as in section 10 and " grandchild ", " parent " and " grandparent " have corresponding meanings.

12. In paragraph 4 (1) of Schedule 1, sub-paragraph (iii) of paragraph (*d*) shall be omitted, together with the " and " preceding it, and after paragraph (*d*) there shall be inserted the words " or if the policy was issued before 6th April 1976, or was issued before 6th April 1979 and is in substantially the same form as policies so issued before 6th April 1976.".

Premiums payable to friendly societies and industrial assurance companies

12–118 **13.**—(1) Where a policy is issued by a registered friendly society or a policy to which paragraph 11 above applies is issued by an industrial assurance company, paragraphs 4 and 5 above shall apply in relation to premiums payable under the policy subject to the following modifications.

(2) References to the deductions authorised under paragraph 5 shall be construed as including references to any amount retained by or refunded to the person paying the premium under any scheme made by the society or company in accordance with regulations made under this paragraph.

(3) The appropriate authority may make regulations authorising—

(*a*) the adoption by registered friendly societies and industrial assurance companies of any prescribed scheme for securing that in the case of policies or contracts to which the scheme applies amounts equal to $17\frac{1}{2}$ per cent. of the premiums payable are retained by or refunded to the person paying the premiums or that, in the case of such policies or contracts issued or made before 6th April 1979, the amounts expressed as the amounts of the premiums payable are treated as amounts arrived at by deducting $17\frac{1}{2}$ per cent. from the amounts payable and that the amounts of the capital sums assured or guaranteed are treated as correspondingly increased; or

(*b*) the adoption by any such society or company of any special scheme for that purpose which may, in such circumstances as may be prescribed, be approved by the appropriate authority.

(4) Increases treated as made in pursuance of regulations under this paragraph shall not be treated as variations of a policy or contract and shall be disregarded for the purposes of section 332 of and paragraph 4 of Schedule 1 to the Taxes Act and section 7 (6) of the Finance Act 1975; and the regulations may include such adaptations and modifications of the enactments relating to friendly societies or industrial assurance companies and such other incidental and supplementary provisions as appear to the appropriate authority necessary or expedient for the purpose of enabling such societies or companies to adopt the schemes authorised by the regulations.

(5) Subsections (4), (5) and (7) to (11) of section 6 of the Decimal Currency Act 1969 shall, with the necessary modifications, apply in relation to regulations made under this paragraph.

Supplementary provisions as to relief under section 19

2–119 **14.** Where it appears to the Board that the relief (if any) to which a person is entitled under section 19 has been exceeded or might be exceeded unless the premiums payable by him under any policy were paid in full, they may by notice in writing to that person and to the person to whom the payments are made exclude the application of paragraph 5 above in relation to any payments due or made after such date as may be specified in the notice and before such date as may be specified in a further notice in writing to those persons.

15.—(1) Where in any year of assessment the relief to which a person is entitled under section 19 has not been fully given in accordance with the preceding provisions of this Schedule, he may claim relief for the difference, and relief for the difference shall then be given by a payment made by the Board or by discharge or repayment of tax or partly in one such manner and partly in another; and where the relief given to any person in accordance with the preceding provisions of this Schedule exceeds that to which he is entitled under section 19, he shall be liable to make good the excess and an inspector may make such assessments as may in his judgment be required for recovering the excess.

(2) The Taxes Management Act 1970 shall apply to any assessment under this paragraph as if it were an assessment to tax for the year of assessment in which the relief was given and as if—

(a) the assessment were among those specified in sections 55 (1) (recovery of tax not postponed) and 86 (2) (interest on overdue tax) of that Act; and

(b) the sum charged by the assessment were tax specified in paragraph 3 of the Table in section 86 (4) of that Act (reckonable date).

2–120 **16.**—(1) The Board may make regulations for carrying the preceding provisions of this Schedule into effect.

(2) Without prejudice to the generality of sub-paragraph (1) above, regulations under this paragraph may provide—

(a) for the manner in which claims for the recovery of any sum under paragraph 5 (b) above may be made;

(b) for the furnishing of such information by persons by or to whom premiums are payable as appears to the Board necessary for deciding such claims and for exercising their powers under paragraph 14 or paragraph 15 above; and

(c) for requiring persons to whom premiums are paid to make available for inspection by an officer authorised by the Board such books and other documents in their possession or under their control as may reasonably be required for the purpose of determining whether any information given by those persons for the purposes of this Schedule is correct and complete.

(3) In section 98 of the Taxes Management Act 1970 (penalty for failure to furnish information etc.) the following shall be added in the second column of the Table:

" Regulations under paragraph 16 of Schedule 4 to the Finance Act 1976 ".

(4) The following provisions of the Taxes Management Act 1970, that is to say—

    (*a*) section 29 (3) (*c*) (excessive relief);

    (*b*) section 30 (recovery of tax repaid in consequence of fraud or negligence);

    (*c*) section 88 (interest); and

    (*d*) section 95 (incorrect return or accounts);

shall apply in relation to the payment of a sum claimed under paragraph 5 (*b*) above to which the claimant was not entitled as if it had been income tax repaid as a relief which was not due.

17. A notice given to a person under section 8 of the Taxes Management Act 1970 may require him to include in the return of his income particulars of premiums paid by him or his wife living with him under policies of life insurance or contracts for deferred annuities and of deductions made from the premiums payable.

Consequential amendments

18.—(1) In section 5 after the words " who makes a claim in that behalf " there shall be inserted the words " (or, in the case of relief under section 19 below, who satisfies the conditions of that section) ".

(2) In section 25 (2) the words " section 19 or " shall be omitted.

(3) The proviso to section 27 (2) shall have effect as if the amount of any relief to which an individual is entitled under section 19 were an amount by which his liability to income tax is reduced.

(4) In section 39 (1) (*c*) the words " 19 or " shall be omitted.

19.—(1) In section 7 (5) of the Finance Act 1975 for the words " the basic rate of income tax in force " there shall be substituted the words " the percentage found by doubling that mentioned in paragraph 5 (*a*) of Schedule 4 to the Finance Act 1976 as in force ".

(2) In section 8 (2) of the Finance Act 1975 for the words " one half of the basic rate of income tax in force " there shall be substituted the words " that mentioned in paragraph 5 (*a*) of Schedule 4 to the Finance Act 1976 as in force ".

(3) In paragraph (*b*) of section 9 (4) of the Finance Act 1975 for the words from " income tax " where they first occur to " liability " there shall be substituted " section 19 of the Taxes Act as a sum paid by that person in satisfaction of his liability " and in the words following the paragraph the words " increase in " shall be omitted.

(4) In paragraph 7 (1) of Schedule 2 to the Finance Act 1975 there shall be substituted—

    (*a*) for the words " the conditions of paragraphs (*a*) and (*d*) (iii) of that sub-paragraph are satisfied " the words " the condition of paragraph (*a*) of that sub-paragraph is satisfied ";

    (*b*) for the words " they are not " the words " it is not "; and

    (*c*) for the words " those conditions " the words " that condition ".

20. In section 20 the following shall be omitted:—

    (*a*) in subsection (1), paragraph (*a*) and the words " on the amount of the premium paid by him or ";

    (*b*) subsection (2);

    (*c*) in subsection (4), the words " premiums or other ";

    (*d*) in subsection (5), the words " premiums or " and the proviso; and

    (*e*) subsection (6).

21.—(1) Section 21 shall be amended as follows.

(2) In subsection (1) for the words " sections 19 and 20 " there shall be substituted the words " section 19 " and for the words " one-sixth of that person's total income " there shall be substituted the words " £1,500 in any year of assessment or one-sixth of that person's total income, whichever is the greater ".

(3) Subsection (1A) shall be omitted.

(4) In subsection (3) for the words " the said sections " there shall be substituted the words " sections 19 and 20 above ".

(5) In subsection (4) for the words " one-half of the basic rate " there shall be substituted " $17\frac{1}{2}$ per cent." and the words " premiums or " in paragraph (*b*) and the words following that paragraph shall be omitted.

12–122

Table I

TRANSFERS AT OR WITHIN THREE YEARS OF DEATH

Portion of value		Rate of tax	Cumulative tax at upper limit in column (2)
(1) Lower limit	(2) Upper limit	Per cent.	
£	£		£
0	15,000	Nil	Nil
15,000	20,000	10	500
20,000	25,000	15	1,250
25,000	30,000	20	2,250
30,000	40,000	25	4,750
40,000	50,000	30	7,750
50,000	60,000	35	11,250
60,000	80,000	40	19,250
80,000	100,000	45	28,250
100,000	120,000	50	38,250
120,000	150,000	55	54,750
150,000	500,000	60	264,750
500,000	1,000,000	65	589,750
1,000,000	2,000,000	70	1,289,750
2,000,000	–	75	–

12–123

Table II

TRANSFERS INTER VIVOS

Portion of value		Rate of tax	Cumulative tax at upper limit in column (2)
(1) Lower limit	(2) Upper limit	Per cent.	
£	£		£
0	15,000	Nil	Nil
15,000	20,000	5	250
20,000	25,000	$7\frac{1}{2}$	625
25,000	30,000	10	1,125
30,000	40,000	$12\frac{1}{2}$	2,375
40,000	50,000	15	3,875
50,000	60,000	$17\frac{1}{2}$	5,625
60,000	80,000	20	9,625
80,000	100,000	$22\frac{1}{2}$	14,125
100,000	120,000	$27\frac{1}{2}$	19,625
120,000	150,000	35	30,125
150,000	200,000	$42\frac{1}{2}$	51,375
200,000	250,000	50	76,375
250,000	300,000	55	103,875
300,000	500,000	60	223,875
500,000	1,000,000	65	548,875
1,000,000	2,000,000	70	1,248,875
2,000,000	–	75	–

Based on the tables in F.A. 1975, s. 37.

CAPITAL TRANSFER TAX—PENSION SCHEMES

Inland Revenue Statement of May 7, 1976

2–124   1. This note has been prepared at the request of the National Association of Pension Funds primarily to enable the administrators of pension schemes to answer enquiries about the capital transfer tax liability of benefits payable under such schemes.

2. No liability to capital transfer tax arises in respect of benefits payable on a person's death under a normal pension scheme except in the circumstances explained below.

3. Such benefits are liable to capital transfer tax if:

(a) they form part of his freely disposable property passing under his will or intestacy. (This applies only if his executors or administrators have a legally enforceable claim to the benefits: if they were payable to them only at the discretion of the trustees of the pension fund or some similar persons they are not liable to capital transfer tax) or

(b) he had the power, immediately before his death, to nominate or appoint the benefits to anyone he pleased.

In these cases the benefits should be included in the personal representatives' account (schedule of the deceased's assets) which has to be completed when applying for a grant of probate or letters of administration. The capital transfer tax (if any) which is assessed on the personal representatives' account has to be paid before the grant can be obtained.

4. On some events other than the death of a member information should be given to the appropriate Estate Duty Office. These are:

(i) the payment of contributions to a scheme which has not been approved for income tax purposes;

(ii) the making of an irrevocable nomination or the disposal of a benefit by a member in his lifetime (otherwise than in favour of his spouse) which reduces the value of his estate (*e.g.* the surrender of part of his pension or his lump sum benefit in exchange for a pension for the life of another).

If capital transfer tax proves to be payable the Estate Duty Office will communicate with the persons liable to pay the tax.

Capital Transfer Tax On Benefits Under Superannuation Schemes

These notes replace those that were issued to explain the practice of the Estate Duty Office regarding liability to estate duty on benefits payable under the rules of employees' retirement benefits schemes and superannuation funds and under retirement annuity contracts and trust schemes approved under section 226 of the Taxes Act.

They outline the effect on such benefits of the capital transfer tax introduced by the Finance Act 1975 in the case of lifetime transfers on and after March 27, 1974, and deaths on and after March 13, 1975, and refer in particular to paragraph 16 of Schedule 5 to that Act.

A. Payments to the deceased's legal personal representatives

1. Payments that are legally due to the legal personal representatives and cannot be withheld from them at the discretion of any person exercisable after the death form part of the deceased's estate and are taxable as such (subject to any " spouse " exemption under para. 1, Sched. 6 having regard to the devolution of the deceased's estate under his will or intestacy). Payments made to the legal personal representatives in exercise of a discretion exercisable after the death are not treated as part of the deceased's estate for tax purposes on his death.

2. Payments which are taxable as at 1 above are not regarded as property comprised in a settlement and where they are paid over to duly constituted legal personal representatives those representatives (not the trustees of the fund) are liable for any tax. They should include the value of the payments in the personal representatives' account of the deceased's estate.

3. Where payments are made to the duly constituted legal personal representatives the person making them need not send a separate notification to the Estate Duty Office.

B. Where the deceased had a general power of nomination

1. Where the deceased had a general power to nominate a benefit to anyone he wished and had not exercised his power irrevocably in his lifetime the benefit forms part of his estate for capital transfer tax purposes and is taxable as such subject again to any " spouse " exemption under paragraph 1, Schedule 6.

2. The legal personal representatives are liable for any tax.

3. Where the deceased's power of nomination is restricted to a specified class of persons which does not include himself failure to exercise the power irrevocably in his lifetime will not give rise to a tax liability on death unless under the rules of the fund or scheme the benefit then forms part of his estate.

4. Where the deceased had at the time of his death an option to have a sum of money paid to his legal personal representatives that sum of money will normally be taxed as part of his estate. Where however an annuity is payable to the deceased's widow, widower or dependant under a contract or trust scheme approved under section 226 or section 226A of the Taxes Act or (before the commencement of that Act) under section 22 of the Finance Act 1956 and the deceased had an option to have a sum of money paid to his legal personal representatives tax is not charged (para. 2, Sched. 7 to the Finance Act 1975).

C. Annuities which continue to be payable after the deceased's death

1. Provided that the scheme or fund under which it is payable is one mentioned in paragraph 16 (1), Schedule 5 a pension or annuity continuing after the deceased's death will not give rise to a tax liability in connection with his death unless the continuing pension or annuity results from the settlement or other application of a lump sum benefit (see para. 16 (2) (*b*)).

2. If however the continuing pension or annuity is payable as of right to the deceased's legal personal representatives it will be taxable (see para. A above).

D. Gratuitous transfers of value

1. Capital transfer tax is not considered to be chargeable under section 20 (2) of the Finance Act 1975, as a gratuitous transfer of value, on the contributions (made either directly or by a reduction in the remuneration which he would otherwise have received) by a member to provide any benefit to another person payable under retirement benefit or superannuation schemes, trusts, contracts or arrangements the main or a substantial object of which is to make provision for a person on his own retirement. (As to the surrender of part of a benefit to which the member would himself have been entitled, see E below).

2. The statement in paragraph 1 above does not extend to any *separate* provision made by a member for his dependants or others, for example under a group life insurance scheme operated in conjunction with superannuation arrangements, even if the scheme or other provision is arranged and administered by or in co-operation with the employer. Nor does it extend to an annuity contract under section 226A of the Taxes Act.

Premiums paid by the member on a policy on his life effected under a scheme of this kind or under such an annuity contract may be chargeable to tax as gratuitous transfers of value although the transfers will commonly qualify for exemption under paragraph 5, Schedule 6 to the Finance Act 1975 as normal expenditure out of income.

3. In practice contributions (other than those provided as at E) payable under ordinary pension or superannuation schemes for members of the kind referred to in paragraph 1 above will automatically be regarded as covered by the statement in that paragraph if the scheme is one to which paragraph 16 applies (see para. 16 (1)). The tax position of contributions to and benefits arising from any other scheme will be considered individually when a transfer of value occurs.

E. Dispositions by nomination or surrender of benefits

1. Where
   - (a) a member provides for a pension to another
       - (i) by irrevocably surrendering part of his own pension, or
       - (ii) by giving up a right to receive a lump sum (or part of it) payable to him on retirement or to his legal personal representatives on his death

or
   - (b) he irrevocably nominates such a lump sum

he will prima facie have made a chargeable transfer if his disposition is after December 9, 1974. The value transferred will be determined by the " loss " to the member at the date the disposition is made and therefore will normally be less than the value of the pension or lump sum ultimately paid to the beneficiary.

A disposition of this nature could in appropriate circumstances be an exempt transfer under:
   - (a) Paragraph 1, Schedule 6
     (Transfers between spouses);
   - (b) Paragraph 2, Schedule 6
     (Values not exceeding £1,000 [1]);
   - (c) Paragraph 4, Schedule 6
     (Small gifts to same person);

---

[1] The figure of £1,000 was increased to £2,000 by F.A. 1976, s. 93 (1), in relation to transfers of value made after April 5, 1976.

(d) section 46 (3)
     (Dispositions for maintenance of family).

Where it is clear that the disposition falls within (a) above, there will be no necessity to notify it to the Estate Duty Office.

2. The *revocable* exercise of a power of nomination over a lump sum benefit will have the same capital transfer tax consequences except that the disposition will be treated as taking effect at the latest time at which the member could have revoked his nomination (*e.g.* his retirement or his death).

F. Termination of a pension or annuity

1. Paragraph 16, Schedule 5, provides exemption on the termination on death or otherwise of a pension or annuity payable under a scheme or fund to which paragraph 16 (1) applies. For this purpose a pension payable without proportion to the date of death is regarded as terminating on the death.

2. Paragraphs 16 (2) (*b*) and (3) make it clear that the exemption does not extend to the termination of an interest under a trust of a *lump sum* benefit payable under a scheme or fund and paragraphs 16 (5) and (6) that it does not extend to capital distributions made out of a benefit which, having become payable, becomes comprised in a settlement. If a lump sum benefit is settled (for example, in the exercise of discretionary powers as to the disposal of a death benefit) claims for tax may arise on the termination of an interest in possession under the settlement or, if there are no interests in possession in the settled property, on the various chargeable events described in paragraphs 6 to 15 of Schedule 5.

3. Where a lump sum benefit is converted into a pension under the rules of the scheme or fund then normally neither the conversion nor the cesser of that pension will give rise to a tax charge. If however the lump sum benefit is surrendered to provide a pension for some other person then paragraph E above will apply.

G. Payments made in exercise of a discretion

Where a lump sum benefit payable under a scheme or fund within paragraph 16 (1) of Schedule 5 is distributed or settled in exercise of a discretion neither such distribution nor the making of the settlement will give rise to a liability to tax.

INDEX

261